British Settler Colonialism since 1530

British Settler Colonialism since 1530

Indigenous Peoples in an Imperial World

Susan Kingsley Kent

BLOOMSBURY ACADEMIC
LONDON · NEW YORK · OXFORD · NEW DELHI · SYDNEY

BLOOMSBURY ACADEMIC

Bloomsbury Publishing Plc, 50 Bedford Square, London, WC1B 3DP, UK
Bloomsbury Publishing Inc, 1385 Broadway, New York, NY 10018, USA
Bloomsbury Publishing Ireland, 29 Earlsfort Terrace, Dublin 2, D02 AY28, Ireland

BLOOMSBURY, BLOOMSBURY ACADEMIC and the Diana logo are
trademarks of Bloomsbury Publishing Plc

First published in Great Britain 2025

Copyright © Susan Kingsley Kent, 2025

Susan Kingsley Kent has asserted her right under the Copyright,
Designs and Patents Act, 1988, to be identified as Author of this work.

For legal purposes the Acknowledgments on p. ix constitute an
extension of this copyright page.

Cover design by Akihiro Nakayama / A2creative
Cover image: Fight between Fengu and Gcaleka, Fengu-Gcaleka War, 1877–79,
From British Battles on Land and Sea, by James Grant (© history_docu_photo via
Alamy Stock Photo)

All rights reserved. No part of this publication may be: i) reproduced or transmitted in
any form, electronic or mechanical, including photocopying, recording or by means of
any information storage or retrieval system without prior permission in writing from the
publishers; or ii) used or reproduced in any way for the training, development or operation
of artificial intelligence (AI) technologies, including generative AI technologies. The rights
holders expressly reserve this publication from the text and data mining exception as per
Article 4(3) of the Digital Single Market Directive (EU) 2019/790.

Bloomsbury Publishing Plc does not have any control over, or responsibility for,
any third-party websites referred to or in this book. All internet addresses given
in this book were correct at the time of going to press. The author and publisher
regret any inconvenience caused if addresses have changed or sites have ceased
to exist, but can accept no responsibility for any such changes.

A catalogue record for this book is available from the British Library.

A catalog record for this book is available from the Library of Congress.

ISBN:	HB:	978-1-3502-9167-6
	PB:	978-1-3502-9166-9
	ePDF:	978-1-3502-9168-3
	eBook:	978-1-3502-9169-0

Typeset by Integra Software Services Pvt. Ltd.
Printed and bound in Great Britain

For product safety related questions contact productsafety@bloomsbury.com.

To find out more about our authors and books visit www.bloomsbury.com
and sign up for our newsletters.

To Phil Deloria, friend and scholar extraordinaire.

CONTENTS

List of Figures viii
Acknowledgments ix

1 The Nature of Settler Colonialism 1

2 The Colonization of Ireland, 1530–1780s 11

3 The Decimation of Indian Peoples in Colonial North America, 1607–1783 35

4 The Expansion of Anglo-American Settlement, 1783–1830s 59

5 Liberal Empire, 1830s–70s 83

6 Expansion, Intensification, and Resistance, 1860s–1914 113

7 Indigeneity and War, 1914–45 147

8 Cold War Developments, 1945–65 173

9 Land Back, 1960s–Present 197

Index 223

FIGURES

1.1 *Map of Ireland, sixteenth and early seventeenth centuries* 14
3.1 *Map delineating the Royal Proclamation of 1763* 50
4.1 *1834 Carey Map of South Africa Cape of Good Hope Capetown Colony* 77
5.1 *Signing the Treaty of Waitangi, 1840* 107
6.1 *Native Americans at Carlisle Indian School* 116
6.2 *Lands designated for African by Native Lands Act of 1913* 130
7.1 *Soldiers of the King's African Rifles on patrol in German East Africa, 1917* 149
8.1 *Sign of Apartheid* 182
9.1 *Australians demanding land back for Aboriginal peoples in Melbourne, 2023* 208

ACKNOWLEDGMENTS

I am beholden to a number of people who helped me to think about and write this book. A wide-ranging and synthetic treatment such as this cannot be produced in isolation: the scholars whose writings I depend upon and draw from deserve recognition and credit for their superb work. Not all of them appear in the notes and Further Readings, alas, but I am indebted to a broad array of historians and theorists. Sue Keaveney and Butch Rovedo provided the idea for the vignette that opens the Colonial America chapter (Chapter 3); I thank them for their hospitality and inspiration. The external reviewers of my proposal and the reader of the final manuscript gave invaluable advice, improving it immeasurably; I appreciate their input and wish I could tell them so to their faces. Maddie Smith and Megan Harris at Bloomsbury supported this project from the start and have worked hard to make it a reality. Thank you for all you have done.

Lil Fenn, Peter Wood, and Carol Byerly, as is always the case, offered scintillating conversation and cogent commentary about a whole slew of things I wasn't clear about, keeping me on track and facilitating my understanding of American history. Myles Osborne graciously allowed me to use material he contributed to our co-authored book on British imperialism in Africa, without which this book would have been considerably impoverished. Bonnie Smith and Peggy Burns provided encouragement of and enthusiasm for this and other ventures into settler colonialism. The presence of all these dear friends in my life enriches it profoundly. My partner, Anne Davidson, makes my scholarship possible as readily as she does our personal life together, continuing to bring me tea and make me laugh. I am deeply grateful to you all.

Finally, my heartfelt thanks to Phil Deloria, whose contributions to this book are legion. I, like countless others, have been the beneficiary of his subtle and nuanced understandings of culture and power, his fresh, original, and critical approaches to conventional historical developments, his capacious knowledge of history and theory. Our discussions over the past thirty years have never not left me more than a bit awed, and better able to appreciate the complexity of historical and contemporary dynamics. He has been a generous colleague and, more importantly, a steadfast friend. In some small measure of my admiration, respect, regard, and gratitude, I dedicate this book to him.

1

The Nature of Settler Colonialism

In the spring of 1856, as a teenaged Xhosa girl named Nongqawuse chased birds out of her uncle's cornfields in southern Africa, two men appeared from out of nowhere with a message for her people. A new world was coming, they told her, one in which the Xhosa would be rejuvenated and white people cast into the sea. Before that could happen, however, the Xhosa people would have to purify themselves by sacrificing their very means of existence. "Kill your cattle," one of them instructed her to tell them, "consume your corn," and do not "cultivate any more." Nongqawuse told her uncle of the visions she received from her long-dead ancestors, and he, convinced of their truth, spread the word. At first, many people doubted her message, but as 1856 turned into 1857, more and more came to believe the prophecy. Ultimately, the Xhosa slaughtered 400,000 of their cattle; another 40,000 animals died of starvation. Some 80,000 Xhosa perished as a result.

The Xhosa cattle-killing came about in response to British settler colonialism in South Africa. Seventy years of contact with white settlers had devastated Xhosa communities. A series of frontier wars with the British had undermined the political and economic structures that ordered their society; British missionaries seemed to be luring people away from long-held beliefs; and, most recently, an epidemic of bovine pleuropneumonia had swept through the country, decimating the cattle herds upon which the community based itself. As the Xhosa saying went, "cattle are the race, they being dead the race dies."[1] When ancestors promised that the slaughter of their cattle would pave the way for the renewal of their world, the desperate Xhosa paid heed.

The British reaction to these events helped determined the final outcome for the Xhosa people. The governor-general of the Cape Colony, Sir George Grey, claimed that the chiefs had concocted the cattle-killing to inspire their people to a final massive effort to drive out the colonizers. He refused to stop the cattle killing when he had opportunities to do so and rejected the entreaties of Xhosa chiefs in 1857 who pleaded with him for food as thousands of their people starved. The cattle-killing marked the collapse of the Xhosa polity. Grey's inaction stemmed from a specific agenda: he wanted the entire region of British Kaffraria, as the territory was called, rid of the Xhosa living in it, and looked to settle whites on their lands. As the Xhosa collapsed, he set about implementing his vision. He confiscated the lands of a number of chiefs and gave out 300,000 acres to some 200 white settlers. In 1865, British Kaffiria became incorporated into the Cape Colony.

***

The tragedy of the Xhosa encapsulates many of the themes addressed in this book, which treats the territories settled by British men and women in Ireland, North America, Australia, New Zealand, South Africa, Kenya, and Rhodesia. Long described as "white colonies of settlement," the histories of these lands told the stories of triumphant white colonists prevailing over disease, starvation, inhospitable environments, and hostile "natives" to establish Anglo social and political systems, "building better Britains," as one historian put it.[2] Beginning in the early twenty-first century, scholars inspired by the theorizing of Australian anthropologist Patrick Wolfe began to focus their attention on the impact settlers had on Indigenous peoples in the white colonies and dominions, whose lands they took and whose populations they disrupted and even eradicated. These new studies, collectively examining what we now call "settler colonialism," emphasize the ongoing depredations against Indigenous communities and cultures right up to our own time.

Settler colonies differed from colonies of trade and exploitation in a number of ways. In places like India and Nigeria, for instance, agents of British imperialism did not go there to obtain land and settle; rather, they sought to extract the resources of the colonies, utilizing the labor of the local population. In settler colonies, by contrast, Britons sought to obtain the land of the Indigenous peoples who occupied it and carried out campaigns to oust local peoples from their homelands. They aimed to establish their own societies and their campaigns to do so frequently turned murderous. Indeed, Wolfe argued that settler colonialism rests upon a logic of elimination, on the impulse to get rid of Indigenous peoples. Policies of eradication did not always go so far as to effect the physical destruction of Indigenous peoples; sometimes they were "merely" cultural in nature, as in the efforts to assimilate Indigenous peoples by destroying their lifeways and languages and stealing their children. In all cases, the impetus was the seizure and possession of Native land, no matter what rationales settlers might put forth to justify their policies and actions.

In many places, such as Ireland, South Africa, Rhodesia, and Kenya, settlers also required the labor of the Indigenous people whose land they appropriated. Some Indigenous folks facilitated and benefited from white settlement; everywhere, others resisted and fought back, sometimes forcing settler societies and their governments to enact reforms. In the long run, however, they could not undo the damage wreaked upon their communities.

For one major distinguishing feature of many settler colonies lies in the ongoing impact of the phenomenon. In the period of decolonization following the Second World War, local inhabitants in colonies of exploitation gained their independence from Britain and compelled colonial officials to leave; settler colonists, for the most part, did not go back to Britain, and in all but a few cases their domination of Indigenous peoples and cultures continues to this day. The attitudes, actions, policies, institutions, laws, and cultures put in place by white settlers structured—then and now—the societies they created in the lands they expropriated from Native peoples. This long-lasting impact, the continued existence of profound inequities between Native and settler populations—even in places where Indigenous people have gained control of their governments—is why Wolfe described settler colonialism as "a structure, not an event." It wasn't a one-off occurrence that then stopped. It lasted, and lasts still.

Wolfe asserted that the elimination of Native peoples stands as an "organizing principle" of settler colonialism, the means by which the land on which they lived would be seized and their displacement effected. By elimination he did not necessarily mean genocide, though outright genocide certainly did take place in many instances, as we shall see in subsequent chapters. Elimination might mean assimilation, biological and/or cultural, into the society of whites. Biologically, assimilation entailed the dilution of racial distinctions through sexual intercourse with white settlers; often that contact was not consented to by Indigenous women and girls. Australia and New Zealand had formal biological assimilation policies designed to "whiten" their First Nation populations. Culturally, assimilation involved a wide array of practices designed to destroy Indigenous groups as a people, including—but not limited to—the banning of Native languages or Native religions; removing children from their families and placing them in boarding schools; forbidding Native dress or hairstyles; eliminating Native land-holding practices, and replacing them with land tenure policies based in private property.

Wolfe's theories, derived from his studies of Australia and extrapolated to the situation of Native peoples in America, have enabled us to see things differently and have illuminated a great deal about various nations' histories that we might not have seen before. But they shouldn't be regarded as complete or universal. Robin Kelley, for example, pointed out that Wolfe's insistence on the physical removal of Indigenous people from the land as the *sine qua non* of settler colonialism went only so far; it failed to take into account the experiences of African peoples in the southern part of the continent—South Africa, Rhodesia (modern-day Zimbabwe), and Kenya. We should add to Kelley's critique the example of Ireland. In these instances, settlers appropriated the land of Native peoples, to be sure, but they also required the labor of millions of Indigenous men and women to work the land and make it productive. As Kelley put it, settlers "wanted the land *and* the labor, but not the people."[3] By that he meant that settlers determined to turn Native farmers and grazers into proletariats, into landless laborers and mine workers who had no relationship with or claim to the land or the fruits of their labor.

Settler colonialism displayed many different faces, depending upon where and when it took hold, but it also involved a number of shared attitudes and practices in the territories under scrutiny here. The "Doctrine of Discovery," issued by Pope Alexander VI in 1493, underpinned virtually all settler regimes. It declared that any territory that was not occupied by Christians could legally be claimed and inhabited by Christians. When Britain underwent the reformation of its churches and embraced various iterations of Protestantism, settler justifications for their depredations adapted the Catholic focus of the pope's bull to the notion of the providential nature of their enterprise. As US Chief Justice John Marshall put it in 1823, "the principle of discovery gave European nations an absolute right to New World lands."[4]

In almost all cases, the way Indigenous communities utilized the land—or, in the minds of the English, did not utilize it—provided settlers with justifications for taking it. Local Native communities that relied on the land for their material and spiritual sustenance, but did not farm it in ways that looked familiar to the English, could readily be discounted: collective ownership of the land, as distinct from the private property ideals that undergirded English law, politics, and social structure, marked Aboriginal peoples as backward and lazy, undeserving of any consideration when it came to land seizures. Commentators saw in the pastoral ways of Irish and African people driving their cattle to grazing lands, or in the seasonal lifeways of American Indians, Māoris, and Australian Aboriginal peoples proof that they were "nomadic," allowing the English to invoke the principle of "terra nullius," that is, to claim that the "empty" lands were fair game for whomever settled on and cultivated them. The English regarded the absence of cultivation as the epitome of incivility, a characterization that incorporated traits of savagery, wildness, and barbarity, in marked contrast, they asserted incessantly, to their superior civilization based in the possession and productivity of land. Convictions of English or Anglo superiority over colonized peoples took on increasingly racial tones as Irish or Native American or Aboriginal or African peoples resisted settler encroachment on their lands.

Ideas about race informed settler colonialism in myriad ways. In medieval and Renaissance times, European understandings about race drew upon the contrast of darkness and light, which in turn connoted good and evil. Long before the British came into contact with peoples whose skins were dark, they used terms of black and white that carried deep meaning for them: "black" might signify death, mourning, evil, sin, and danger, while "white" might stand for purity, innocence, goodness, and beauty. As England became involved in overseas colonization, and especially as it engaged in the trade of enslaved Africans, the term "black" proved to be a ready means of distinguishing English "civilization" from "barbarism." Contemporaries began to ascribe blackness to virtually any group of people who fell under English control—Irish, Native Americans, Aboriginal Australians and New Zealanders, and South Africans. They used race to justify coercive and violent measures against the Indigenous communities whose lands they took by rendering them different, inferior, unruly, savage, and in need of British colonizing efforts. Race undergirded the settler colonial enterprise.

But it isn't all that clear-cut, a fact that requires us to appreciate the complexity and protean nature of settler colonialism. It wasn't always a case of white settlers imposing their dominance over people of color. Not all settlers were white or European; not all Aboriginal groups colonized by settlers were people of color. Inter-racial unions, sometimes consensual and often compelled, produced mixed-race populations that settler governments regarded in different ways—many of the Métis of Canada, for instance, considered themselves "native," while the government did not classify them as such in legislation dealing with First Nations people. In Australia, mixed-race Aborigines were seen as the means by which the Indigenous population could be "whitened." Colonists who settled in North America and New Zealand, moreover, often depended heavily upon the assistance of Native peoples for their very survival, a circumstance that led them and then their governments to enter into agreements with those whose help they sought. As we will see in subsequent chapters, the existence of treaties made a difference, even if slight, in the conditions in which Indigenous people lived under regimes of settler colonialism.

In almost every instance, settlers found themselves in a triangular relationship with local Indigenous populations, on the one hand, and, on the other, with the more distant metropolitan government, whether in London or, after 1783, Washington. In every instance, bar none, the seizure of Native lands involved settler violence against the local Indigenous communities, depredations that required colonial officials to intervene in order to keep the peace. That could entail great expense, and colonial authorities worked hard to keep settler despoliation of Native lands and peoples at a minimum. Settler groups often rebelled against the metropolitan government's efforts to control their actions against Indigenous populations or restrict their expansion. In some instances, rebellion turned into something more permanent: as one prominent theorist of settler colonialism, Lorenzo Veracini, noted, "settlers are founders of political orders." He distinguishes settlers—who "carry their sovereignty with them"—from migrants, who ask to be members of "a political order that is already constituted."[5] We might complicate his position a bit by suggesting that actions endemic to settler colonialism actually created sovereign political orders. As we will see in the case of the US, American settlers constituted their new political order at least partly in response to a metropole that would not permit them to expand westward onto Indian lands. In effect, rather than bringing it with them, settlers actually established their sovereignty as a new nation through their efforts to eliminate Native peoples. We don't see as direct a connection in places like Canada, South Africa, Australia, or New Zealand, but it is certainly the case that the prospect of self-government in those dominions excited major concerns in the metropole for the well-being of Indigenous peoples.

Settler societies told themselves stories that rationalized and validated their seizure of Native lands and the elimination of Native cultures and peoples. The Doctrine of Discovery instantiated Christianity as the moral ground on which they stood as interlopers; it justified rule over Indigenous peoples and the destruction of their cultures by asserting that "the Catholic faith and the Christian religion be exalted and be everywhere increased and spread, that the health of souls be cared for and that barbarous nations be overthrown and brought to the faith itself."[6]

Settlers invoked fantasies of a purported past, present, and future—for both themselves and for the Indigenous societies they exterminated–that justified their murderous actions and/or depicted them as part of a larger divine plan. Bringing civilization and true Christianity to poor benighted barbarians; establishing a particularly gendered social order; pursuing a manifest destiny to populate the farthest regions of the earth; providing a "soft pillow" for Indigenous peoples who were purported to be "vanishing"—these narratives served to erase settler culpability in the elimination of Native communities and to assuage whatever misgivings settlers might have. They worked to establish an identity in contradistinction to those whose lives, families, communities, and wholesale cultures they destroyed. Ironically, and unselfconsciously, settlers frequently conjured up a past that established *themselves* as the first people, the Aborigines of the lands they stole from Indigenous people.

Just who are the "Indigenous" people—also referred to throughout as "Native" and "Aboriginal"—who are the subjects of settler colonialism, the people on the receiving end of attempts to eliminate them? They are the very people whose existence as Indigenous was in fact called into being by settler colonialism itself, people who would not be destroyed by settler colonial regimes, whose cultures would not be entirely eliminated. Until very recently, they referred to themselves in local terms, according to the band, the clan, the village, the confederacy, the tribe to which they belonged—the term "Indigenous" was not part of their self-identification until late-twentieth-century global developments brought it into use. As we will see in Chapter 8, the collective impact of decolonization and international activism produced a world-wide movement linking various Aboriginal groups to one another on the basis of their shared experiences. As Sam Deloria, a Standing Rock Sioux, and Ranginui J. Walker, a Te Whakatōhea Māori, suggested at a 1974 meeting of activists from around the globe held in Georgetown, Guyana, "the term 'Indigenous People' refers to people living in countries which have a population composed of differing ethnic or racial groups who are descendants of the earliest populations living in the area and who do not, as a group, control the national government of the countries within which they live." The delegates to the conference accepted the definition offered by Deloria and Walker, tying the notion of indigeneity directly to the relationship of Native peoples to settler colonial regimes. It did not include or exclude any group on the basis of race, geography, population size, culture, or social ethos or organization; rather, as one scholar has put it, "it is a shared history of invasion, colonialism or outside settlement and a shared experience of marginalization that made you *Indigenous*."[7] The term "Indigenous" enabled them to come together as a single global entity with common interests, to draw attention to their situation and demand change. Once expected to be wiped off the face of the earth, the Indigenous survivors of settler colonialism emerged to become a force in international conversations. In 2007, in fact, the United Nations (UN) issued a wide-ranging Declaration on the Rights of Indigenous Peoples (UNDRIP), a document that recognized the impact of settler colonialism and put forward a set of ethical precepts for addressing its ills. As we will see in Chapter 9, the interventions of the global Indigenous community have produced some impressive victories in its struggle to recoup land lost under settler colonialism. Much, much more remains to be done, but the recovery of land constitutes a requisite first step in the campaign to regain sovereignty.

Different groups of Indigenous peoples refer to themselves as collective entities and individuals in various ways. Most prefer to be addressed by their particular and specific clan names as a means both of respecting their self-defined identities and of recognizing the fact that Indigenous peoples do not constitute a monolithic assemblage of indistinguishable cultures, languages, communities, societies, or nations. Settler colonial states frequently behaved as if they did, and often imposed offensive names upon them that demeaned, undermined, and diminished them. I have tried throughout what follows to conform to the naming practices advanced by Indigenous peoples themselves in each locale under consideration, even as the sometimes broad nature of the narrative militates against using culturally-specific band names. Thus, I use the term "First Nations people" and "Aboriginal peoples" in my discussions of Native peoples in Canada and Australia; "Native Americans" and "American Indian" or "Indian people" for the US; "Māori" for New Zealand; and "African peoples" for South Africa, Zimbabwe, and Kenya when I don't identify groups or individuals by their ethnicity. In Africa, unlike in the US, African peoples tend not to use the term "tribe" to refer to the collective groupings to which they belong, it being an unwelcome holdover from the colonial period that fails to account for the often-fluid composition of ethnic groups rendered static and unchanging by the word. Native Americans, by contrast, do often use the term, interchangeably with "nation." Use of the word "Native" or "Aborigine" or "Indian" as a noun to indicate an individual or a group is regarded as outdated and even offensive by many Indigenous people but utilizing the terms as adjectives or descriptors is generally acceptable.

All of this language variety bespeaks the existence of a great diversity among Indigenous peoples across the world, even as the concept of indigeneity enabled the growth of a powerful political movement of resistance to the impacts of settler colonialism. The complexity of naming practices across time and space may introduce a degree of confusion among readers, especially as what is regarded as appropriate and what is not may change as political contexts change. But the fraught history of colonial power and Aboriginal peoples requires us to be respectful of the desires of Indigenous peoples to define themselves. It is the responsibility of the historian to endeavor to conform to acceptable naming practices, even as she is cognizant that she may fall short.

Primary Source

The Doctrine of Discovery, 1493

Pope Alexander VI.

Demarcation Bull Granting Spain Possession of Lands Discovered by Columbus

Rome, May 4, 1493.

Alexander, bishop, servant of the servants of God, to the illustrious sovereigns, our very dear son in Christ, Ferdinand, king, and our very dear daughter in Christ, Isabella, queen of Castile, Leon, Aragon, Sicily, and Granada, health and apostolic benediction. Among other works well pleasing to the Divine Majesty and cherished of our heart, this assuredly ranks highest, that in our times especially the Catholic faith and the Christian religion be exalted and be everywhere increased and spread, that the health of souls be cared for and that barbarous nations be overthrown and brought to the faith itself. Wherefore inasmuch as by the favor of divine clemency, we, though of insufficient merits, have been called to this Holy See of Peter, recognizing that as true Catholic kings and princes, such as we have known you always to be, and as your illustrious deeds already known to almost the whole world declare, you not only eagerly desire but with every effort, zeal, and diligence, without regard to hardships, expenses, dangers, with the shedding even of your blood, are laboring to that end; recognizing also that you have long since dedicated to this purpose your whole soul and all your endeavors ... we therefore are rightly led, and hold it as our duty, to grant you even of our own accord and in your favor those things whereby with effort each day more hearty you may be enabled for the honor of God himself and the spread of the Christian rule to carry forward your holy and praiseworthy purpose so pleasing to immortal God. We have indeed learned that you, who for a long time had intended to seek out and discover certain islands and mainlands remote and unknown and not hitherto discovered by others, to the end that you might bring to the worship of our Redeemer and the profession of the Catholic faith their residents and inhabitants ... chose our beloved son, Christopher Columbus, a man assuredly worthy and of the highest recommendations and fitted for so great an undertaking, whom you furnished with ships and men equipped for like designs, not without the greatest hardships, dangers, and expenses, to make diligent quest for these remote and unknown mainlands and islands through the sea, where hitherto no one had sailed; and they at length, with divine aid and with the utmost diligence sailing in the ocean sea, discovered certain very remote islands and even mainlands that hitherto had not been discovered by others; wherein dwell very many peoples living in peace, and, as reported, going unclothed, and not eating flesh. Moreover, as your aforesaid envoys are of opinion, these very peoples living in the said islands and countries believe in one God, the Creator in heaven, and seem sufficiently disposed to embrace the Catholic faith and be trained in good morals. And it is hoped that, were they instructed, the name of the Savior, our Lord Jesus Christ, would easily be introduced into the said countries and islands. Also, on one of the chief of these aforesaid islands the said Christopher has already caused to be put together and built a fortress fairly equipped, wherein he has stationed as garrison certain Christians, companions of his, who are to make search for other remote and unknown islands and mainlands. In the islands and countries already discovered are found gold, spices, and very many other precious things of divers kinds and qualities. Wherefore, as becomes Catholic kings and princes, after earnest consideration of all matters, especially of the rise and spread of the Catholic faith, as was the fashion of your ancestors, kings of renowned memory, you have purposed with the favor of divine clemency to bring under your sway the said mainlands and islands with their residents and inhabitants and to bring them to the Catholic faith. Hence, heartily commending in the Lord this your holy and praiseworthy purpose, and desirous that it be duly accomplished, and that the name of our Savior be carried into those regions, we exhort you very earnestly in the Lord and by your reception of holy baptism, whereby you are bound to our apostolic commands, and by the bowels of the mercy of our Lord Jesus Christ, enjoy strictly, that inasmuch as with eager zeal for the true faith you design to equip and despatch this expedition, you purpose also, as is your duty, to lead the peoples dwelling in those islands and countries to embrace the Christian religion; nor at any time let dangers or hardships deter you therefrom, with the stout hope and trust in your hearts that Almighty God will further your undertakings. And, in order that you may enter upon so great an undertaking with greater readiness and heartiness endowed with benefit of our apostolic favor, we, of our own accord, not at your instance nor the request of anyone else in your regard, but out of our own sole largess and certain knowledge and out of the fullness of our apostolic power, by the authority of Almighty God conferred upon us in blessed Peter and of the vicarship of Jesus Christ, which we hold on earth, do by tenor of these presents, should any of said islands have been found by your envoys and captains, give, grant, and assign to you and your heirs and successors, kings of Castile and Leon, forever, together with all their dominions, cities, camps, places, and villages, and all rights, jurisdictions, and appurtenances, all islands and mainlands found and to be found, discovered and to be discovered towards the west and south, by drawing and establishing a line from the Arctic pole, namely the north, to the Antarctic pole, namely the south, no matter whether the said mainlands and islands are found and to be found in the direction of India or towards any other quarter .... And we make, appoint, and depute you and your said heirs and successors lords of them with full and free power, authority, and jurisdiction of every kind ... Moreover we command you in virtue of holy obedience that, employing all due diligence in the premises, as you also promise—nor do we doubt your compliance therein in accordance with your loyalty and royal greatness of spirit—you should appoint to the aforesaid mainlands and islands worthy, God- fearing, learned, skilled, and expeienced men, in order to instruct the aforesaid inhabitants and residents in the Catholic faith and train them in good morals ... We trust in Him from whom empires and governments and all good things proceed, that, should you, with the Lord's guidance, pursue this holy and praiseworthy undertaking, in a short while your hardships and endeavors will attain the most felicitious result, to the happiness and glory of all Christendom. Given at Rome, at St. Peter's, in the year of the incarnation of our Lord one thousand four hundred and ninety-three, the fourth of May, and the first year of our pontificate.

Notes: Translation from https://www.gilderlehrman.org/history-resources/spotlight-primary-source/doctrine-discovery-1493

Notes

1. Quoted in Noel Mostert, *Frontiers: The Epic of South Africa's Creation and the Tragedy of the Xhosa People* (New York: Alfred A. Knopf, 1992), pp. 1181, 1187.
2. Cecilia Morgan, *Building Better Britains? Settler Societies in the British World, 1783–1920* (Toronto: University of Toronto Press, 2016).
3. Robin D.G. Kelley, "The Rest of Us: Rethinking Settler and Native," *American Quarterly*, Vol. 69, No. 2 (June 2017), pp. 267–76, p. 269.
4. "The Doctrine of Discovery, 1493," The Gilder Lehrman Institute of American History Collection. https://www.gilderlehrman.org/history-resources/spotlight-primary-source/doctrine-discovery-1493.
5. Lorenzo Veracini, *Settler Colonialism* (Basingstoke: Palgrave Macmillan, 2010), p. 3.
6. "The Doctrine of Discovery, 1493."
7. Quoted in Jonathan Crossen, "Another Wave of Anti-Colonialism: The Origins of Indigenous Internationalism," *Canadian Journal of History/Annales canadiennes d'histoire*, Vol. 52, No. 3 (2017), pp. 533–59, pp. 545, 546.

Further Reading

Jonathan Crossen, "Another Wave of Anti-Colonialism: The Origins of Indigenous Internationalism," *Canadian Journal of History/Annales canadiennes d'histoire*, Vol. 52, No. 3 (2017), pp. 533–59.
Robin D.G. Kelley, "The Rest of Us: Rethinking Settler and Native," *American Quarterly*, Vol. 69, No. 2 (June 2017), pp. 267–76.
Steffi Retzlaff, "What's in a Name? The Politics of Labelling and Native Identity Constructions," *Canadian Journal of Native Studies*, [s. l.], Vol. 25, No. 2 (2005), pp. 609–26.
Lorenzo Veracini, *Settler Colonialism* (Basingstoke: Palgrave Macmillan, 2010).
Patrick Wolfe, "Settler Colonialism and the Elimination of the Native," *Journal of Genocide Research*, Vol. 8, No. 4 (2006), pp. 387–409. https://doi.org/10.1080/14623520601056240

2

The Colonization of Ireland, 1530–1780s

In 1586, Grace O'Malley mounted the scaffold built purposely for her execution by the English governor of the Irish province of Connaght, Sir Richard Bingham. Considering her to be "a notable traitress and the nurse of all rebellions in the province for forty years," Bingham charged O'Malley with rebellion against the English crown and "drawing in of Scots" to aid in that rebellion. Some tales have it that he had had the rope placed around her neck when suddenly his hand was stayed at the last moment by a mounted messenger carrying orders from Queen Elizabeth to release O'Malley, "the most notorious woman on all the western coasts," as the infamously brutal and bloody-minded governor styled her. No doubt seething with frustration, Bingham let O'Malley go; within weeks, she and her extended clan members were back at it, bringing in Scots from Ulster province to resist English rule in Ireland.

Queen Elizabeth's reprieve of O'Malley's execution for seditious revolt against her very person seems illogical at best. Things become even more confusing for us when we learn that in 1593 O'Malley requested—and received—an audience with the queen to plead for protection against Bingham's depredations against her, and for the release of her son Tibbot, and her half-brother Donal, taken prisoner following the killing of her kinsman, Owen O'Flaherty, at the hands of the governor. She also requested an income to compensate for the loss of the cattle, horses, and ships Bingham's troops had seized, rendering her and her kin destitute. Following a discussion in Latin, the only language the two women shared, during which O'Malley pledged her loyalty to the crown, Elizabeth directed her privy council to look into Bingham's actions. Some weeks later, she ordered him to release Tibbot and Donal, and leave O'Malley in peace in return for her "many most earnest promises that she will, as long as she lives, continue a dutiful subject, yea, and will employ all her power to offend and prosecute any offender against us." She also instructed the governor to arrange a regular income for O'Malley from the funds paid by her sons to the English crown. We can only imagine Bingham's chagrin at the order that he "protect them to live in peace to enjoy their livelihoods."[1]

How to make sense of this complicated and seemingly contradictory set of relationships? On the one hand, Grace O'Malley fomented and engaged in active revolt against English rule in western Ireland. She and her family suffered mightily at the hands of English authorities during a number of rebellions. On the other, she seems to have provided those same English authorities with intelligence and assistance against other Irish rebels sufficient to earn leniency and even rewards from the English. Part of the explanation lies in the dynamics of the period during which she lived: English settlement of Irish lands was, in the late sixteenth century, sporadic and patchy, leaving open the opportunity for frequent challenges to English efforts to impose their laws, language, and culture on Irish lands and Irish people. Clans often took advantage of the English presence to enhance their positions against their Irish rivals or to protect their interests by temporarily siding with the interlopers. Shifting alliances and inter-clan conflicts occurred frequently, both facilitating and blocking English colonial settlement. It was not until the defeat of Irish rebels at the end of the Nine Years' War in 1603 that the English conquest of Ireland can be said to have been completed.

The relationships of the descendants of English settlers in Ireland to the Native peoples of the island changed dramatically and continually over time. What has tended to be portrayed as a constant, centuries-long conflict between "Irish Catholics" and "English Protestants" in fact involved many iterations of factions, sometimes working together against groups that might once have been in alliance with them. What did remain constant in the period under consideration was dissatisfaction with, and often resistance against, the English colonial regime in Ireland, though not necessarily the English monarch her- or himself.

***

In the twelfth century, England's Henry II seized Ireland and rendered it a "lordship" of the English crown. Led by descendants of the Normans who had conquered Anglo-Saxon England in 1066, English lords set up a number of towns in the provinces of Connacht and Ulster and from their positions of strength there, compelled the Native Gaelic population to pay rents for the lands it worked. This settlement did not last very long: economic and demographic crises combined with military defeats in the late thirteenth and early fourteenth centuries to drive out the English lords. The disasters of the Black Death in the mid-fourteenth century sealed their fate, and Native Irish lords re-established themselves in the lands they had lost to the English. The small number of English who had managed to hold on to their lands became almost fully integrated into Gaelic society and culture. In Galway on the west coast, by contrast, and towns in eastern Ulster province, and in areas around Dublin, the English maintained their domination. The four counties next to Dublin became known collectively as the English Pale. From Dublin, English royal officials taxed and administered the lands that surrounded it. The local populations of Native Irish continued to speak Gaelic and practice Gaelic customs.

When in 1182 Henry declared Ireland a lordship of the crown, he imposed a legal code that explicitly differentiated the English settlers from the Native Gaelic Irish. Irish were not considered subjects of the king; they were "aliens," and as such, outside the protection of the law. That meant that they could not own land, hold governmental or ecclesiastical office, or avail themselves of the royal courts to protect their interests. Bylaws in the towns and cities went even further to distinguish English from Irish: they forbade the wearing of Gaelic dress, limited the admission of Irish to municipalities, and went so far as to expel Irish from cities such as Dublin, which occurred in 1454. In 1494, "Poynings' Law" subordinated the Irish parliament to the English parliament and the English crown. Try as they might, however, the English could not stamp out the stubborn persistence of Gaelic culture, even among the descendants of English settlers, especially in regions far from Dublin. Intermarriage between them and Native Irish, the adoption of Gaelic customs, and even the use of the Irish language among the English characterized late-fifteenth-century settler society outside the Pale and excited much negative comment among English circles.

The situation changed dramatically in the 1530s, when Henry VIII declared England's separation from the Roman Catholic Church. The Native Gaelic Irish, and, importantly, the English descendants of the Norman conquerors, refused to follow the king into Protestantism, remaining adamantly Catholic. People began to speak of two factions of English in Ireland, the Protestant New English and the Catholic Old English. In 1541, fearful that the Catholic powers of Spain and France might use Ireland as a launching pad for an invasion of heretical England, Henry declared himself King of Ireland and began the process of bringing the country under the administrative control of England. The laws imported under Henry II that distinguished between English subjects and Irish "aliens" remained in place formally, but because the Native Irish were now to be considered subjects of the king, they were invited to realize their new status under a policy known as "surrender and regrant." That is, those Gaelic lords who had been able to hold on to their land could declare their submission to the crown and, in return, receive from the king a new grant of land under English law. Sometimes, as in the case of Conn O'Neill, they also received a noble title; O'Neill became the Earl of Tyrone, holding the largest estate in the province of Ulster (see Figure 1.1).

Henry's attempt to integrate the Native Irish into the Tudor state fell short, largely because they would not relinquish their Catholicism. In a bid to secure their power in a now-Protestant state containing a largely Catholic

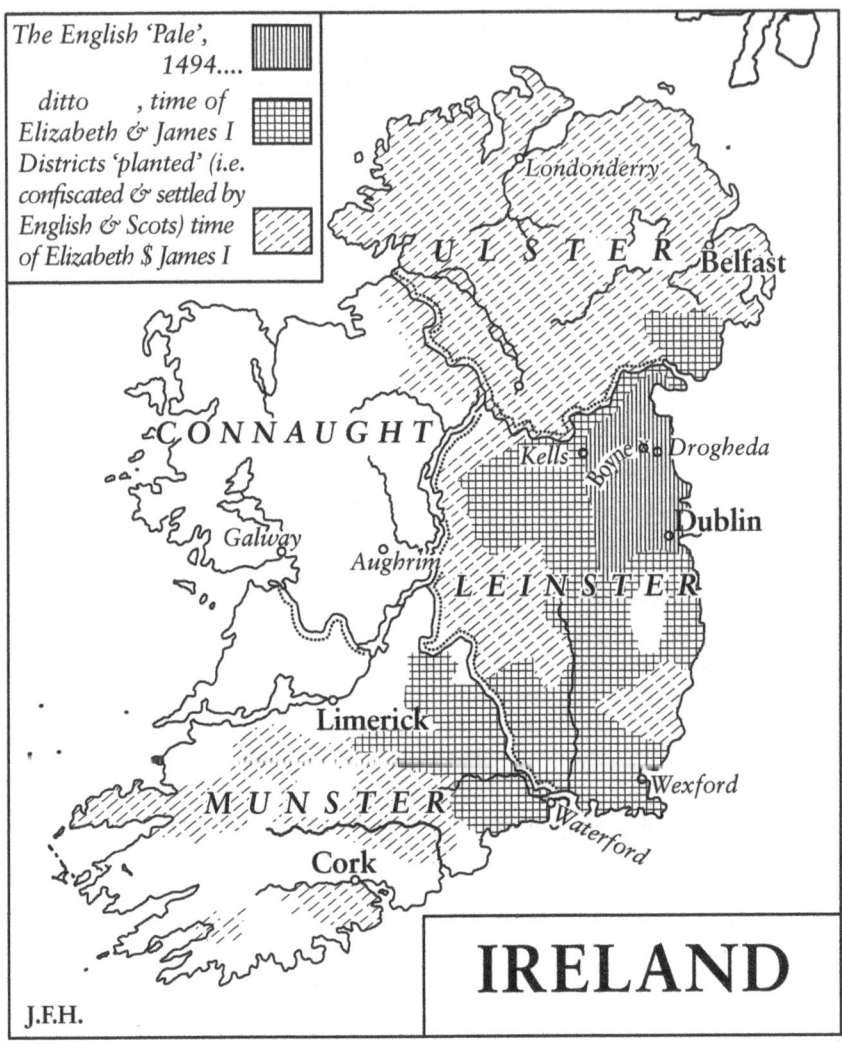

FIGURE 1.1 *Map of Ireland, sixteenth and early seventeenth centuries.*

population, he and his successor, Elizabeth I, established "plantations" of loyal Protestant followers in Ireland, massacring Catholics, confiscating their lands, and granting them to English colonists. In 1565, Elizabeth's government declared its intention to extend English control over all of Ireland, not simply those areas of the Pale. She appointed Sir Henry Sidney as lord deputy of Ireland; he, along with her favorite, Robert Dudley, Earl of Leicester, immediately set out to colonize the provinces of Ulster and Muenster. Eight years later, in 1573, Walter Devereau, First Earl of Essex, brought his considerable resources to bear in Ulster. Although Elizabeth had directed them all to ensure that the Native Irish be "well used," Essex, in particular, chafed under her restrictions. His troops drove Irish men and women into the woods in wintertime, where it was clear that they would starve or die from the cold. One of Essex's lieutenants, Edward Barkley, allowed as "how godly a dede it is to overthrowe so wicked a race the world may judge: for my part I thinke there canot be a greater sacryfice to God."[2] At Christmastime in 1574, Essex's men killed 200 followers of a local ruler, Sir Brian McPhelim O'Neill; O'Neill and his wife and some of their relatives were later executed in Dublin. Sir Humphrey Gilbert, military governor of Muenster, possessed of the powers of martial law, ordered the slaughter of any "manne, woman and childe" who resisted English rule. He commanded

> That the heddes of all of those (of what sort soever thei were) which were killed in the daie, should be cutte of from their bodies and brought to the place where he incamped at night, and should there be laied on the ground by eche side of the waie ledying into his owne tente so that none could come into his tente for any cause but commonly he must pass through a lane of heddes which he used *ad terrorem*, the dedde feelying nothyng the more paines thereby: and yet did it bring greate terrour to the people when thei sawe the heddes of their dedde fathers, brother, children, kinsfolke and friends, lye on the grounde before their faces, as thei came to speake with the said collonell.[3]

The English justified their depredations against the Irish by portraying them as barbarous, primitive, pagan people whose country it was the responsibility of the English to "inhabit and reform." The English regarded enclosure and cultivation of the land as an important feature of civilization; it would become a significant aspect of settlers' justification for the seizure of land in the Americas, Australasia, and southern Africa. The practice among Irish peasants of moving with their cattle to seasonal pasturage, known as transhumance, proved to English settlers that the Irish could only be considered barbaric. One commentator described Irish society as a collection of people living like "beastes, void of lawe and all good order"; they were, he asserted, "more uncivill, more uncleanly, more barbarous and more brutish in their customs and demeanures, then [sic] in any other part of the world that is known." Just as the Romans had once brought civilization to a backward, uncivil, and uncouth England, declared Sir Thomas Smith, so too would the English persuade the Irish to engage "in vertuous labour and in justice, and ... teach them our English lawes and civilitie and leave robbyng and stealing and killyng one of another."[4]

The Irish were dirty, violent, dishonest people who lived under inequitable and unjust laws, the English claimed. The "wild shamrock manners"[5] of women, in particular, both shocked and titillated English travel writers, who saw in their refusal to wear corsets an intentional assertion of sexual invitation. Because Irish women partook of strong drink, presided over public feasts, and greeted strangers with a kiss; because their marriage laws permitted them to retain their names upon marriage and to divorce their husbands with relative ease and material support; because Irish custom permitted sexual relations within degrees of kin affinity far closer than those constituted by either English law or the Catholic clergy, English writers concluded that the women of Ireland held positions of authority over men at home and in public. Unmanly men and aggressive, sensualized, licentious women, they insisted, characterized social relations in Ireland, undermining good order and necessitating English intervention if civilization were ever to be established there. English observations of Irish culture and society contained frequent mention of exotic sexual activities and unconventional gender arrangements in languages of sexuality and gender that would later serve to legitimate the English conquest of Native peoples in the Americas. Catholic Ireland served as a model of Indigenous peoples in need of British "civilization."[6]

The seizure of Irish lands and the slaughter of Irish men, women, and children sparked violent resistance. The earls of Desmond led a revolt in the 1580s, supported by the Spanish, but it failed to dislodge the English. Instead, Queen Elizabeth seized the lands of the rebels and settled some 4,000 English on ninety formerly Irish estates. She stipulated that all those holding the confiscated lands must be English born and must take on as tenant farmers only those who "descended of an English name and ancestor."[7] These new settlers did not have much time to consolidate their gains, as rebellion led by Hugh O'Neill, Earl of Tyrone, spread across a good part of Ireland in the 1590s. In the course of what has come to be called the Nine Years' War, Irish rebels prevailed at the Battle of Clontibret in 1595 and at the Battle of the Yellow Ford in 1598, but they were unable to oust the English, even with Spanish support. Following the siege of Kinsale in 1601–2, they had to concede defeat. Soon the English gained control over the entirety of Ireland, marking the end of the Gaelic order in Ireland. As if to punctuate the collapse, O'Neill and a great many other Gaelic lords and their armed servitors fled to the continent in 1607, in what has been styled the flight of the earls; their hopes of returning to recover their lands and positions never materialized.

The Nine Years' War proved devastating. It cost the English some 30,000 lives, a number far exceeded by Irish deaths. Perhaps as many as 60,000 Irish men and women died famine-related deaths in Ulster alone; historians believe that a total of 100,000 Irish deaths is well within reason. The economic impact proved equally damaging. Despite the natural gifts of climate and fertility the country possessed, Ireland could barely feed itself. The great majority of the population, living almost entirely in rural areas, faced starvation on a regular basis. Their diet consisted of milk, cakes made of oats, and potatoes, which had been introduced in the late 1500s from the Americas by Spanish fishermen who had dried their catch on the western coast of the island. The tuber quickly became a mainstay. Irish peasants worked the unimproved fields of their landlords with rudimentary tools, eking out a barely sustainable existence in the good years. In the bad ones, which occurred with increasing frequency, they died in large numbers.

Upon Elizabeth's death in 1603, James VI of Scotland succeeded her, becoming James I of England. James continued the Tudor practice of settling colonists in Ireland: in what is known as the Plantation of Ulster, he ousted Gaelic landowners in five counties in the northern reaches of Ireland and transferred the land to Scottish and English Protestants. More than 10,000 Scots ultimately came to settle in Ulster province. English officials sought purposefully to segregate the province along ethnic and religious lines: they gave 40 percent of the land to English and Scottish settlers who were directed to place only English, Welsh, or Scottish tenants on their lands. Some 12 percent of the area, largely located on the peripheries of the province, was given over to soldiers and royal officials as a reward for their service in the Nine Years' War. These so-called "servitors" were given leave to tenant their lands with Native Irish, if they so chose. Another 20 percent of the territory was granted to Native Irish lords who had not rebelled against the English, but the estates they received were located far away from the lands their families had held in the past. English officials hit upon this policy both as a means to ensure that Gaelic elites could not re-establish or consolidate their traditional power bases in the province and to physically separate Irish lords and tenants from English and Scottish settlers. State-sponsored plantation combined with the unprompted migration of Britons to northern Ireland to dramatically alter the ethnic complexion of the region. By the 1630s, some 80,000 Protestants had settled in Ulster. Altogether by that time, Ireland's population reached perhaps one million people. The Gaelic Irish constituted the vast majority of them, followed in number by the Old English descendants of the Norman invaders, the New English Protestant settlers from the plantations of the Tudors and the Stuarts, and Scottish Presbyterians. Almost half of the settlers, English as well as Scottish, were women.

Intense divisions plagued the country, preventing the kind of economic growth seen in England and parts of Lowland Scotland. Seventy-five percent of the Irish people worshipped as Catholics; they lived predominantly in the provinces of Leinster, Munster, and Connacht, where they made up 95 percent of the population. The remaining 25 percent counted themselves Protestant, either Anglican (the established Church of England and of Ireland) or Presbyterian. Protestants comprised half the population in Ulster province, and probably half of those were Presbyterian. Almost half of the landowners were Protestant, having gained their estates through the forcible and violent confiscation of Irish Catholic property. Almost 40 percent of the land was owned by Protestants. In contrast, most of those who worked the land were Catholic, some of whom had once owned the property they now had to lease from their hated landlords. Thus, economic and political power was inextricably entwined with religious divisions, to the benefit of Protestants. Some dispossessed Catholics turned to banditry as a way to express their rage and rebellion against Protestants. Landlords often found themselves isolated in a sea of hostile Catholics who spoke a language they could not understand and harbored long-standing and deep-seated resentments. They had little incentive to try to improve agriculture or better the conditions of their angry tenants.

The province of Ulster proved the exception to this rule. There, Presbyterian landowners worked to bring agriculture into the capitalist system, growing food for market and increasing their output wherever they could. They invigorated the cattle trade and raised sheep and grew flax for woolen and linen manufacture. Ulster prosperity facilitated the growth of towns there, as did a regular flow of goods, ideas, and people between the northern counties of Ireland and Lowland Scotland, a mere thirteen miles away across the Irish Sea.

Even amidst formal divisions, however, accommodations between the four groups that made up the Irish population could be found. Gaelic elites still held a variety of offices—those of sheriff, justice of the peace, and member of parliament—even in Ulster; their families interacted socially and even intermarried with New Protestant elites. Lower down the social scale, settlers and Native Irish lived amongst one another in urban areas. Perhaps most importantly for what was to come, Irish and Old English lords, who shared a common Catholic identity, began to soften their animosities toward one another, in part through social intercourse and in part owing to the actions of English administration. In 1628, England found itself at war with France and Spain. Strapped for cash and seeking it among Irish elites, Charles I issued what came to be called the "Graces," a number of concessions to Catholics that, among other things, protected Old English lands from being confiscated by royal officials. The very next year, however, peace between England and the continental powers allowed Charles to delay putting the "Graces" into effect, an action that deeply embittered Catholic elites, Irish as well as Old English. The appointment in 1632 of Thomas Wentworth as lord deputy caused further resentment: he threatened Catholics with additional seizures of land for plantations of Protestants and disregarded their presence in parliament. Gradually, the Old English elites joined with the Native Catholic lords in resentment against their English overlords.

In 1637, Scottish Presbyterians rebelled against Charles I's efforts to impose Anglicanism on Scotland, setting off what would come to be called the War of the Three Kingdoms. Two years later, Wentworth declared martial law in Ireland in order to forestall any spread of Scottish revolt across the Irish Sea to Ulster. His actions, combined with economic distress, the continued loss of Catholic lands, diminished influence in parliament, and ongoing persecution of Catholics at the hands of the English administration, finally provoked the Irish to revolt. In late October 1641, Sir Phelim O'Neill, a Gaelic landowner, justice of the peace, and member of parliament, led his armed followers to the home of Sir Toby Caulfield, the governor of Charlemont Fort in County Armagh, and took it over, setting off a war against English colonial rule that would last for more than ten years. The spark set off by O'Neill's raid spread rebellion throughout Ulster and Leinster provinces, which soon reached Munster province as well. Led by Native Irish lords who declared fidelity to Charles, the rebels insisted that their actions derived from unfair policies enacted by royal officials serving as colonial masters, and should not be construed as a rising against the king. Tenant farmers and wage laborers working the land of Protestant landlords joined the Gaelic elite; driven by poverty and their many grievances against the settler population, they began to attack Protestants, especially those in Ulster.

What began as attacks on property soon turned lethal. In one of the worst incidents of Native Irish violence against settlers, Protestants were massacred in County Armagh in November 1641. One hundred lost their lives in the initial assault; those who could sought to escape to far-off garrison towns but were regularly preyed upon by local rebels, who took whatever food and clothing they were carrying. Some 5,000 Protestants died on the side of the road from starvation and exposure to the elements. An equal number of Catholics lost their lives to reprisals committed by royal forces. For the colonial administration responded to the rebellion with fury, directing attacks against not just insurgent Catholics but also against Catholics in general. As the lords justice—deputies to the governor of Ireland—declared after O'Neill's raid on Charlemont Fort, the treachery was the action of "evil affected Irish papists." The Catholic Old English protested their innocence vociferously, in one instance petitioning the king to condemn his colonial administrators for failing to distinguish rebellious Catholics from peaceable ones. They cited the case of innocent Catholics in Dublin who had been "murdered in their beds, and many hanged by martial law without cause." Many, Gaelic and Old English alike, feared that the indiscriminate violence against Catholics indicated "that the extirpation of the Catholic religion and the nation, not the punishment of men's particular crimes, was the end [the colonial administration] aimed at."[8]

Fed by decades of stories about wild, savage, barbarian Irish Catholics, the English government sent ten thousand English and Scottish troops to Ireland to put down the rebellion. The lords justice gave them leave to "execute to death or otherwise by martial law any pillager, or any rebel or traitor," conflating combatants with civilians and putting the latter at great risk of death. The lords particularly trained their sights on priests and on women, whom they regarded as "being manifestly very deep in the guilt of this rebellion, and, as we are informed, very forward to stir up their husbands, friends and kindred."[9] Atrocities against Irish Catholics of all walks of life made it difficult to believe the lords justice's adamant declarations that they did not intend to exterminate the entire Irish nation. The conviction that that was precisely what they did have in mind led the Old English to bury their centuries-old antagonisms against the Gaelic Irish and join with the Native Irish rebels in a confederacy in defense of their property, their religion, and their lives at the hands of English and Scottish soldiers. Faced with greater insurgency now, the English government sent more troops in 1647. At Dungan's Hill, near Dublin, English forces massacred between three and five thousand Catholics.

At the end of January in 1649, parliamentary forces in England led by Oliver Cromwell executed King Charles I after years of civil war there between royalists and parliamentarians struggling for supremacy in the governing of their country. The victory of Cromwell's armies left parliament in the hands of some of the most extreme Protestants, men determined to subdue Catholic Ireland and take revenge on those who had massacred Protestants in County Armagh in 1641. Cromwell landed in Ireland in August 1649, and marched his troops to Drogheda, some 30 miles north of Dublin, in early September. He laid siege to the town and began bombarding it on September 8. Two days later, more than 2,500 Catholic officers and men lay dead; the number of civilians killed in the massacre is not known. As Cromwell explained, "our men ... were ordered by me to put them all to the sword ... being in the heat of the action, I forbade them to spare any that were in arms in the town." His army moved on to Wexford soon thereafter, massacring troops and civilians there as well. "The blood lust of soldiers flooded the streets and houses," one clergyman noted in a report.[10] Ireland's Catholic forces could not withstand the might of Cromwell's armies. A decade of war between Native Irish Catholics and settler English and Scottish Protestants devastated the country. Some 20 percent of the Irish population perished from fighting, disease, and/ or famine, a figure that far outweighs the 3 percent who were lost during England's decade of civil war. Farms were destroyed, villages and towns reduced to rubble. Ireland could not feed itself and became dependent upon imports from abroad.

The parliament at Westminster passed an Act of Settlement in 1652, stripping all Catholic landowners of all or part of their lands and exiling them to Connacht. Cromwell's government used the confiscated lands to repay so-called "adventurers," men who had loaned it money to prosecute the war against Charles, and to reward soldiers who had fought on the side of parliament. As it turned out, many of the beneficiaries sold their newly received lands to others rather than move to Ireland to occupy their holdings, but some 200 adventurers did take possession of their estates, while about 7,500 soldiers did likewise. When he came to the throne following the restoration of the monarchy in 1660, King Charles II upheld Cromwell's settlement in the so-called "Gracious Declaration," leaving Protestants in possession of 80 percent of Ireland's land. Only in Connacht did Irish Catholics elites continue to own land. Protestants also dominated in the towns and cities, places where Old English Catholics had once prevailed.

In 1660, following twenty tumultuous years of civil war and revolution that involved the beheading of a king, military conquest of Ireland and Scotland, the creation of a republican form of government, and the abolition of the Church of England and of parliament, English elites asked Charles II to return to the throne. The restoration of the monarchy included, perforce, that of the Church of England as well, an act that had serious repercussions for dissenting and nonconformist congregations. Charles's failed attempts to impose toleration for Catholics and nonconforming Protestants through royal prerogative did little to soften the persecution against those who refused to swear an oath to the Anglican Church. Religion continued to play a central role in questions of governance, especially as people suspected that Charles, having spent his formative years in the royal court of France, had come to embrace Catholicism, if only in the privacy of his own quarters. Charles's brother, James, openly practiced Catholicism, creating anxiety and consternation among the political classes of England.

In Ireland, an Act of Settlement threatened civilians and soldiers who had rebelled in 1641 with execution. Catholic soldiers fled to the continent but local groups of insurgents continued to operate against English and Scottish forces. Unable to put down these armed bands, the colonial administration ordered the disarming of all Catholics thoughout Ireland; it also relocated peasants and farmers in the countryside into small villages of thirty families each, a measure designed to keep them under observation and control. The Act of Settlement also envisaged the execution of all Catholic clergy; in the event, however, most of them ended up in exile instead.

Upon the death of Charles II in 1685, James II ascended the throne of England and Scotland. As he had no son to succeed him, and as both of his daughters by his first wife, Mary and Anne, were committed Protestants, James was perceived to pose no permanent threat to the Protestant nation. Eager to prevent any recurrence of another civil war, MPs swallowed their fears and agreed to let things take their course, confident that a Protestant succession would follow upon James's death. But then, in January 1688, the court announced that James's wife of fifteen years, Mary of Modena, was pregnant, shocking all of James's subjects. The potential of a Catholic heir now loomed ominously, compelling a group of parliamentary leaders to bury their political differences at the prospect of an unlimited Catholic line of succession if the baby were to be a boy. They began to hatch a plan to invite William, Prince of Orange, the husband of the Protestant Mary, to invade England, oust James, and set himself upon the throne. At the same time, rumors that the queen's pregnancy was fraudulent began to circulate, claiming alternately that her "great belly" was fake. In what became known as the warming pan scandal of 1688, Queen Mary was accused of having had her newborn son smuggled into her bedchamber in a warming pan rather than having given birth to him herself. The Prince of Wales's birth provided a powerful justification for William's invasion of England, allowing him to defend the hereditary rights of his wife Mary to succession. As he asserted in his 1688 *Declaration ... of the Reasons Inducing him to Appear in Arms in the Kingdom of England*, "the just and visible grounds of suspicion [that] the Pretended Prince of Wales was not born by the Queen" compelled him to act.[11] The Glorious Revolution set off by the birth of a Catholic heir to the throne would have momentous consequences for all of the lands encompassed by the British empire.

In Ireland, news of William's landing in November 1688 sparked a protracted and bloody civil war between factions organized along religious lines. By this time, some two million people inhabited the island, a large majority of whom were Catholic. Perhaps 25 percent of the Irish counted themselves as Protestants, and among those were a large number of Presbyterians of Scottish heritage living in the northern counties of Ulster province. Protestants of the established Church of Ireland regarded themselves as the English-in-Ireland, or the Anglo-Irish, as historians have come to call them, and it was only the common threat of Catholicism that bound the two sectarian groups together. Protestants had felt themselves under threat in the years of James II's reign, as he imposed Catholic administrators and military commanders on the country and instituted land policies that gave Catholics land formerly held by Protestants. The predominance of Catholic power in Ireland in the three years preceding the Glorious Revolution strongly influenced the response of Protestants to William's invasion of England.

Catholic Ireland gave its loyalty to James. In the countryside, poverty-stricken Catholic farmers rose against their Protestant landlords, killing thousands of cattle. Protestants in Derry (which Protestants always called Londonderry) in Ulster closed the city gates against the army led by the Catholic Earl of Tyrconnel and declared their allegiance to the Prince of Orange. Irish Protestants in London persuaded William that a promise to give land confiscated from the Catholics to Protestants would supply him with an eager military force with which to confront the Catholic rebels, a move that forced the compromise-minded Tyrconnel to turn to France for assistance. By March 1689, when James returned to Ireland from France, Tyrconnel had placed virtually all of Ireland outside Ulster under Catholic administration.

James sought to make his stand against William from Ireland, which he regarded as the jumping off point from which to secure Scotland. His attitude towards Irish Catholics, despite his own Catholicism, proved ambivalent, as he needed to present a reasonable face to English and Scottish Protestants if he hoped to regain his throne. That and his own interests led him to resist many of the efforts of Irish Catholics in the Irish parliament of 1689 to restore the Catholic Church to a position of supremacy or to separate the country from England. His hopes of reconciliation with Protestants created a great many anxieties for his Catholic supporters. In the meantime, in Derry, 30,000 Protestants determined to withstand a siege by Jacobite forces (so-called because *Jacobus* is the Latin term for James). For three months the Derry Protestants held their ground, staving off starvation by consuming the dog, cat, and rat population of the city, until they were relieved by forces loyal to William.

In August 1689, a Williamite army of some 20,000 led by the German Protestant Marshal Schomberg arrived in Ireland, causing tensions between Catholics and Protestants in Dublin to intensify. But little military confrontation ensued throughout the fall and winter, as weather conditions made it difficult for both the Jacobite and Williamite armies to successfully position themselves. In the spring of 1690, French troops reinforced James's army; frustrated by the inaction of his general, William himself landed near Belfast in June with 15,000 additional soldiers, intent upon defeating his rival once and for all. The armies met at the Boyne river, northwest of Dublin, on July 1, 1690. After extensive bombardment and fierce hand-to-hand fighting, William's forces prevailed, sending James's troops—and James himself— scurrying south. James's commanders fired on their soldiers in order to regain control and establish an orderly retreat, though James continued his headlong flight, overnighting in Dublin on his way to Duncannon, whence he embarked to France, never to return to his kingdoms. War continued without him, though the Battle of the Boyne has been seen as the decisive campaign in the Jacobite wars against William. Dublin fell to the new king, as did Athlone a year later, which opened up Galway to English depredations. The final battle between Jacobite and Williamite troops took place in Aughrim in July 1691, resulting in horrific casualties for the Irish army. Retreating to Limerick, where it could still assemble a force of 20,000, the soldiers awaited French aid. When it was not forthcoming, the Jacobites, more demoralized than defeated, sued for peace. The Treaty of Limerick, signed on October 3, 1691, ended the conflict between Ireland and England.

Three distinct groups emerged from the maelstrom of late-seventeenth-century politics as they played out in Ireland: a minority Episcopalian elite that looked toward England and established itself as the Anglo-Irish Ascendancy; a minority Presbyterian culture, deeply suspicious of the established Episcopal Church and the Anglo-Irish Ascendancy, that looked to Presbyterian Scotland for inspiration and support; and a Catholic, Gaelic majority that looked toward France for its redemption. The established and dissenting Protestants had joined forces against Catholicism during the Glorious Revolution, but once William and Mary's victory was secured, fissures among the two groups reappeared, and it wouldn't be long before the dissenting Presbyterians found themselves at a disadvantage relative to Episcopalians under the law and in holding political and administrative offices. In many respects, they were treated not much better than Irish Catholics, who were subjected to harsh penal laws designed to ensure that they would never again threaten Anglo-Irish interests.

Protestants' relations with England often did not go smoothly. Appointments of Englishmen rather than Anglo-Irishmen to prominent positions in the Irish established church, the legal system, and the armed forces, and the granting of Irish peerages to Englishmen who had no relationship with the country caused deep resentment among the Anglo-Irish. England's viceroy to Ireland, Henry Sidney, reported with alarm in 1692 that Irish MPs spoke of "freeing themselves from the yoke of England, of taking away Poynings' Law, of making an address to have a habeas corpus bill, and twenty other extravagant discourses."[12] (Poynings' Law of 1494, as we saw earlier, had subordinated the Irish parliament to that of Westminster.) Commercial interests in England regarded Ireland as a threat to their trade, and were sufficiently well placed to push through legislation in 1696 that prohibited goods of any kind from the American colonies from landing in Ireland. England treated Ireland not as a partner or a sister kingdom, but as a colony. It rankled.

In 1697, two events provoked a showdown between the Irish and English parliaments. In the first instance, MPs representing the woolen manufacturers in the West Country of England introduced a bill that would make it difficult for the Irish wool traders to export their goods to England. In the second, England questioned the right of the Irish House of Lords to act as an appellate body, as it did in England. These provocations led the Bishop of Derry to declare that England had reduced Ireland to a state of slavery; they also compelled MP William Molyneux to write *The Case of Ireland's being Bound by Acts of Parliament in England Stated*, in which he argued that if union with England could not be achieved ("an Happiness we can hardly hope for"[13]), Irish parliamentary rights must be strengthened and protected. Ireland should not be lumped in with those "colonies of outcasts in America," he insisted;[14] rather, it should be recognized as a crucial component within England's empire, an equal to England, with Irish representation in the English parliament as a means of defending Irish interests. Molyneux's treatise raised the hackles of the English, who pretended to hear in his writings a call for separation from England. They painted him and those many others who thought the same way he did with the brush of "independency" and "Jacobitism," levying charges that the Anglo-Irish could not possibly allow to stand. Though support for Molyneux's position was fairly widespread, the Anglo-Irish community backed off from his demands.

The union of England and Scotland in 1707 added insult to injury, striking Protestant Ireland like a hammer blow. Protestants, especially the Episcopal Anglo-Irish, would have dearly loved to form a union with England. Jonathan Swift (1667–1745), the Anglo-Irish satirist, penned *The Story of the Injured Lady, Being a true Picture of Scotch Perfidy, Irish Poverty, and English Partiality* in response to the slap in the face he and others experienced with the Act of Union. For now, in light of the Scottish and English union, Ireland looked more and more like a colony, a position the Anglo-Irish could do little to improve. Conflicts and contests between the two parliaments continued, until in 1720, with the Declaratory Act— "An Act for better securing the dependency of Ireland"—the now-British parliament explicitly established that it had every power to enact legislation for Ireland. As it turned out, the Declaratory Act was rarely invoked, as Westminster knew very well that Ireland could not be governed by force; a significant amount of cooperation from the Anglo-Irish was necessary for things to run as smoothly as they did after 1720. Nevertheless, the Anglo-Irish sense of wounded pride, economic deprivation, political oppression, and cultural disrespect remained high throughout the eighteenth century.

The Anglo-Irish who so resented their colonial status vis-à-vis England established their own colonial-style rule over Catholic and, to a lesser extent, Presbyterian Irish men and women. The Anglo-Irish Ascendancy secured both power and wealth in Ireland on the basis of a penal code directed at Catholics, which over time came also to be applied to dissenting Presbyterians. The penal code emerged from a number of laws passed by the Irish and English parliaments between 1695 and 1704: in 1695, the Irish parliament made it illegal for Catholics to own a horse worth more than £5, to carry firearms, or to attend foreign universities; two years later, it banished Catholic clergy from the country and made intermarriage between a Protestant and a Catholic grounds for disinheriting the Protestant under the law. In 1704, an English Act "to prevent the further growth of popery" extended the English law that forbade Catholics to buy or inherit real estate to Ireland; it abolished the rights of Catholics to inherit from each other; and it prohibited them from taking up a profession or participating in public life. "Test" clauses in the act made it impossible for Catholics—or for dissenters—to hold office. Catholics also lost ownership of their land under laws finalizing the Treaty of Limerick in 1703: while they constituted between 75–80 percent of the population, they owned only 14 percent of the land. Fifty years later, that figure would fall to 5 percent.

The penal code probably sought more to destroy Catholic economic power than to eliminate "popery." The prohibition against priests, for example, was softened by the 1704 act's tacit recognition of them in the clause that required them to be registered, and Irish people of all faiths resisted "priest-catching," even though it carried a monetary reward. And one could always find a priest saying mass on any given Sunday in the myriad mass-houses that existed across the country. But whatever the Anglo-Irish motives, the Catholic Irish never ceased to consider themselves a colonized people whose fortunes were governed by a cruel imperial master of alien culture and religion. Nor did the English or the Anglo-Irish conceive of them in anything other than these terms.

The deprivations inflicted upon the mass of Irish peasantry propelled an outbreak of widespread rural unrest by people known as Houghers in 1711 and 1712; across five western counties of the country, a determined group conducted a campaign of slaughter of cattle and sheep belonging to stockholders who took peasant land to pasture their animals. In the 1720s and 1730s, anti-tax riots and assaults upon tax collectors occurred in all four of Ireland's provinces. By and large, however, the Irish peasantry remained relatively quiet in the first half of the eighteenth century, despite poor economic conditions and actual famine in the 1740s. That changed in 1761, when a series of peasant risings, known as the Whiteboy movement, broke out; named after the white smocks participants wore over their jackets, the revolt catalyzed the establishment of agrarian unrest as an almost permanent condition of late-eighteenth-century Irish life.

The Whiteboys, comprised largely of landless and land-poor men and women, first appeared in Tipperary in the fall of 1761; soon thereafter other branches of the movement sprang up in surrounding counties. Obliged to pay heavy tithes for their potatoes and kicked off common lands they had long been accustomed to using to grow crops by landlords who now wished to graze their livestock on it, hard-pressed and dispossessed peasants gathered at night, took loyalty oaths to one another, armed themselves with whatever weapons they could amass, and set out to vandalize or destroy property of those responsible for their plight. They knocked down fences and gates, tore up hedgerows, broke up fields to make them useless for grazing, cut down fruit trees, and burned manor houses. They would appear at the site of evictions, 100 or more strong, to prevent their neighbors from being thrown off land they had worked for decades; if unsuccessful in that effort, they would threaten and intimidate the new occupants of the farm until they left. Mobs of them would seize the horses, cattle, and tools of tenants being sold for non-payment of rent. Sometimes they went after people, intimidating them with kidnapping and threats of violence, and eventually actually committing it against their persons. Whiteboys might seize a particularly egregious target of their grievance, beat him, and bury him up to his neck in a pit of briars. Rarely did they kill offenders outright, but when they did, as in the murder of a well-connected magistrate, Ambrose Power in November of 1775, they provoked the incandescent wrath of the Anglo-Irish Ascendancy.

Up to that time, authorities could do little to stem the Whiteboy movement, despite passing legislation that made any number of actions a capital offense. The Whiteboy Act of 1765 failed to quell the rising, largely owing to a lack of witnesses willing to testify against them and because local jurors either would not convict or would treat the charges as falling outside of the act, and therefore not subject to the death penalty. Official ineffectiveness buoyed Whiteboy morale and spurred them to greater efforts. In 1775, however, the tide began to turn. Dublin Castle ordered more troops to southeastern Ireland, where the rebellion was still in full swing; locally, targets of Whiteboy violence started to fight back, literally, forming volunteer militias to move against the rebels. In County Wexford, the proctor of Killann and his brother killed and wounded a number of Whiteboys as they were attacking their house, prompting one observer to comment, wryly, that a "few such warm receptions [would] have a greater effect on the minds of the lower classes than hanging them up by dozens." But hang them up by dozens the Ascendancy did, especially after the murder of Power, hoping that the spectacle of public hanging accompanied by the drawing and quartering of rebels would deter the Whiteboys from further actions. "After hanging for a few moments," recorded an official who watched one such proceeding against two rebels, "they were cut down whilst life still remained, after which they were quartered and beheaded, the streets being lined by three troops of the 2d regiment of horse, three companies of foot and all the gentlemen of the county ... properly armed."[15]

Legislation that strengthened magistrates' hands; increased military presence; and the emergence of volunteer militias organized and captained by the landed gentry proved effective in hamstringing the Whiteboy movement after 1775. Because these measures were not accompanied by any changes in land policy that might have addressed the difficulties faced by the Irish peasantry, however, they would not prevent further agrarian violence from re-emerging in the 1780s and 1790s, as we will see in Chapter 4.

Counterpoint: New Spain

Two decades before Henry VIII of England declared himself King of Ireland and began planting Protestants there, the Spanish conquistador, Hernán de Cortés, conquered the lands in Central America that would be called New Spain. In the course of his bloody campaigns against a number of Indigenous empires such as the Aztecs, he amassed great riches, while his soldiers received little in the way of payment for their efforts. They made known their unhappiness with this state of affairs in no uncertain terms, and he had little choice but to accede to their demands for payment. They received *encomiendas*—grants not of land, which the crown reserved for itself, but of tribute and labor from Indian people. *Encomenderos*, as these recipients of the grants were called, were expected to protect and to Christianize their Indigenous workers, but few of them took that obligation seriously. Instead, looking to raise their social station to the level of "lords of vassals," most of them exploited Indian people mercilessly, often enslaving them and seizing their lands. These first settlers in New Spain sought not to become farmers; on the contrary, they aimed to establish themselves as gentlemen of wealth and leisure, not unlike the English owners of Irish estates. The status of these settlers as lords depended upon the labor of the Indigenous people. It also depended on the dispossession of Indians from their land, a process made infinitely easier by the near-total annihilation of them through diseases introduced by Europeans. Prior to the arrival of Columbus in the "new world," at least 25 million Indigenous people populated the central regions of New Spain, according to scholars' estimates. By the early part of the seventeenth century, fewer than a million remained, a staggering decrease of 95 percent. The exploitation and abuse of Indian people contributed to the decline as well, and those who survived often left their communities and farms and pastures in order to escape rough treatment at the hands of the new settlers, who seized the abandoned lands for themselves.

As late as 1650 or so, Indians still possessed 44 percent of New Spain's territory, while Spanish settlers held 26 percent of it (the crown owned the rest of the land, which was largely desert or highlands). But over the next century and a half, when New Spain won its independence and became Mexico, Indian land-holding fell to only about 8 percent of Mexico's total territory. Conflicts over land gave rise to frequent uprisings, as Indian people sought redress for their grievances. In the seventeenth century, eight serious revolts took place, especially in the northern frontier areas where settlers were few. The 1680 Pueblo revolt in modern-day New Mexico left twenty-one Franciscan missionaries and more than 400 settlers dead.

The demise of the Indigenous population of New Spain left settlers without the labor force they required to work their plantations, ranches, and mines. Spaniards turned to enslaved Africans to replace it; some 200,000 of them arrived in New Spain between the 1540s and the 1820s, when the colonial period ended. As Indian people became increasingly immune to European diseases, their numbers began to recover. By 1620, in fact, Indigenous people began to increase in number, though not sufficiently to reestablish themselves as dominant, as they would remain in places like Guatemala and Bolivia. In every colony we treat in this book, sexual abuse carried out by settlers produced a mixed-race population; in New Spain, the absence of Spanish women until well into the seventeenth century allowed for especially aggressive male sexual behavior that continued long after their arrival. As a result, New Spain featured a disproportionately large mixed-race population. In general terms, society consisted of Spaniards (who never amounted to more than 20 percent of the total population), mixed-race men and women (called *castas*), Indians, and Blacks, but so complex was the demographic breakdown that one estimate claims that sixteen different racial categories existed in the years following conquest. As decades passed, race mixing became ubiquitous until it was difficult to discern racial makeup; most settlers were categorized simply as *castas*.

New Spain differed from Ireland and subsequent Anglo-American settler colonies in the efforts by the metropolitan and colonial governments to incorporate Indigenous people into the general life of the colony. Even while Indian land was being seized by settlers, the Spanish government officially recognized Indian ownership of lands they placed in cultivation. Officials turned to Indian elites to organize labor for agricultural production and the operation of mines, and to establish order among Indian communities. High-status Indian women might marry into Spanish families, bringing land and labor with them. Over time, Spaniards became less dependent on Indian elites, whose social status then often declined, but the increasingly central place of the Catholic Church in the lives of Indian people generally brought a kind of integration of Indians into New Spain's social order that would not be matched anywhere in the Anglo-American settler world.

Primary Source Document

Irish Penal Laws

English Statute 1 Ann c.26 (1702):

An Act for the Relief of the Protestant Purchasers of the forfeited Estates in Ireland

Sec. 7: *To the end that none of the aforesaid purchased forfeited estates may ever descend to any Papist but shall remain to be held and enjoyed by Protestants for the strengthening of the English interest and Protestant religion,* if any person educated in the popish religion, or professing the same, and being under the age of 18, shall not, within 6 months of attaining the age of 18, take the oaths of allegiance and supremacy, and the declaration against transubstantiation in the courts of Chancery or Kings-bench in England or Ireland, or in the quarter-sessions where such person shall reside, and continue to be a protestants, such person in respect of himself only, and not his heirs or posterity, shall be disabled to take by decent, devise, or limitation, any of the forfeited estates purchased in Ireland, and during the life of such person, or until he shall take the oaths etc., the protestant next of kin shall enjoy the premises.

English Statute 1 Ann c.26 (1702):

An Act for the Relief of the Protestant Purchasers of the forfeited Estates in Ireland

Sec. 8: Such papist shall also be disabled to purchase any of the forfeited premises, and all estates and interests in the premises for the benefit of such person shall be void.

English Statute 1 Ann c.26 (1702):

An Act for the Relief of the Protestant Purchasers of the forfeited Estates in Ireland

Sec. 9. All leases of the said forfeited estates shall be made to such persons only as are of the protestant religion, and any lease made to or in trust for any papist shall be void, and both the person making such lease and the person for whose benefit the lease shall be made, shall forfeit treble the yearly value of the lands, one half to her Majesty, the other to such protestant who will sue for the same.

English Statute 1 Ann c.26 (1702):

An Act for the Relief of the Protestant Purchasers of the forfeited Estates in Ireland

Sec. 10. Nothing in this act shall make void any lease of any cottage or cabin under the yearly value of 30 shillings to any day-labourer.

English Statute 1 Ann c.26 (1702):

An Act for the Relief of the Protestant Purchasers of the forfeited Estates in Ireland

Sec. 15. No papist, during the time of his professing the popish religion, shall be capable to inherit, take or enjoy any other forfeited estates or interest therein, and if any person educated in the popish religion, or professing the same, shall not, within 6 months after the accruing of his title, or of attaining the age of 18, take the oaths of allegiance and supremacy, and the declaration against transubstantiation in the courts of Chancery or Kings-bench in England or Ireland, or in the quarter-sessions where such person shall reside, and continue to be a protestants, such person in respect of himself only, and not his heirs or posterity, shall be disabled to inherit or take any of the premises, or any trust or interest in the same, and during the life of such person, or until he shall take the oaths etc., the next of kindred who shall be a protestant, shall enjoy the premises.

English Statute 1 Ann c.26 (1702):

An Act for the Relief of the Protestant Purchasers of the forfeited Estates in Ireland

Sec. 16–17. All leases of any of the premises shall be made to protestants and none other, and any lease made to or in trust for any papist shall be void, and both the person making such lease and the person for whose benefit the lease shall be made, shall forfeit treble the yearly value of the lands, one half to her Majesty, the other half to such protestant who will sue for the same. Same proviso excepting cottages.

English Statute 1 Ann c.26 (1702):

An Act for the Relief of the Protestant Purchasers of the forfeited Estates in Ireland

Sec. 20. In all acts which have passed this session of parliament relating to the forfeited estates in Ireland, which injoin the taking the oaths of allegiance, the person injoined to take oaths of allegiance, shall be obliged at the same time to take the oath of supremacy, under the like penalties.

English Statute 1 Ann c.26 (1702):

An Act for the Relief of the Protestant Purchasers of the forfeited Estates in Ireland

Sec. 21. There shall not be let with any cabin or cottage to any day labourer (as by any act of this session relating to the forfeited estates in Ireland is permitted) above 2 acres of land, and not above one cottage or cabin with such land to any one day-labourer. Or such lease will be void, and both the person making and the person taking such lease, or occupying such cottage or lands, shall forfeit treble the yearly value, to be recovered and distributed as any other penalties by the said acts.

2 Ann c.6 (1703):

An Act to prevent the further Growth of Popery

Sec. 6. Every papist shall be disabled to purchase any lands, or any rents or profits of lands, or any lease of lands, other than for a term not exceeding 31 years, whereon a rent not less than two thirds of the improved yearly value, at the time of making such lease, shall be reserved during such term.

And all estates or terms or other interests acquired after the 24th of March, 1703, other than such 31-year leases, by or on behalf of papists, shall be void.

2 Ann c.6 (1703):

An Act to prevent the further Growth of Popery

Sec. 7. No papist shall inherit or take any other interests in land owned by a Protestant, unless the papist shall conform to the protestant religion within six months of the time at which he would be entitled to said lands. But during the life of such papist the nearest protestant relation shall enjoy such land without being accountable for the profits, subject only to charges for the maintenance of the children of such disabled papist as the chancellor shall see fit to allow until they reach the age of 18.

2 Ann c.6 (1703):

An Act to prevent the further Growth of Popery

Sec. 8. Provided that if any papist that would be entitled to the same by virtue of this act, or the disability of another papist, shall afterwards become protestant, and continue as such, he shall be intitled to enjoyment of the land as he would have been if he had been a protestant when the disability fell on such other papist. And the person enjoying the same may lease the land, or any part thereof, for 21 years or less, without fine, reserving the best improved rent that can be got, but if such person commit waste on the said lands, the disabled party may recover damages for the waste.

2 Ann c.6 (1703):

An Act to prevent the further Growth of Popery

Sec. 9. Provided that the protestant wife of such disabled papist shall have her dower and thirds as at common law.

2 Ann c.6 (1703):

An Act to prevent the further Growth of Popery

Sec. 10. All lands owned by a papist, and not sold during his lifetime for valuable consideration, really and bona fide paid, shall descend in gavelkind, that is to all of his sons, share and share alike, and not to the eldest son only, and lacking sons, to all his daughters, and lacking issue, to all kin of the papist's father in equal degree, etc.; notwithstanding any grant, settlement or disposition made by such papist, by will or otherwise, subject however to all debts and incumbrances charging such estate.

2 Ann c.6 (1703):

An Act to prevent the further Growth of Popery

Sec. 11. Provided such papist may charge his estate with reasonable maintenances and portions for his daughters.

2 Ann c.6 (1703):

An Act to prevent the further Growth of Popery

Sec. 12. If the eldest son or heir at law of a papist be a protestant at the time of the decease of such papist, the lands of the papist shall descend to that eldest son or heir at law according to the rules of the common law, provided that the bishop's certificate of his being protestant be enrolled within 3 months after the decease of such papist,

And if that eldest son or heir at law become a protestant within one year after the decease of such papist, he shall be entitled to the real estate of such papist, as he might have done had he been a protestant at the time of such papist's decease.

And the estate shall be chargeable with such sums for the maintenance and portions of the daughters and younger sons of such papist as the court of chancery shall appoint, not to exceed the value of one third of the estate.

2 Ann c.6 (1703):

An Act to prevent the further Growth of Popery

Sec. 13. Provided that such lands, during such time as any protestant shall be seized thereof in fee-simple or fee-tail, shall from such protestant be descendable according to the rules of the common law.

2 Ann c.6 (1703):

An Act to prevent the further Growth of Popery

Sec. 14. All debts and incumbrances that a papist may contract to encumber his real estate must be publicly recorded in the court of exchequer within six months after the making thereof, or the same shall not encumber the estate during such time as it shall belong to a protestant.

2 Ann c.6 (1703):

An Act to prevent the further Growth of Popery

Sec. 23 and 28. No papists shall take or purchase any house or tenement or inhabit the cities of Limerick and Galway, or the suburbs thereof, and all papists now inhabiting said cities or suburbs, shall before the 24th of March next ensuing before the chief magistrate become bound to her Majesty with two sufficient sureties, in a reasonable penal sum to be set by the chief magistrate, sheriff or recorder, with condition of faithfully bearing himself toward her Majesty, and in default of giving such security, such papists shall depart from the said city before the 24th of March, 1705. Provided that seamen, fishermen, and day labourers in houses worth 40 shillings a year or less are excepted.

Notes

1 This vignette is drawn from Judith Cook, *Pirate Queen: The Life of Grace O'Malley, The True Story of the Legendary Rebel* (Edinburgh: Birlinn, 2021; originally published 2004), pp. ix, x, 154–7.
2 Quoted in Nicholas Canny, "Ideology of English Colonization: From Ireland to America," *The William and Mary Quarterly*, Vol. 30, No. 4 (October 1973), pp. 580, 581.
3 Canny, "Ideology of English Colonization," p. 582.
4 Quoted in Thomas Metcalf, *The New Cambridge History of India, III: Ideologies of the Raj* (Cambridge: Cambridge University Press, 1994), p. 2.
5 See R.F. Foster, *Modern Ireland, 1600–1972* (London: Penguin, 1989).
6 Quoted in Richard Ned Lebow, *White Britain and Black Ireland: The Influence of Stereotypes on Colonial Policy* (Philadelphia: Institute for the Study of Human Issues, 1976), p. 41.
7 Quoted in S.J. Connolly, "Settler Colonialism in Ireland from the English Conquest to the Nineteenth Century," in Edward Cavanagh and Lorenzo Veracini, eds., *The Routledge Handbook of the History of Settler Colonialism* (London: Routledge, 2017), p. 53.
8 Quoted in Micheál Ó Siochrú, *God's Executioner: Oliver Cromwell and the Conquest of Ireland* (London: Faber and Faber, 2008), p. 26.
9 Quoted in Ó Siochrú, *God's Executioner*, p. 31.
10 Quoted in Ó Siochrú, *God's Executioner*, pp. 84, 97.
11 From Robert Beddard, ed., *A Kingdom Without a King: The Journal of the Provisional Government in the Revolution of 1688* (Oxford: Phaidon Press, 1988), pp. 124–8, 145–9.
12 Quoted in R.F. Foster, *Modern Ireland, 1600–1972* (London: Penguin, 1988), p. 161.
13 Quoted in Jacqueline Hill, "Ireland Without Union: Molyneux and His Legacy," in John Robertson, ed., *A Union for Empire. Political Thought and the British Union of 1707* (Cambridge: Cambridge University Press, 1995), p. 277.
14 Quoted in Thomas Bartlett, "Ireland, Empire, and Union, 1690–1801," in Kevin Kenny, ed., *Ireland and the British Empire* (New York: Oxford University Press, 2004), p. 70.
15 Quoted in J.S. Donnelly, "Irish Agrarian Rebellion: The Whiteboys of 1769–76," *Proceedings of the Royal Irish Academy: Archaeology, Culture, History, Literature*, Vol. 83C (1983), pp. 324, 327.

Further Reading

Nicholas Canny, "Ideology of English Colonization: From Ireland to America," *The William and Mary Quarterly*, Vol. 30, No. 4 (October 1973), pp. 575–98.

S.J. Connolly, "Settler Colonialism in Ireland from the English Conquest to the Nineteenth Century," in Edward Cavanagh and Lorenzo Veracini, eds., *The Routledge Handbook of the History of Settler Colonialism* (London: Routledge, 2017), pp. 49–64.

John Patrick Montano, *The Roots of English Colonialism in Ireland* (Cambridge: Cambridge University Press, 2011).

Micheál Ó Siochrú, *God's Executioner: Oliver Cromwell and the Conquest of Ireland* (London: Faber and Faber, 2008).

Jane H. Ohlmeyer, "Civilizinge of those Rude Partes: Colonization within Britain and Ireland, 1580s–1640s," in Nicholas Canny, ed., *The Oxford History of the British Empire, Volume 1: The Origins of Empire, British Overseas Enterprise to the Close of the Seventeenth Century* (Oxford: Oxford University Press, 1998).

3

The Decimation of Indian Peoples in Colonial North America, 1607–1783

On June 27, 1689, four Penacook women made their way to four different garrisoned homes in Cochecho, near Dover, New Hampshire. They asked for shelter for the night, a request made frequently enough by local Indian people that it aroused no comment or suspicion. Early the next morning, each of the women opened the doors of their respective dwelling places to hundreds of warriors led by their sagamore (chief) Kancamagus, who proceeded to massacre the English settlers within. The Penacook men paid particular attention to Major Richard Waldron, one of the town's most prominent citizens, visiting terrible violence upon him and mutilating his body. Over the course of the day, twenty-three settlers lost their lives; another twenty-nine fell captive to the Penacooks. Many of the latter were sold to the French in Montreal. In the short space of a single day, fifty years of generally amicable dealings between Native Americans and white settlers came to a bitter and bloody end. Dover lost fully a quarter of its settler population and its inhabitants' relationship with Native people would never be the same again.

What came to be called the Cochecho massacre was a revenge attack more than a decade in the making. Thirteen years earlier, in 1676, Kancamagus and other Penacooks had witnessed an act of betrayal by Waldron that festered within them for years. In nearby Massachusetts, King Philip's war against English settlers had been raging for more than a year. Some 200 Wampanoag people seeking to escape the violence and threat of capture by the English moved north to the area around Cochecho, setting up a small community among the Penacooks, with whom they were friendly. On September 8, 1676, two companies of Massachusetts soldiers arrived to capture the refugee Wampanoags. Waldron, an officer in the local militia and the town's representative to the General Assembly in Boston, faced a dilemma. He had just signed a pact of non-violence with the Penacook sagamore Wonalancet but was duty-bound to accede to the orders of the Massachusetts governor to give up the Wampanoags living among them. He devised a plan that he believed would resolve his difficulty. In the short run it worked, but it would ultimately lead to his torture and death.

Waldron invited the Native Americans to engage in a friendly mock battle against the Massachusetts and Cochecho militias. While the warriors prepared for "battle" in a field just outside of town, the militia companies, including that commanded by Waldron, encircled and captured them. The Penacooks were allowed to go free; the young Kancamagus and other Penacooks watched in dismay as the Massachusetts militia marched 200 Wampanoags to Boston. There they were hanged or sold into slavery.

Waldron believed he had hit upon a righteous solution; the Penacooks felt otherwise. They saw his actions as a betrayal of their allies, a perception aided by prior experiences with the prominent settler. He had been accused in the past of selling liquor to the local Indian people and was widely believed to place his thumb on the scale when trading with the Penacooks. Kancamagus and his followers had reason to believe the worst of Waldron and the settlers in the Dover area, especially as encroachments on their lands by English settlers continued apace in subsequent years. Tensions between Native Americans and European newcomers increased markedly in the 1680s, until the Penacooks could tolerate no more depradations. When the time came to exact their revenge in 1689, they singled out Waldron as an especial target of their anger. After they forced him to fall on his sword, they made their particular displeasure with his cheating known by cutting off the offending hand that had disadvantaged them in their commercial dealings with him.

The story of the Cochecho massacre offers a concise picture of virtually all of the elements that characterized settler colonialism in North America between 1607 and 1783. Indian/settler relations started off fairly peaceably, with both sides gaining advantages from the other. Without the help of Native peoples, in fact, the Jamestown and Plymouth colonists would not have made it. Over time their relationships soured, as more English arrived and pushed aggressively on to Native lands. Disease, violence, and then war broke out in both Virginia and New England, devastating tribal populations and requiring surviving individuals to seek community and belonging with other Native groups, a process historians call ethnogenesis. As we've just seen, Indian people resisted stoutly and often successfully, but ultimately, all of the ills white settlers inflicted upon Native peoples, which included enslavement, brought about their demise.

***

Many of the figures behind efforts to colonize North America cut their teeth in Ireland. Some of them, like Sir Walter Raleigh, who was instrumental in establishing the failed colony of Roanoke in the 1580s, played crucial roles in the implementation of the Irish plantation schemes. Others, such as the merchant Thomas Smythe, invested financially in colonial undertakings in Ireland and North America, while still others, like Thomas Hariot and Theodore De Bry, provided through their writings the justifications for taking Native American lands by comparing the Indigenous peoples to Irish Catholics. The experiences of settler colonialism in Ireland, in other words, provided templates, models, and the language for the settling of the North American continent.

The first (ultimately) successful English settlement began its life in 1607, when some 100 colonists came ashore at Chesepiooc, a Powhatan town on "a big river" that the English would name after their king, James I.[1] Recruited and sponsored by the Virginia Company, a joint-stock commercial venture out of London, the colonists initially appeared non-threatening to the Native inhabitants of the area. The fact that all of them were men implied that they were there to trade, something that appealed intensely to the Powhatan leader, Wahunsenacawh, who eagerly sought the firearms the English possessed. Wahunsenacawh presided over a vast territory stretching from the Atlantic Ocean to the Appalachians; he commanded the fealty of some 15,000 people and expected the same kind of deference to his authority from the new arrivals. Instead, the colonists immediately set about building a fortified settlement and sent out emissaries to a number of surrounding Powhatan villages, seeking to ally with them. Their actions constituted a challenge to Wahunsenacawh's leadership, which the paramount chief could not allow to stand.

Wahunsenacawh sent 200 warriors to capture Captain John Smith and two other colonists. He ordered the deaths of the other two, and ritually "killed" Smith with a simulated clubbing; his daughter, who has come down to us as Pocahontas, then ritually brought Smith back to life, symbolically bringing the Englishman and his followers into kinship with the Powhatan. Smith read the ritual as a sign of "how well Powhatan loved and respected me," but the chief was of a different mind. He regarded the ceremony as an act that incorporated the English into his larger empire and facilitated the trade in goods—fabrics, copper and iron goods, beads, and, above all, guns—that would enhance his control over his sprawling domain.[2]

The colonists had chosen an inauspicious place to establish their settlement. Located on a peninsula that seemed to them to offer effective defense against any enemies—Spanish or Indian—that might seek to attack them, the site instead isolated them from gaining access to the inland hunting grounds that might have sustained them. For the colonists would not work, not even to grow the corn to keep themselves from starving: they had come to the New World to enrich themselves, not to do manual labor. The salty water of the James River produced agonizing intestinal distress, while mosquitos carrying malaria plagued them in the summer months. Before 1607 was out, all but thirty-eight of the original 100 colonists had perished from disease and starvation. The Virginia Company sent out more settlers, but nothing changed. Over the next two years, during the so-called "starving time" of 1609–10, colonists who eschewed work for searching for precious metals were compelled to feed on horses, cats, rats, and dogs. (In 2022, archeologists found the DNA of ancient Indigenous dogs among the remains of the Jamestown dead, indicating that dogs living among the local Indian peoples had either been shared with or stolen by the colonists in their efforts to stay alive.) Still the settlers balked at providing for themselves, leading Smith to lament, "There was no talk, no hope, no work, but dig gold, wash gold, refine gold, load gold."[3] In these circumstances, it is perhaps not surprising that some settlers turned to cannibalism. As George Percy, one of Jamestown's leaders, described the horrifying situation, "And now famine beginning to look ghastly and pale in every face that nothing was spared to maintain life and to do those things which seem incredible, as to dig up dead corpses out of graves and to eat them, and some have licked up the blood which hath fallen from their weak fellows. And among the rest this was most lamentable, that one of our colony murdered his wife, ripped the child out of her womb and threw it into the river, and after chopped the mother in pieces and salted her for his food."[4] Percy had the offender executed.

The Virginia Company sent more colonists in 1612, who fared no better and behaved worse than their predecessors. Their depredations against the Powhatan peoples seemingly knew no bounds: they murdered children and adults alike, destroyed villages, and put Indian cornfields to the flame. Their actions shocked and disgusted many of their countrymen, who joined the Powhatan in order to dissociate themselves from such savagery. Settlement leaders ordered that these English malcontents be tracked down and burnt at the stake or crushed by an execution wheel. Fearful that the Powhatan would retaliate, the English took Wahunsenacawh's beloved Pocahontas captive and held her hostage until an agreement with the chief could be secured. She was married off to a Jamestown settler, John Rolfe. In return for peace, Wahunsenacawh gained access to a variety of trade goods that he and others coveted, including liquor. Rolfe, auspiciously, began to grow a strain of tobacco that found favor back in England, a development that would assure the success of the flailing colony.

Tobacco transformed the Jamestown project from a sinkhole of men and treasure into a going venture. Having spent large amounts of capital on the failed search for gold and silver, the Virginia Company sought to take advantage of the demand for the stimulant by sending young men—and women now, too—to permanently settle the colony. Hundreds of settlers arrived over the next few years, along with their pigs and cows; by 1620, the settler population reached 1,000. More than half of the new arrivals were indentured servants who had contracted with sponsors to provide four to five years of servitude in return for their passage to the colony. In 1619, the first enslaved Africans were brought to the colony to work the tobacco fields, producing a yield of 370,000 pounds of the lucrative commodity. Former indentured servants who had fulfilled their contracts and newly arrived immigrants seeking to enhance their share of the trade in tobacco invaded and seized Powhatan lands, burning villages and slaughtering Native peoples who stood in their path. English settlement grew apace, gobbling up the lands of the Indigenous peoples of the Tidewater region. Expansion roused deep resentment among the Powhatan, as did Virginia Company efforts to educate Native youths and to convert the Indian people to Christianity.

In 1622, the Powhatan, under the leadership of Wahunsenacawh's brother, Opechancanough, determined to end the English assaults on their lands, their livelihoods, and their lifeways. On March 21, a large group of them made their way to a number of English villages under the guise of friendly socializing with their neighbors. The next morning, in a coordinated attack, the Powhatans seized tools and weapons from the settlers and set upon their tormentors, killing nearly 350, fully a third of all the colonists. They crammed the mouths of the dead with bread in a message meant to warn the English not to "eat up all the land,"[5] and slaughtered the livestock that the settlers allowed to roam free through Powhatan fields, destroying their crops. Whatever sympathy settlers might have shown through efforts to educate and Christianize Powhatans immediately gave way to an impulse to exterminate them. As one English commentator put it, "conquering them is much more easier than of civilizing them by fair means."[6]

War ensued for the next ten years, with settlers destroying Powhatan crops in order to starve them and the Powhatans retaliating with guerrilla attacks on the English. In 1632, the antagonists established a tentative peace, but it broke down quickly under the continued seizure of Indian territory by land-hungry settlers. In 1644, Opechancanough, now nearly ninety years old, rallied one last attack on Jamestown, killing over 400 soldiers. With both sides exhausted, physically and materially, the newly established Virginia General Assembly in 1646 brokered a peace accord that ended hostilities. For the Powhatans, it marked the end of their existence as a coherent society; for the English, the defeat of the Powhatan empire confirmed them in their belief that God had destined them for the occupation and exploitation of the "New World."

Virginia continued to attract settlers from England, who were promised fifty acres of land there for immigrating. Most of them, however, could not afford the price of the Atlantic crossing, and were compelled to indenture themselves—in effect, mortgage themselves—to elite farmers in return for payment for their passage. Indentured servitude commonly entailed seven years of toil for no pay, but for impoverished Britons who could see no other prospect for improvement, the tradeoff was worth it. Upon gaining their release from servitude, immigrants scrambled to obtain land, hoping to make their living by growing tobacco or trading in furs with local Indians. By the early 1640s, however, tobacco prices had fallen to rock bottom, and the governor of Virginia, William Berkeley, sought to curb the creation of new tobacco farms in order to boost the price of the commodity. He also controlled the fur trade, limiting the possibilities for newcomers. New settlers, as a result, turned to the seizure of Indian lands as a means of achieving their dreams, which inevitably set up clashes between them and the Native Americans who inhabited the border regions of the Virginia colony.

Keeping the peace between settlers and Indians required the expenditure of scarce colonial resources. Berkeley sought to reduce conflict, and therefore costs, by recognizing the rights of friendly Native peoples to their land. In so doing he necessarily curtailed the land available to aspiring settlers, who seethed against his policies of protecting Indian people at their expense. Land-hunger spurred an already full-throated hatred of Native Americans to virulent extremes: before too long, settlers began to call for the extinction of all Indian people, making no distinction between friendly and hostile. In 1675, war broke out between the colony and Susquehanna peoples on Virginia's northern and western borders. Berkeley sought to contain the war to that area, but settlers, led by wealthy landowner Nathaniel Bacon, insisted on an all-out war against all Native people. Bacon accused Berkeley, his cousin by marriage, of failing Virginians through policies that "defended and protected" the "darling Indians," who were no more than "barbarous outlaws" and "delinquents," and of doing so contrary to the interests of "his Majesty's loyal subjects."[7] In 1676, in a defiant rebuke of Berkeley's authority, he led militia volunteers on a campaign of indiscriminate slaughter of any Indian people they could find. In one battle against the Ocaneechi, he recounted, "wee destroyed about 100 men and 2 of their kings, besides women & children," providing "satisfaction to the people."[8] When he couldn't find enemy Susquehannas or Ocaneechis, he set his sights on friendly Powhatan groups who posed no threat to Virginians. Supporters in the legislature aided the rebellion against British colonial authorities, passing laws making it legal to drive Indian people from their lands and to enslave them.

Then Bacon died suddenly, probably of dysentery, and the rebels crumpled. Berkeley hanged twenty-three of them and went back to London to face the wrath of royal officials. King Charles II replaced him with Colonel Herbert Jeffreys and an additional thousand British troops, who reestablished royal authority and brought order to the colony. Jeffreys held talks in 1677 with the remaining survivors of the Powhatan groups and in the Treaty of Middle Plantation pledged to protect them by drawing a three-mile cordon around every Indian settlement, within which settlers were banned. The treaty called upon the Powhatans to recognize the English king as their suzerain, but it also recognized that "each Indian King, and Queen have equal power to Govern their own people and none to have greater Power then [sic] other, except the Queen of Pamunkeys to whom several scattered Nations do now again own their ancient Subjection."[9]

Bacon's Rebellion has gone down in US history as a first instance of colonists' defiance of Britain in a line of events that would lead to the American Revolution. It has also been seen as a critical inflection point in the development of a racist society: shocked and alarmed by the prospect of a possible coalition of lower-class whites and enslaved Africans, elite planters ceased to use indentured servants to till their fields and turned exclusively to the African slave trade to provide their laborers. Certainly the rebellion had profound effects on the American colonies going forward. What we need to keep in mind is that it took place because and in a process of white settler conquest of Native American land and lifeways.

***

Where Jamestown had begun as a commercial venture and only after 1620 evolved into a colony of settlement, the English who landed in what would become the Plymouth colony in that year intended to establish a permanent settlement from the very start. In the dozen years before their arrival on the tip of Cape Cod, perhaps as many as 90 percent of the Native inhabitants had perished from diseases introduced by European fishermen and traders, against which the Indians lacked immunity. The Pilgrims thus came ashore to a landscape cleared of people and immediately chalked up their situation to the providential hand of God.

They thanked God again when they stumbled across corn supplies stashed by sick Wampanoag men and women who had died before they could consume them; without these foodstuffs, they would not have survived the winter. As it was, half of them died. In the spring, a Patuxet man named Squanto, who had been kidnapped earlier by a sea captain and returned to find that all of his people had perished from disease, showed the colonists how to plant corn. They did so on lands that had so recently been worked by Indians that the fields required little in the way of tilling. God, it seemed to the Pilgrims, had destined them to succeed in the "New World." Colonization proceeded apace: in 1629, Puritans established the Massachusetts Bay Colony, and between 1630 and 1633, in what historians have styled "the great migration," 3,000 settlers made their way to the area. They invoked their status as "chosen people" over and over in the next decades as they expanded further and further onto Indigenous lands, destroying Native hunting grounds, trampling Native croplands, undermining Native cultures, and, ultimately, destroying New England's Indigenous societies.

Indian people resisted settler depredations even as some tribes sought alliances with the English in order to protect themselves from their enemies. Massasoit, for instance, "great sachem" of the Wampanoags who had been significantly reduced in number by disease, allowed the Pilgrims to settle in Plymouth in hopes of recruiting them to his defense against the Narragansett and other Native peoples of the region. Through intermediaries like Squanto and an Eastern Abenaki sachem named Samoset, Massasoit negotiated a pact with the Plymouth settlers for mutual defense. He assumed that the agreement acknowledged the colonists' tributary status; the settlers, for their part, sought to make Massasoit and his people Christian subjects of England's King James. When the chief instead decried and scorned Christianity, Plymouth Colony governor William Bradford denounced the Wampanoags as evil savages.

As settlers sought more and more Indian land and a larger share of the trade in New England, they sometimes ran into obstacles that caused them to question their position in the eyes of God. This was especially so in the case of their failed efforts to subjugate the Pequot peoples of what would become Connecticut, a large confederacy that controlled the lucrative trade in furs and wampum. Try as they might, the Puritans could not force the Indian people they regarded as savage and sinful to bow to their demands or to cede commercial ground. In making it difficult to enlarge their land holdings or trade, it appeared that God was expressing his dissatisfaction with the Puritans. Then, in 1633, God revealed his plans for them, or so they thought, when a terrible smallpox epidemic struck New England, killing as many as 80 percent of the Indian people in the region. The Pequots, numbering some 30,000 or so, suffered an enormous loss, reducing their population to about 4,000 souls. Puritan settlers saw in the devastation God's hand at work, opening a path to subjugating the Connecticut Valley Indian communities to English rule. They demanded tribute payments and land along the commercially vibrant Mystic River, convinced that the weakened Pequots would have to give in. Colonists began filtering into Connecticut in 1634, establishing settlements; in their compromised state, the Pequots turned to their long-standing enemies, the Narragansetts, to form an alliance against the colonists' encroachments. The overture had the opposite effect, as the Narragansetts felt it necessary to ally, however reluctantly, with the English against their long-time foes.

Angered by continued settler expansion, the Pequots launched a series of raids on English towns and villages in 1637. John Winthrop, governor of the Massachusetts Bay Colony, beseeched the Plymouth colonists to join with him "against the common enemy, who, if he were not subdued, would prove as dangerous to them as to us, and, he prevailing, would cause all the Indians in the country to join to root out all the English." They did, and in the war that followed, the English, with Narragansetts and Mohegans at their side, fought with an uncommon brutality. Their campaign of violence peaked in May, when they launched a pre-dawn attack on a Pequot town on the Mystic River, setting it ablaze and killing nearly 400 Indians, most of them women, children, and old men. The ferocity of the attack shocked many of the colonists and upset their Indian allies, who protested "*mach it, mach it*; that is, it is naught, it is naught, because it is too furious, and slains too many men."[10] Following the massacre, the colonists tracked down whatever remaining Pequots they could find, killing the men and selling the women and children into slavery in the West Indies.

The Pequot War marked the end of the Pequot peoples. By the Treaty of Hartford of 1638 they lost their lands. Those who escaped death at the hands of the settlers became incorporated into the Narragansett or Mohegan communities. Settlers flooded into Connecticut, and in a burst of expansion, into New Hampshire and Rhode Island as well. By 1650 or so, the New England colonies could boast over forty towns with a population exceeding 23,000. Some of those towns had been established as "praying towns" by the Reverend John Eliot, who in 1644 began an effort to Christianize Indian people in and around the Massachusetts Bay Colony. Some Native men and women whose communities and lifeways had been devastated by European diseases and warfare found in Christianity a way forward. Membership in the praying towns required them to adopt "civilized" European practices, such as English methods of farming, dress, family organization, and gender roles. Many of the roughly 2,500 Indians who joined the mission towns by 1670 adapted by incorporating Christian ways into their traditional practices and beliefs.

Settlers continued to arrive in New England in the 1650s and 1660s, doubling the English population between 1650 and 1670 to 50,000. Disease, warfare, enslavement, and the disruption of Indigenous commerce and farming had reduced the number of Native peoples to about a third of the white population. As settlers poured in, in ever greater numbers, driving an economy that could compete now with that of London, they sought more and more land, pushing ever nearer to Indian villages and encroaching on Native cornfields. They insisted that because, as they saw it, Indian people failed to use the land properly by improving it, it was theirs for the taking. They cut down trees to clear the land for farming and to provide wood for fencing and for the burgeoning shipbuilding industry, denuding the forests and disrupting the habitats of the deer that Native Americans relied on for hunting. Perhaps most galling of all, the settlers' animals roamed freely across Indigenous cropland, their cattle and pigs ripping up fields that had taken Native women weeks to establish and cultivate. In earlier years, colonial governments would have required the owners of the beasts to pay for the damage; now, with settler/Native population differentials so great, they felt no need to do so. The Indian communities had no redress; the arrogance of the English settlers and the destruction of Indigenous lifeways finally reached a breaking point.

Under the leadership of Metacom, the Wampanoag son of Massasoit, who had welcomed the Pilgrims in 1620, a coalition of Indian groups prepared for war against the colonists. When in June 1675 the Wampanoags were ordered to surrender their weapons to Plymouth authorities, Metacom, known as Philip to the English, led an attack on Swansea, a town on Narragansett Bay. His forces killed dozens of settlers and then moved on to other towns around the bay. Raids turned into all-out war, as the violence proliferated inland and other Indigenous groups such as the Narragansetts and the Mohegans joined the Wampanoags in a larger effort to push the settlers out of New England altogether.

The fighting was bloody and savage. Half of all the English towns came under attack from the Indigenous forces; more than ten of them were totally destroyed. English troops seemed able to do little to repel the furious assaults of enraged Wampanoags and Narragansetts, and it looked as if the Native warriors might succeed in destroying English rule. Over the winter of 1675–6, however, the momentum shifted. The colonial soldiers turned to a kind of guerilla warfare, destroying Native crops and foodstuffs and weakening the Indigenous armies. The Mohawks joined the fight on the side of the English in the spring of 1676, attacking Metacom's forces from the west; their intervention allowed the colonists to successfully counter the Indian attacks, which they did with a vengeance. By late summer, what became known as King Philip's War had come to an end. A mission Indian man shot Metacom dead in August 1676; colonial authorities chopped off his head and mounted it on a watchtower at Plymouth, where it remained for another twenty-five years, a graphic symbol of the destruction of Indigenous political sovereignty.

New England's victory in King Philip's War owed much to the intervention on the settler side of Mohawk warriors, members of the Iroquois Five Nations Confederacy (also known as the Haudenosaunee, or "people of the completed longhouse") that dominated vast territory south of the Great Lakes when European settlers arrived. Indeed, Britain's alliances with the Confederacy—Seneca, Oneida, Mohawk, Cayuga, and Onondaga—ensured its ability to sustain its North American colonies and to prosper from its trade, especially as France sought to expand its own presence on the continent. Haudenosaunee power and influence also ensured that up until the outbreak of the American Revolution, Iroquois peoples fared fairly well in their dealings with settlers.

King Philip's War devastated New England, Indigenous and settler alike. Almost 70 percent of the Native population—at least 3,000 men, women, and children—died in the violence; another 2,000 Indians fled to other areas. Those who remained in New England found themselves in dire straits; some joined the praying towns, which became little more than dumping grounds for distressed Indian people. Hundreds of Native Americans became enslaved to West Indian planters. On the victors' side, 1,000 colonists and some 600 white soldiers were killed by Indian warriors. Over 1,000 settler homes were lost, and property damage in the raided towns reached unprecedented levels: it would take until 1700 for the geographical area held by settlers prior to the war to again be inhabited. Such losses shocked and traumatized the Puritans, who had always been fearful that their piety might not meet their God's expectations. Now their anxieties skyrocketed, leading to a profound questioning of themselves and one another. Did the rage and savagery they had displayed during King Philip's War bespeak a dreadful lack of civility and morality? Could their failings be forgiven? Deep introspection gripped the mind of Puritan New England at the end of the seventeenth century, manifest in many written accounts of the conflict and in community campaigns to drive the devil out of their lives, the most notable taking place in Salem in the early 1690s.

***

The southeastern region of North America experienced its counterpart to King Philip's War and Bacon's Rebellion in the Tuscarora War of 1711–12 and the Yamasee War of 1715–16, which emerged out of settlers' involvement in slavery. The enslaving of Indian peoples constituted a key element of settler colonialism in North America from its earliest days. When colonial forces defeated Native Americans in war, as they did the Pequots in 1633, the Wampanoags in 1676, and the Powhatans in 1644 and 1676, English officials often sold the surviving men, women, and children into slavery, especially in the West Indies. Enslaving Indian people had multiple advantages, as the settlers saw things: it rid the lands of Native Americans, making it available to European settlers, and the profits garnered from the sale of human beings helped to offset the costs of war and expansion. To be sure, Indian people across North America had long engaged in the taking of captives, but more often than not they did so either to gain advantage from their foes through hostage-taking, to redress wrongs committed against them by their foes, or to replenish their ranks. The latter consideration, for example, drove the Iroquois peoples to conduct a wide-ranging series of "mourning wars" across the Great Lakes Region in order to replace the many thousands of Iroquois who had lost their lives to European diseases in the seventeenth century. Captivity generally did not render the subject a chattel slave, as it did in the North American and Caribbean systems of slavery.

The advent of settler colonialism changed the nature of Indigenous captive-taking in the late seventeenth and early eighteenth centuries, bringing it into a global network of trafficking in human beings and turning it into an all-out struggle between Native communities to enslave or be enslaved themselves. This was especially the case in the southeastern region of the American continent following the colonization of the Carolinas in 1670. The so-called "proprietors" who established the colony did not intend for it to become the hub of the Indian slave trade, but many of its settlers, elites hailing from Barbados who had benefited enormously from slavery and the slave trade there, almost immediately incorporated the territory and its Native American inhabitants into their networks. Indian traders who had engaged in a wide-ranging and lucrative commerce in deerskins with settlers were encouraged to shift their focus to capturing and selling Indigenous people instead, "commodities" that proved far more materially valuable on the global market. Carolina and other settler elites urged friendly Indian groups to wage war against other Native tribes in order to gain captives that could be sold into slavery; this strategy proved so effective that warfare soon became endemic in the area, as various tribes in alliance with settlers sought to gain from the all-encompassing violence.

The Tuscarora people resided in what is today North Carolina. They lived too far from the slave-trading center at Charleston to benefit from it themselves, but not far enough away to avoid being the object of raiding for slaves, which caused deep distress and hardship. When German and Swiss immigrants began to encroach on their lands, they fought back. In 1711 they attacked Europeans and killed over a hundred of them. South Carolinians turned to their Yamasee allies, and with their help laid waste to their Tuscarora rivals. By 1713, the Tuscarora peoples had lost over a thousand dead and some 700 enslaved; 2,500 of them escaped: homeless because virtually all of their villages had been burned to the ground, they became refugees, migrating north to New York and seeking safety and belonging with the Iroquois. The Tuscaroras became the sixth member of the Iroquois Confederacy.

Despite giving assistance to South Carolina in its war against the Tuscaroras, the Yamasees faced extreme difficulties of their own. They had lost a significant amount of territory under a 1707 Carolina law that seized their land, and now planters and cattle ranchers began to trespass on what remained. Many of them owed money to white traders, who often recouped their losses by enslaving their debtors. Under considerable pressure and believing they had few alternatives, Yamasees joined with Creek warriors and in 1715 went to war against the English, who were themselves aided by Cherokees. The Yamasee War proved deadly and devastating to Indian communities and settlers alike, depopulating vast regions of the southeast entirely. Some 7 percent of the British population of the Carolinas had been killed, while the surviving members of various Indian tribes were compelled to join together to form new communities. Three complex multiethnic groupings—the Cherokees, the Creeks, and the Choctaws—emerged from the wreckage of the early eighteenth century. The wars also destroyed the economy for many years, including the commerce in enslaved peoples. The Tuscarora and Yamasee Wars persuaded the surviving Indigenous peoples of the southeast to end their participation in the global slave trade, a decision that had much to do with the colonists' turn to African slavery almost exclusively.

***

By the early eighteenth century, the eastern seaboard of North America looked very different than it had some hundred years earlier when the first British colonists arrived. White settlement had expanded dramatically; in 1730, perhaps 600,000 British settlers lived on and farmed the lands formerly held by Native Americans (twenty years later, that number had doubled). Though gradations of wealth and status certainly existed, the settlers had, relatively speaking, prospered as a consequence of their involvement in a robust global trade. Though initially very much a part of that international trade—and benefiting from it—Indian people did not fare as well, as disease, warfare, reduced hunting grounds, and a voracious settler hunger for land vastly decreased their ranks and/or compelled their migration to new places. British settler colonialism had decimated Native populations, economies, societies, and cultures, necessitating a reconstituting of Native communities from the remnants of those individuals and groups that had survived the overall depredations. People known as "Iroquois," or "Creek," or "Cherokee" were in fact made up of a variety of ethnic groupings displaced in what historians came to call "the shatter zones" of the mid-Atlantic and southeastern regions of North America. Still, in the first half of the eighteenth century, they held their own—and were recognized as sovereign nations—by playing off the British, French, and Spanish empires against one another. In the context of an intense imperial rivalry, no European power could afford to offend potential Indian allies for very long. They needed their trade and they needed their warriors. For their part, Native communities depended heavily on Europeans purchasing their trade goods, especially furs.

At the same time, ironically, racial antagonisms were on the rise. Settler hatred of Indian peoples dated back to King Philip's War and Bacon's Rebellion in the 1670s; it grew more virulent as more colonists arrived seeking land and met with pushback from Indian communities resisting encroachment. Indigenous antipathy for whites was a more recent phenomenon, arising from a variety of Nativist renewal movements seeking to reestablish ancient rituals, ceremonies, and identities that had been lost in the chaos of the shatter zones. Especially in what were called Ohio Country—territory ranging from modern-day Pittsburgh through West Virginia, Kentucky, and eastern Ohio—and the *pays d'en haut*—an area incorporating Michigan, Wisconsin, northern Indiana, and northern Illinois, where French traders engaged with Native people on a daily basis—renewal movements sought to create a kind of pan-Indian unity that would bring dispossessed and hard-done-by communities together, reestablish a balance with the cosmos, and enable Indian people to eliminate Europeans from their lives altogether. Increased settler expansion out of Pennsylvania and Virginia only further heightened Nativist efforts to create a world without Europeans, driving up an already intense anti-settler sentiment.

The outcome of the war between the European empires that began in 1754 destroyed the imperial framework within which Native communities had been able to operate. Called the French and Indian War by Americans and the Seven Years' War by Europeans, it broke out first in North America in 1754 and then spread in 1756 to the European continent, the Mediterranean, West Africa, and India. American colonists had long feared the spread of French influence on the continent as they and their Indian allies ventured deeper into the interior; now, with the French building forts on the shores of the Great Lakes and along the Ohio River, concern turned into something resembling panic. In 1754, Virginia commissioned a militia troop under the direction of an inexperienced officer named George Washington to march north to modern-day Pittsburgh, where the French had ensconced themselves in Fort Duquesne. Washington's little force ill-advisedly attacked the entrenched French and Indian army and got itself captured, forcing Britain's hand. It had now to step in and take over what had become a war. Most of the Native peoples of the Ohio country sided with the French, taking advantage of French-supplied weapons to strike against settlers who had pushed them westward from the Pennsylvania and Virginia frontiers. In response, Pennsylvania authorities put a hefty cash bounty on the scalps of any Indian male over the age of ten, ratcheting up the violence and bloodshed.

In 1755 the newly appointed British prime minister, Lord Newcastle, dispatched the Royal Navy to the mouth of the St. Lawrence River in order to block the arrival of additional French troops, and ordered General Edward Braddock to Fort Duquesne to avenge the hapless Americans. Braddock's efforts proved no better than those of the colonists; he was killed in the July battle, and the blockade of the St. Lawrence largely failed, allowing French reinforcements to land in French Canada. Shortly thereafter, in an event that provides a sharp reminder that settler colonialism is an often protean phenomenon that cannot be said to have a universal character, the British embarked on a campaign that would result in the deportation of 7,000 French Canadians from Acadia, on the shores of the Bay of Fundy. The Acadians, who had inhabited their territory since the early 1600s, found themselves caught between a rock and a hard place when in 1713 the Treaty of Utrecht following the War of the Spanish Succession gave Nova Scotia to Britain. The British did little with the territory until 1749, when they established the town of Halifax at the end of the War of the Austrian Succession. Under the governorship of Edward Cornwallis, the British began to harass the French settlers in the region. Now situated between the British to the east and the French to the north, the Acadians tried to negotiate a neutral path between the belligerent powers, an effort that proved doomed to fail when British troops and Massachusetts militiamen invaded the small colony in August 1755. Over the next three years, they carried out a policy of terror, capturing and deporting every Acadian they could find. Wrested from their land and their homes and their livelihoods, Acadians, like thousands of Native Americans before them, found themselves refugees in a number of locations across the French-, Spanish-, and British-held worlds. The group most familiar to Americans landed in Spanish Louisiana, where later generations of Acadians became known as Cajuns.

The British and American settlers fared badly for the first few years of the Seven Years' War, suffering defeats at the hands of the French in Quebec. In late summer of 1758, however, they began to take French forts in the *pays d'en haut* and Ohio Country, forcing the Indian people there to agree to cease their attacks. In return, the so-called Easton Treaty of 1758 called for Pennsylvania to abandon its claims to land west of the Appalachian mountains. When Montreal fell to British-American forces in 1760, the American portion of the Seven Years' War effectively came to an end.

For Indian people who had been able to create some semblance of sovereignty and security against settler depredations by playing off one imperial power against the other, everything changed with the defeat of the French. No longer did the victorious British need to sustain friendly relations with Native Americans in order to counterbalance French incursions; they could dispense with the diplomatic efforts of the past and treat Indian people as subordinates rather than commercial or military partners. The British commander in America, Sir Jeffrey Amherst, thus decreed that henceforth all trade in furs in the Great Lakes region and the Ohio Country could only take place at military forts; he also forbade the sale of liquor and weapons to Indian people. Finally, for cost-cutting purposes as well as an expression of British superiority, he ordered that the gift-giving that always accompanied diplomatic forays in Indian country be discontinued. The slights as well as the material deprivations Indian people experienced caused great resentment among many Indigenous leaders.

Worse still, the British did not honor pledges they had made since the Treaty of Easton in 1758: they had promised to keep settlers from encroaching on lands west of the Appalachians and undertaken not to build new forts or occupy those held by the French. In both instances, they failed to keep their word, constructing a line of military outposts running from Fort Pitt through Detroit up to Michilimackinac, and doing little to halt the steady stream of colonists flowing into Indian territory. Distrustful of English intentions, inspired by Nativist prophets who insisted that their lands be cleansed of Europeans and their ways, and hoping that the French would regroup and resume their struggle against the British, a number of Native groups led by the Ottawa chief Pontiac besieged Detroit in 1763. Other Indian forces followed their example, seizing British fortifications across the *pays d'en haut*. "Drive them out, make war upon them," urged Neolin, a Delaware prophet.[11] Across Ohio Country, Senecas, Shawnees, Delawares, and a host of other Indian peoples heeded his call and resumed the attacks on settlers they had quit under the terms of the Easton Treaty. For two months in the summer of 1763, they laid waste to squatter homes and killed their inhabitants, leading other settlers to flee to the east. Tellingly, they left African Americans alone, leading historians to see in Pontiac's Rebellion a determined effort by Native Americans to ethnically cleanse their lands.

It appeared that they might succeed, but by the fall, the inability to resupply themselves with weapons from the French and an epidemic of smallpox, likely the result of Amherst's sending of blankets contaminated with smallpox to Fort Pitt to infect the Delawares laying siege there, weakened the Indian forces. In October, Pontiac learned that the Treaty of Paris had conclusively brought the Seven Years' War to an end; with no

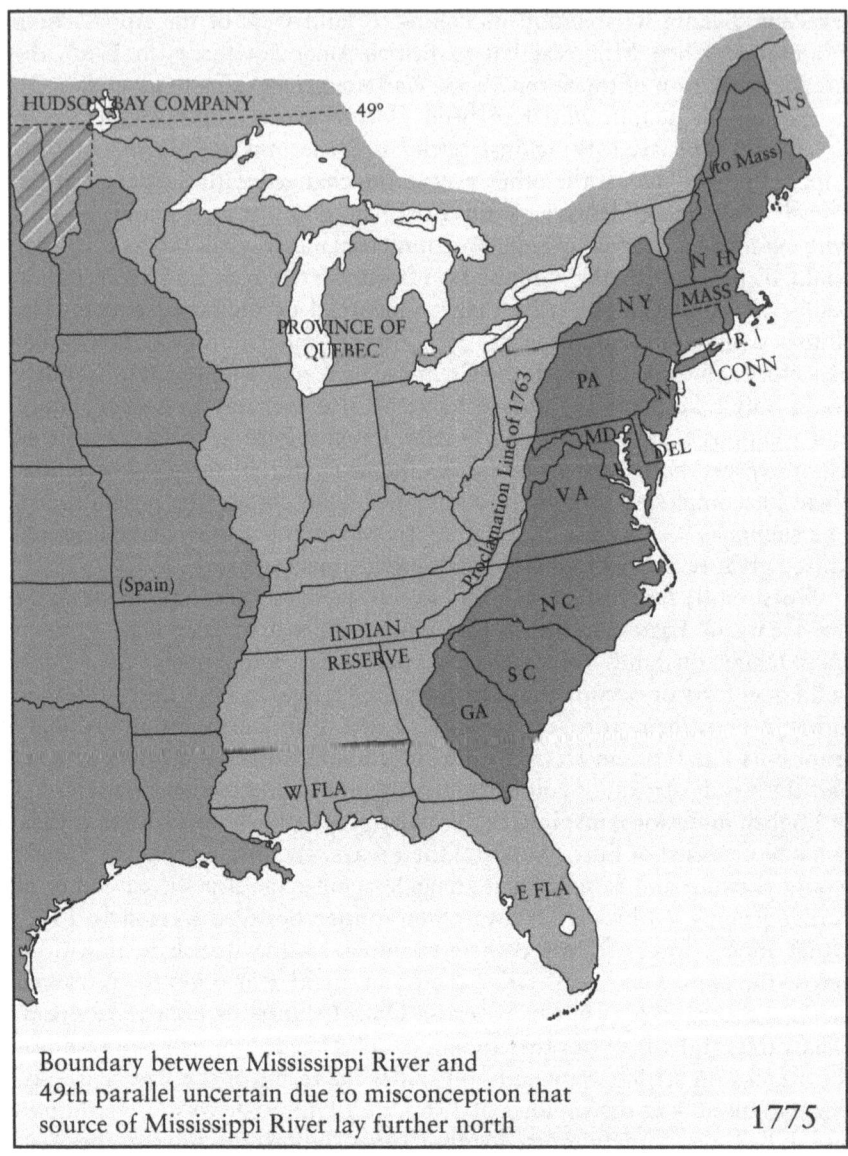

FIGURE 3.1 *Map delineating the Royal Proclamation of 1763.*

hope of the French taking over his position in Detroit, he and his warriors retreated to the Maumee River. By the end of December, his rebellion had come to an end.

By the Treaty of Paris of 1763 the French ceded all their holdings in North America to the British except Louisiana, which they gave to the Spanish. (Louisiana at the time made up almost a third of today's continental US, so considerable territory remained out of British hands.) The Peace of Paris proved a disappointment for North American colonists. They had been asked to contribute men and treasure to the war, and had done so expecting to reap rich rewards. Instead they found that the treaty guaranteed the rights of French Catholics in Canada, which enraged Protestants. Moreover, Britain expected them to help pay for the expenses of policing the new empire, especially as the colonists themselves often instigated conflicts with Indian groups as they moved westward onto lands held by Iroquois, Shawnees, Delawares, Ottawas, Cherokees, and many other tribes. In 1765, parliament extended the Stamp Act, a tax on paper that Britons at home already paid, to the American colonies. The tax itself amounted to very little, but to the Americans it constituted an attempt to impose the rule of parliament over that of their own colonial legislatures. They determined to resist it and any other effort to tax them without their consent. "No taxation without representation," they cried.

Worse still, as they saw it, a royal proclamation issued in October 1763 barred colonists from settling lands west of the Appalachian mountains (see Figure 3.1). It announced "that the several nations or tribes of Indians, with whom we are connected, and who live under our protection, should not be molested or disturbed in the possession of such parts of our dominions and territories as, not having been ceded to, or purchased by us, are reserved to them." The lands protected by the Treaty of Easton five years earlier, which a number of tribes had long sought to preserve, fell under the scope of the proclamation. Little could have infuriated settlers more: in the conflict they referred to as the French and Indian war, their aim had been to obtain more Indian land, not less. When the British signed the Quebec Act of 1774, declaring that lands north and west of the Ohio River belonged to Quebec and therefore were off limits to Virginian and Pennsylvanian settlers, dissatisfaction turned into potential for revolt. Among those unhappy with British policies were hundreds of veterans of the Seven Years' War, who had been promised land in the west in return for their military service, and speculators such as George Washington and Thomas Jefferson, who had been given land charters by Virginia officials. The following year, American colonists went to war against Great Britain.

The Americans articulated a number of high-minded universal principles in defense of their revolt against King George III and memorialized them in the Declaration of Independence, signed in July 1776. Among the twenty-seven particular "injuries and usurpations" they adduced to support their rebellion were the king's actions in "raising the conditions of new Appropriations of Lands"—a direct reference to the Royal Proclamation of 1763 and to the Quebec Act of 1774, which Virginia delegate Richard Henry Lee insisted was the "worse grievance of all."[12] American rebels cited numerous reasons for casting off British rule, but one of their most pressing ones concerned Britain's perceived refusal to allow them to expand onto and seize Indian lands.

In an effort to bind western squatters—who were subject during the Revolutionary War to destructive Indian attacks on their homesteads—to the American cause and keep them from turning to the British for protection, the Declaration of Independence also denounced the king's efforts "to bring on the inhabitants of our frontiers, the merciless Indian Savages, whose known rule of warfare, is an undistinguished destruction of all ages, sexes and conditions." Certainly, the British, like the Americans, sought to enlist Native communities to their side. Most tribal leaders, however, worked hard to stay out of the fight, which would prove to be the single most destructive war against Indian people to date, far outdistancing the losses suffered during the Seven Years' War or any other. They feared, as they had for a number of years now, that the Americans sought not just to take their lands but to destroy them as a people; staying neutral seemed to be the best way forward in the midst of catastrophic warfare and uncertainty. A few chiefs, like Cherokee Dragging Canoe and Mohawk Joseph Brant thought differently, however, seeing in the conflict between the whites the possibility of regaining territory they had lost to settlers. Just a month following the signing of the Declaration of Independence, 600 Cherokee warriors attacked settlements in the western regions of Virginia, the Carolinas, and Georgia, burning buildings and killing some settlers. Five thousand militiamen responded by burning down over fifty Cherokee towns, killing men, women, and children, destroying their crops, and killing or driving off their livestock. Many of those who survived the killings died of starvation or were sold into slavery.

The onslaught of American militias in the summer of 1776 convinced many Cherokees to abandon their fight with settlers. Dragging Canoe, however, continued his campaign, and with his followers built new towns on Chickamauga Creek. Virginia and North Carolina sent another force against the Chickamaugas, as they called themselves, attacking them and other Cherokees living on the Tennessee River. "There was no withstanding them," recounted The Raven, a Cherokee who had opposed Dragging Canoe's efforts, "they dyed their hands in the Blood of many of our Women and Children, burnt 17 towns, destroyed all our provisions by which we & our families were almost destroyed by famine this Spring."[13] The American attacks on the Cherokees persuaded the British to abandon their western forts, which in turn led to an immense influx of settlers onto Cherokee lands.

The Haudenosaunee peoples—the Iroquois—fared even worse. Long the allies of the British in their conflicts with the French, most of the Haudenosaunee at first hoped to stay neutral in the fight with American colonists. The course of the war made that impossible, for battles between the British and the American forces took place on the very territory the Iroquois occupied. Following a number of skirmishes in the spring of 1779, the goal of which, George Washington instructed his generals, was "the total destruction and devastation of their settlements and the capture of as many prisoners of every age and sex as possible," the Americans sent a huge army to take on the Haudenosaunee. Vastly outnumbered and outgunned, the Haudenosaunee decided to sacrifice their towns in order to save their people. The Americans fired over forty settlements and their surrounding croplands. As Sayengeraghta, the Seneca chief, pointed out, "We lost our Country, it is true, but this was to secure our Women & Children."[14] Many Haudenosaunee fled north to Canada; others sheltered at the British Fort Niagara, where many of them perished from starvation and disease. All in all, the Haudenosaunee may well have lost a third of their population during the Revolutionary War.

The American War for Independence ended with the 1783 Treaty of Paris, which ceded to the new United States a vast region between the Appalachian mountains and the Mississippi River, lands belonging to and occupied by Native Americans, none of whom had been involved in or consulted about the crafting of the peace terms. Victory meant that the terms of the Royal Proclamation of 1763, which, at least on paper, established constraints on settler encroachment on Indian territory, no longer applied. As we'll see in the next chapter, those constraints barely existed in Canada either, despite the proclamation remaining in force there.

Counterpoint: The Dutch in Southern Africa

In 1652, the Dutch East India Company (Vereenigde Oost-Indische Compagnie, or VOC), landed three ships on the coast of what became Cape Town in southern Africa. The company built a refreshment station to supply its ships sailing to the East Indies with meat and fresh produce. Dutch and French employees and then their descendants, together with enslaved people brought from regions of the Indian Ocean, established themselves in the rapidly expanding Cape Town; over time, many of them moved eastward from the city. There, on lands in the dry Karoo desert and its margins, they set themselves up as ranchers, eking out a living selling hides or wool. Hardy pioneers, they traveled by wagon and on horseback, professed a fervent Calvinism, and disdained education. As they moved east during the course of the eighteenth century, they became physically and culturally separate from those they left behind in Cape Town. They even developed a new language—later known as Afrikaans—that was based on Dutch, but included a series of loan words in Malay, French, English, and a variety of African languages.

Before the 1760s, the passage eastward of these "trekboers" (the term "Boer" means "farmer") had proceeded in relatively simple fashion, for the land was almost empty. Apartheid-era historians would later argue that the vacant land justified white settlement in South Africa. But their pronouncements neglected to explain why the land was unoccupied, for this was, in fact, a recent phenomenon. The original inhabitants—Khoikhoi pastoralists known to the Dutch as "Hottentots"—had ceased to possess any sort of social or political independence; they had fallen prey to a series of VOC-sanctioned cattle raids by Dutch farmers and ranchers who insisted that they needed the stock and the land to establish themselves and survive. Raids by other Khoikhoi groups who seized upon the weak, and by San "hunter-robbers" who carried off many thousands of cows in the late seventeenth century, compounded the disaster, making it impossible for the Khoikhoi to continue their centuries-old practices. Many sold their sheep and cattle to the company or to the settler farmers, who after 1700 had few limits on their activities from the company.

Khoikhoi society in the Cape had gone through cycles of prosperity and decline in the past, but now the presence of the Dutch settlers prevented regeneration. Many men went to work for the settlers, their opportunities to participate in the renewal of Khoikhoi society now closed off. They earned wages paid not in cattle—which would have allowed them to rebuild their herds—but in food, a place to live, and goods. The final blow came in 1713, when a smallpox epidemic swept through the Khoikhoi population. They enjoyed no immunity to the disease, and perhaps 90 percent of them died. Those who remained often took on jobs as servants for the trekboer pioneers, for few other options existed.

Where the Khoikhoi suffered decline owing to loss of land and cattle, the San people faced out-and-out extermination at the hands of settlers and the VOC administration. In the early days of Dutch settlement, the San, whose mobility and adaptability as hunter-gatherers gave them more resiliency against dispossession than the pastoralist Khoikhoi, were better able to survive the efforts of the Dutch to control them. That changed over time as more and more settlers moved into the territory: in the middle of the eighteenth century, the trekboers numbered no more than 600 or so; some fifty years later they had increased to 15,000. The San responded to the incursions on their hunting grounds and water holes with attacks on settlers and their livestock, prompting the formation of settler "commando" units to hunt down the guerrillas and kill them. Commandos comprised of between forty and 100 settlers would swoop down on San camps before first light, set them on fire, kill the men right there on the spot, and either enslave the women and children or kill them outright. The VOC attempted for a while to keep the killings in check, but in 1777 it authorized a formal policy of eradication of San peoples.

In the 1760s, the trekboers on the eastern frontier of the Cape came into extended contact with a larger and more resilient population of Africans, the Xhosa. Part-agriculturalist, part-pastoralist people, the Xhosa lived in a series of loosely-knit chiefdoms extending from the Fish River eastwards. This region—known as the Zuurveld—provided excellent conditions for pastoralism, and both Xhosa and Boer grazed their cattle there seasonally. The two groups shared similar modes of life and their initial interactions were positive. Boer pastors traveled unmolested into Xhosa lands to preach the gospel; both sides traded with one another; and intermarriage took place as well. But by the following decade, the benevolent interactions had devolved into a series of often violent conflicts. Though the Xhosa possessed greater numbers, the trekboers had more modern firearms. Neither side could achieve dominance, and thus a protracted stalemate ensued. A series of "Frontier Wars" broke out periodically over the following century.

Primary Source Document

The Royal Proclamation of 1763

King George III

A Proclamation. 1763.

By the KING,

A PROCLAMATION.

GEORGE R.

WHEREAS We have taken into Our Royal Consideration the extensive and valuable Acquisitions in America, secured to Our Crown by the late Definitive Treaty of Peace, concluded at Paris the Tenth Day of February last; and being desirous, that all Our loving Subjects, as well of Our Kingdom as of Our Colonies in America, may avail themselves, with all convenient Speed, of the great Benefits and Advantages which must accrue therefrom to their Commerce, Manufactures, and Navigation; We have thought fit, with the Advice of Our Privy Council, to issue this Our Royal Proclamation, hereby to publish and declare to all Our loving Subjects, that We have, with the Advice of Our said Privy Council, granted Our Letters Patent under Our Great Seal of Great Britain, to erect within the Countries and Islands ceded and confirmed to Us by the said Treaty, Four distinct and separate Governments, stiled and called by the Names of Quebec, East Florida, West Florida, and Grenada.

...

And whereas We are desirous, upon all Occasions, to testify Our Royal Sense and Approbation of the Conduct and Bravery of the Officers and Soldiers of Our Armies, and to reward the same, We do hereby command and impower Our Governors of Our said Three New Colonies, and all other Our Governors of Our several Provinces on the Continent of North America, to grant, without Fee or Reward, to such Reduced Officers as have served in North America during the late War, and to such Private Soldiers as have been or shall be disbanded in America, and are actually residing there, and shall personally apply for the same, the following Quantities of Lands, subject at the Expiration of Ten Years, to the same Quit-Rents as other Lands are subject to in the Province within which they are granted, as also subject to the same Conditions of Cultivation and Improvement; viz. To every Person having the Rank of a Field Officer, Five thousand Acres.—To every Captain, Three thousand Acres[.—]To every Subaltern or [Staff] Officer, Two thousand Acres.—To every Non-Commission Officer, Two hundred A[cres.]—To every Private Man, Fifty Acres.

...

And whereas it is just and reasonable, and essential to Our Interest and the Security of Our Colonies, that the several Nations or Tribes of Indians, with whom We are connected, and who live under Our Protection, should not be molested or disturbed in the Possession of such Parts of Our Dominions and Territories as, not having been ceded to, or purchased by Us, are reserved to them, or any of them, as their Hunting Grounds; We do therefore, with the Advice of Our Privy Council, declare it to be our Royal Will and Pleasure, that no Governor or Commander in Chief in any of Our Colonies of Quebec, East Florida, or West Florida, do presume, upon any Pretence whatever, to grant Warrants of Survey, or pass any Patents for Lands beyond the Bounds of their respective Governments, as described in their Commissions; as also, that no Governor or Commander in Chief in any of Our other Colonies or Plantations in America, do presume, for the present, and until Our further Pleasure be known, to grant Warrants of Survey, or pass Patents for any Lands beyond the Heads or Sources of any of the Rivers which fall into the Atlantick Ocean from the West and North West, or upon any Lands whatever, which, not having been ceded to, or purchased by Us as aforesaid, are preserved to the said Indians, or any of them.

And We do further declare it to be Our Royal Will and Pleasure, for the present as aforesaid, to reserve under Our Sovereignty, Protection, and Dominion, for the Use of the said Indians, all the Lands and Territories not included within the Limits of Our said Three New Governments, or within the Limits of the Territory granted to the Hudson's Bay Company, as also, all the Lands and Territories lying to the Westward of the Sources of the Rivers which fall into the Sea from the West and North West, as aforesaid; and We do hereby strictly forbid, on Pain of Our Displeasure, all Our loving Subjects from making any Purchases or Settlements whatever, or taking Possession of any of the Lands above reserved, without Our especial Leave and License for that Purpose first obtained.

And We do further strictly enjoin and require all Persons whatever, who have either wilfully or inadvertently seated themselves upon any Lands within the Countries above described, or upon any other Lands, which, not having been ceded to, or purchased by Us, are still reserved to the said Indians as aforesaid, forthwith to remove themselves from such Settlements.

And whereas great Frauds and Abuses have been committed in the purchasing Lands of the Indians, to the great Prejudice of Our Interests, and to the great Dissatisfaction of the said Indians; in order therefore to prevent such Irregularities for the future, and to the End that the Indians may be convinced of Our Justice, and determined Resolution to remove all reasonable Cause of Discontent, We do, with the Advice of Our Privy Council, strictly enjoin and require, that no private Person do presume to make any Purchase from the said Indians of any Lands reserved to the said Indians, within those Parts of Our Colonies where We have thought proper to allow Settlement; but that if, at any Time, any of the said Indians should be inclined to dispose of the said Lands, the same shall be purchased only for Us, in Our Name, at some Publick Meeting or Assembly of the said Indians to be held for that Purpose by the Governor or Commander in Chief of Our Colonies respectively, within which they shall lie; and in case they shall lie within the Limits of any Proprietary Government, they shall be purchased only for the Use and in the Name of such Proprietaries, conformable to such Directions and Instructions as We or they shall think proper to give for that Purpose: And We do, by the Advice of Our Privy Council, declare and enjoin, that the Trade with the said Indians shall be free and open to all Our Subjects whatever; provided that every Person who may incline to trade with the said Indians, do take out a License for carrying on such Trade from the Governor or Commander in Chief of any of Our Colonies respectively, where such Person shall reside; and also give Security to observe such Regulations as We shall at any Time think fit, by Ourselves or by Our Commissaries to be appointed for this Purpose, to direct and appoint for the Benefit of the said Trade; and We do hereby authorize, enjoin, and require the Governors and Commanders in Chief of all Our Colonies respectively, as well Those under Our immediate Government as Those under the Government and Direction of Proprietaries, to grant such Licenses without Fee or Reward, taking especial Care to insert therein a Condition, that such License shall be void, and the Security forfeited, in case the Person, to whom the same is granted, shall refuse or neglect to observe such Regulations as We shall think proper to prescribe as aforesaid.

And We do further expressly enjoin and require all Officers whatever, as well Military as Those employed in the Management and Direction of Indian Affairs within the Territories reserved as aforesaid for the Use of the said Indians, to seize and apprehend all Persons whatever, who, standing charged with Treasons, Misprisions of Treason, Murders, or other Felonies or Misdemeanors, shall fly from Justice, and take Refuge in the said Territory, and to send them under a proper Guard to the Colony where the Crime was committed of which they stand accused, in order to take their Tryal for the same.

Given at Our Court at St. James's, the Seventh Day of October, One thousand seven hundred and sixty three, in the Third Year of Our Reign.

GOD save the KING.

LONDON:

Printed by Mark Baskett, Printer to the King's most Excellent Majesty; and by the Assigns of

Robert Baskett. 1763.

Notes

1 Quoted in Pekka Hämäläinen, *Indigenous Continent: The Epic Contest for North America* (New York: Liveright Publishing Corporation, 2022), p. 59.
2 Quoted in Hämäläinen, *Indigenous Continent*, p. 62.
3 Quoted in Hämäläinen, *Indigenous Continent*, p. 64.
4 See George Percy, *A True Relation of the Proceedings and Occurances of Moment which have happened in Virginia from the Time Sir Thomas Gates shipwrecked upon the Bermudes anno 1609 until my departure out of the Country which was in anno Domini 1612* (London, 1624). http://nationalhumanitiescenter.org/pds/amerbegin/settlement/text2/JamestownPercyRelation.pdf
5 Quoted in Hämäläinen, *Indigenous Continent*, p. 66.
6 Quoted in Hämäläinen, *Indigenous Continent*, p. 66.

7 Quoted in Walter L. Hixson, *American Settler Colonialism, A History* (Basingstoke: Palgrave Macmillan, 2013), p. 32.
8 Quoted in Hämäläinen, *Indigenous Continent*, p.172
9 Quoted in Hämäläinen, *Indigenous Continent*, p. 174.
10 Quoted in Hämäläinen, *Indigenous Continent*, pp. 79, 80.
11 Quoted in Daniel K. Richter, *Facing East from Indian Country. A Native History of Early America* (Cambridge: Harvard University Press, 2001), p. 199.
12 Quoted in Jeffrey Ostler, *Surviving Genocide: Native Nations and the United States from the American Revolution to Bleeding Kansas* (New Haven: Yale University Press, 2019), p. 53.
13 Quoted in Ostler, *Surviving Genocide*, p. 57.
14 Quoted in Ostler, *Surviving Genocide*, pp. 72, 73.

Further Reading

Pekka Hämäläinen, *Indigenous Continent: The Epic Contest for North America* (New York: Liveright Publishing Corporation, 2022).

Walter L. Hixson, *American Settler Colonialism, A History* (Basingstoke: Palgrave Macmillan, 2013).

Jeffrey Ostler, *Surviving Genocide: Native Nations and the United States from the American Revolution to Bleeding Kansas* (New Haven: Yale University Press, 2019).

Daniel K. Richter, *Facing East from Indian Country. A Native History of Early America* (Cambridge: Harvard University Press, 2001), p. 199.

4

The Expansion of Anglo-American Settlement, 1783–1830s

On October 7, 1830, 2,200 British soldiers, free settlers, and convicts amassed in seven towns across the so-called Settled Districts of Tasmania, aiming to create a nearly 120-mile wide continuous "Black Line" to drive Aboriginal Tasmanians out of the region onto the Tasman Peninsula, where they would be held in camps before being shipped off the island. One historian likened it to shooting parties in Highland Scotland, where beaters flushed out the game for upper-class house-guests to blast them out of the sky; Charles Darwin described it as akin to the "great hunting-matches in India." The men who had joined "with hope and excitement, at the prospect of distinguishing ourselves by the capture of even one of the dreaded savages," however, soon found themselves ground down by the rigors of rough terrain and bad weather.[1] The initial foray of the Black Line failed in its objective, and the participants returned home by the end of November having captured only two Tasmanians and killed two others. Two subsequent lines, however, succeeded: some fifteen months later, the last of the Aboriginal Tasmanians had been rounded up and dispatched to transit camps.

When British settlers first arrived in Tasmania in 1804, an estimated 6,000 Aboriginal people inhabited the island. Their numbers declined rapidly under the impact of white settlement as increasing numbers of free settlers and convicts and their animals flooded into the area. White settlers and their convict servants amounted to some 10,000 in 1823, growing to 22,500 in 1830; the numbers of their sheep and cattle had swelled from about 200,000 to almost 1 million in the same time span. Concomitantly, Aboriginal people had been reduced in number to about 1,200 in 1826 and down to about 250 four years later.

The near extermination of the Aboriginal people of Tasmania did not take long. By 1835, all but seven of the 317 full-descent First Nation

Tasmanians had been removed from the island. The others languished in detention camps, where horrific conditions cut their numbers dramatically. When in 1847 Australian authorities allowed the Aboriginal people to return to Tasmania from Flinders Island, forty-seven—forty-seven!—were left. The experiences and fate of the Aboriginal Tasmanians provide only the most extreme example of the impulse toward elimination that characterizes settler colonialism. Less lethal but no less effective methods of destroying the cultures and lifeways of Indigenous peoples played out in the years following the Peace of Paris of 1783, when British and American colonists moved onto lands far beyond Ireland and the newly-created US.

* * *

After the loss of the American colonies, Britain experienced one of the most dynamic periods of its history of settler colonialism, seeing in the relatively short span of about forty years the establishment of a penal colony in Australia, rebellion in and formal union with Ireland, and the acquisition of South Africa. War with Revolutionary France in 1793 made Ireland a potential source of vulnerability for the United Kingdom, offering as it did the possibility of a staging ground from which the enemy could attack Britain. Starting in 1794, Irish rebels sought out the assistance of the French; in 1798, open rebellion against Britain broke out and was bloodily suppressed. Lacking the resources to establish a permanent occupying force in Ireland, the government hit upon a strategy to create a formal union with England, Wales, and Scotland in the United Kingdom of Great Britain. The government promised the right of Catholics to sit in Parliament as a way to sweeten the deal, an undertaking it would not, as it turned out, meet for another thirty years. In the meantime, victory over the French in the Napoleonic Wars resulted in the ceding of the Dutch colony of South Africa to Great Britain in 1815. Five years later, the first British settlers arrived, setting off a complicated and often bloody triangular relationship between Africans, Boers, and British settlers.

Population growth, industrialization, economic downturns, and urbanization contributed to a significant out-migration of Britons to its white colonies of settlement in Canada, South Africa, Australia, and New Zealand in the years following the end of the Napoleonic Wars. In the five years between 1815 and 1820, 170,000 British folks (mostly voluntarily) left their homes to travel to new and faraway lands to seek a new life. More would have gone if they could have, but did not have the funds to make the long and expensive trip. In 1820, for instance, a governmental program to establish 4,000 British settlers in South Africa received 80,000 applications. Twenty thousand Britons settled there by the 1840s. About 180,000 emigrants traveled to Australia and New Zealand between 1828—when the cost of the voyage fell by half—and 1842. Almost 2 million Britons emigrated to Canada between 1815 and 1860. This "explosive colonization" of British and Irish settlers, as one historian has described it,[2] replicated British society in far-flung corners of the world, vastly increased the lands owned or controled by Britons, and, not incidentally, entailed the displacement and even annihilation of the Indigenous peoples who occupied those territories prior to their arrival. Moreover, though we refer to the "white colonies of settlement" as if they were made up of an ethnically homogenous population, Canada, Australia, New Zealand, and South Africa were marked by many of the same ethnic and religious tensions that characterized Great Britain.

***

British troops marched out of New York City on Evacuation Day in late November of 1783, marking the official end of the British presence in what would become the US. Their departure left thousands of Americans who had remained loyal to King George III facing serious difficulties. If they remained, they risked the wrath of people who regarded them as traitors and enemies; if they left, they relinquished everything they had known and would have to begin again in other lands. The violence directed against them before and after the American victory made the decision easy for many Loyalists: 60,000 left, taking 15,000 enslaved African-Americans with them. Half of the white population moved north into Nova Scotia, New Brunswick, and Quebec, turning the once-largely French Catholic region into an English-speaking territory.

The Loyalists arrived with virtually nothing to their names; British authorities had to provide the means for feeding and housing them over the long term. Officials in Quebec turned to the Ojibwe people to purchase land just north of the Great Lakes to settle both white and Iroquois Loyalists there. Whatever their feelings about the matter, the Ojibwes had little leverage in the negotiations owing to their much-reduced numbers: perhaps some 200 of them remained in the area north of Lake Ontario. Colonial officials then parceled out the territory in land grants ranging in size from 200 acres for ordinary citizens and regular troops to 5,000 acres for high-ranking officers. Towns grew up suddenly out of nothing as houses went up quickly; in Saint John, New Brunswick, for example, the new settlers built 1,500 houses in 1783 alone. By the following year, approximately 166,000 whites lived in Nova Scotia and Quebec. That number rose to 392,000 within twenty years. Though provided with tools and raw materials, Loyalists didn't have an easy time of it. Creating farms out of wilderness entailed a long and tiring process of clearing dense forests; it took more than a year to establish ten acres of arable land.

By the time Britain lost the American colonies, the numbers and welfare of Indigenous Canadian peoples in the northeast had been reduced significantly. Over the past century and a half, contact with Europeans had introduced devastating disease to Native communities, depleted their hunting and farming lands, and intensified deadly warfare among them.

When the Loyalists arrived in 1783, First Nations people, as they came to be called, were in no position to resist the new settlers. Indeed, many of them had become dependent upon the British for their livelihoods and even their very presence there, as was the case for the Iroquois in western Quebec. They relied on the fur trade controlled by the Hudson's Bay Company (HBC), which could often be a nasty business involving coercive violence or addiction to alcohol fostered by British traders. Debt entrapped many First Nations people. Those peoples who still sought to expel American settlers from their traditional lands hoped that the British might help them in that endeavor and feared alienating them by resisting white settlement in Canada.

Loyalist settlers arrived in a country dominated by and organized around the fur trade. From the earliest days of exchange, French and British traders had sought out Indigenous women as "country wives," who provided them with sex, companionship, children, and useful contacts through which to build up commercial networks. "Country marriages," some of which were undoubtedly coercive, could provide Aboriginal women with increased status and prosperity and in some instances, lifelong marital stability. The offspring of these unions produced a new people the French called Métis ("mixed," in French); the British referred to them derogatorily as "half-breeds." In the area to the west of Ontario, north of the American border, the Métis, a semi-nomadic group of men and women who prided themselves on their independence in the wilderness, hunted, trapped, fished, and traded along the Red and Assiniboine rivers, over time forming whole communities in what is modern-day Manitoba. They spoke different languages and established separate identities from their Aboriginal or European neighbors. Their in-betweenness facilitated commerce between Native peoples and Europeans, and they came to take a leading role in the fur trade. They also made and sold pemmican, a high-energy food made up of dried beef, marrow, and berries. Indigenous people across North America consumed pemmican as a staple, as did the fur-trading community.

Comprised of decades of Indian, French, Scottish, and Irish intermarriage, most of them espousing a devout Roman Catholicism and speaking a rich patois of French, Cree, Chippewa, and English, Métis did not consider themselves "Canadian," and especially not subjects of the British crown. They lived in close proximity to the only European settlement west of Ontario, the Red River colony, a frontier outpost settled mostly by Scots. At Fort Garry (modern-day Winnipeg), traders carried out a vibrant commerce; along the Red River for some twenty miles or so, farmers homesteaded and established an Anglo-Saxon community very like that they would have found at home in Britain. The two communities clashed with one another on a fairly regular basis, the Anglo-Saxon settlers distrusting the Métis as violent, liquor-fueled, dangerous Catholic aliens, and the Métis regarding the Anglo-Saxons as agents of an expansionist empire that sought to put an end to their way of life.

The Métis lifeways came under challenge when, in 1812, Lord Selkirk, a Scottish member of the House of Lords in Westminster and shareholder in the Hudson's Bay Company, established a settlement colony at Red River. Hoping to provide a home for Scots displaced by the Highland Clearances and to farm the area in order to provide food for HBC employees, Selkirk sent thirty-five settlers to Red River. Their initial attempts to grow wheat fell prey to disease and weather, while the War of 1812 interrupted the flow of foodstuffs to the colony. In 1814, the colonial governor issued the Pemmican Proclamation, prohibiting the export of the foodstuff; the ban hit the Métis particularly hard, threatening a vital aspect of their economy. The Métis responded with a number of raids on the colony and, in 1816, following a winter of starvation, with an attack on the small armed force bringing pemmican to an HBC outpost. Sixty buffalo hunters under the leadership of Cuthbert Grant seized the pemmican and took it to Red River. En route, they encountered about two dozen settlers sent out to intercept them. The Métis killed them all, losing only one of their number in the fracas. Grant's reputation as a freedom fighter rose dramatically and he became known as the "Captain-General of all the Half-Breeds." Métis resistance to efforts by the colonial government to expand settlement by whites would increase in later years.

In 1815 British North America consisted of Newfoundland; Prince Edward Island; Nova Scotia; New Brunswick; Quebec, which in 1791 had been split into English-speaking Upper Canada and French-speaking Lower Canada; and Rupert's Land, a vast territory controlled by the HBC stretching from the lands around Hudson's Bay westward to Manitoba, Saskatchewan, and Alberta. Immigration from Britain, especially among the Protestant Irish, increased significantly over subsequent years, from 3,370 in 1816 to 23,534 three years later. In 1832, 66,000 Britons, half of them Irish, sailed to Canada. Two-thirds of those Irish immigrants were Protestant, a factor that would play a part in later developments of Canadian settler colonialism.

***

Following its victory against Great Britain, the new American nation confronted multiple threats to its survival. On the most basic level, the government owed huge amounts of money—some $75 million—to creditors who had provided the means to prosecute the war and to veterans who had fought it. Both groups expected to be repaid and rewarded. The new democracy, moreover, precisely because it was a democracy, also needed to secure the loyalty and support of its often fractious citizenry. Differences of wealth and status might foment civil unrest among a populace unafraid of rebellion and now, after nearly a decade of war, armed to the teeth. The very stability of the republic depended upon placating a wide array of constituents.

The acquisition and opening up of Indigenous lands, it appeared to American leaders, provided a far-reaching resolution to their immediate problems. Because many Native communities had sided with the British during the Revolutionary War, it was not difficult to construct a legal veneer over outright land seizures from "enemy" Indians; Loyalists to Britain in the conflict had forfeited their property, after all, at the end of the war. Where possible, officials used treaties to obtain Indian land; where that failed, they resorted to forcible appropriation. Always they faced the issue of settlers bent on grabbing Native lands and pushing Indian people westward through violent means of their own. That dynamic drove the passage of a number of acts—the Federal Intercourse Act of 1790, for example—designed to maintain federal control over the settler colonial project and, not incidentally, provided a persuasive rationale to Native leaders reluctant to give up land. If we don't remove you to distant places, government agents warned Indian leaders, truthfully, settlers will kill you. The Gnadenhütten massacre in 1782, during which American vigilantes had literally broken open the heads of nearly 100 Lenape men, women, and children with hammers, was still fresh in the memories of many people, Native and white alike.

In its efforts to impose some measure of control over settler expansion, Congress passed the Northwest Ordinance in 1787, which provided the protocols by which territories in Ohio Country could establish themselves as new states and join the union. Hoping to establish a regular and orderly set of procedures that would transform Indian lands into American states, the federal government lacked the resources to achieve its goals. Instead, tens of thousands of settlers poured onto Native lands in Ohio Country, 6,000 of them in a six-month period of 1787–8 alone. Swamped and pressured, Lenape, Iroquois, and Wyandot peoples agreed to give up a huge amount of territory in the 1789 Treaty of Fort Harmar. Five years later, by the Treaty of Greenville, they and Shawnee, Odawa, Chippewa, Ojibwe, Miami, Kickapoo, Potawatomi, and Kaskaskia leaders were forced to give up some two-thirds of Ohio Country to settlers. Indian people had to content themselves with a 150-mile sliver of land in the northwestern part of what had once been all of theirs. By 1810, 230,000 white people inhabited Ohio.

These depredations spurred both peaceful campaigns to ensure Indian survival and furious Indigenous resistance; the latter would culminate in the War of 1812. Iroquois chief Handsome Lake led a movement designed to accommodate his people and their traditions to white rule. Further south, Shawnee spiritual leader Tenskwatawa, known as the Prophet, called for a purification of Indigenous life and ways that eschewed any contamination by whites. He urged his ever-increasing number of followers to abandon their commercial and hunting contacts with whites and outlawed the selling of Indian land to settlers. In 1808, he founded Prophetstown where the Wabash and Tippicanoe rivers meet, a center of multiethnic living and worship that drew hundreds of Indian people. His brother, Tecumseh, in the meantime, sought to actually implement Tenskwatawa's vision of a vast Native military alliance to battle the Americans and roll back white settlement; he traveled long distances to rally southern Indian peoples to his cause. By 1811, he had readied a large Indian confederacy that, with hoped-for British arms and support, could take on the US and end American expansion for good.

Terrified and panicked by the prospects of an all-out Indigenous assault on their settlements, colonists appealed to the American president, James Madison, for help. William Henry Harrison, the governor of Indiana Territory, took advantage of Tecumseh being away doing more recruiting to march to Prophetstown with an army and burn it down. By this time, war with Britain—the War of 1812—had broken out, in part owing to Britain's support of Tecumseh's confederacy. In the summer of 1812, the Shawnee military leader laid siege to Fort Detroit and by fooling General William Hull into believing he had three times the warriors than he actually had, induced the commander to give up the fort without firing a shot. Tecumseh's allies, with British troops by their side, took Fort Michilimackinac in the far north of what would become Michigan, while others captured Fort Dearborn at the site that would later become Chicago. They then turned their attention to Indiana Territory and to eastern Ohio Country, where their efforts to take American forts fell short. The tide of the war began to turn; after the American victory in the Battle of Lake Erie in September 1813, Tecumseh and his British allies engaged American forces on the Thames River in October. They lost badly, and the Shawnee warrior was killed. Indian resistance in Ohio Country, for all intents and purposes, died with him.

In the southeastern region of the United States, Indian resistance to American settler encroachment appeared most notably among dissident members of the Creeks, a group known as the Red Sticks after the color of their war clubs. Dissatisfied with wealthier and more accommodationist members of their tribe, they sought to purge their ranks of white influences and were eager to engage Americans and accommodating Indians in violence when the War of 1812 broke out. In the summer of 1813, they attacked Fort Mims just north of Mobile, killing some 250 to 300 civilians. Responding in fury, the people of Nashville demanded the extermination of the Creek nation; the Tennessee legislature called for Andrew Jackson, who led the state militia, to take 3,500 men south to prevent the invasion of Tennessee by the Red Sticks. The Red Sticks had no such plan, for they were more than 250 miles from the Tennessee border, but the fiction allowed Jackson, with the approval of President Madison, to embark on a genocidal campaign against the dissident Creeks. With the help of Cherokee and friendly Creeks, Jackson's troops laid waste to Red Stick towns and massacred Red Stick people in spasms of violence and atrocity. When the Indian campaigns ended with treaties in 1814 and 1816, the Creeks had lost 40,000 square miles of territory. Jackson's slaughter of Creek peoples and the annexation of Creek lands set the stage for what up to that time had been an ardent, if unrealizable, aspiration of settler colonists, ridding the eastern portion of the US of all Indian people.

***

In late January 1788, Eora people of what would come to be called New South Wales in Australia watched with incredulity as 1,000 Britons aboard ships under the command of Captain Arthur Phillip came ashore at Botany Bay. Comprised of eleven ships carrying 1,000 people, the First Fleet had sailed from London on May 13, 1787, with 579 male convicts, 193 female convicts, and fourteen children of convicts aboard; seven other children were born during the 15,000-mile, 252-day trip. Misled by Captain James Cook and naturalist Joseph Banks to believe they would find a landscape conducive to relatively easy settlement, the first Britons to go ashore at what would be named Sydney (after the colonial secretary who commissioned the voyage) instead discovered a land of poor soil and little fresh water. Many of them weak from the long and stressful voyage, they faced the immediate problem of building shelter and finding food in an inhospitable environment. Without obtaining permission, they moved onto land the Eora had occupied for millennia, carrying unrecognizable supplies, animals, and equipment. Strange-looking beings pitched tents, cleared out underbrush, and cut down trees, behaving in ways disrespectful of and offensive to the Indigenous people watching anxiously from a distance. British actions regarded as barbaric by the Eora multiplied over the next weeks and months, as men dressed in scarlet and white marched other men from one end of the settlement to the other, inflicted punishments on their charges, and even hanged some of them. Those self-same scarlet-and-whites desecrated Aboriginal graves, an especial abomination. These were beings to stay away from, the Eora determined, and stay away they did.

Lacking the materials and tools necessary to build proper accommodations, and suffering from malnutrition owing to insufficient rations of food, the prisoners of the First Fleet barely made it through their first year. Without the local knowledge of the Indigenous inhabitants of the region, who had thrived by fishing, hunting, and gathering, the British floundered as the crops they planted failed and starvation loomed. Phillip tried hard to establish friendly relations with the Eora people, hoping to gain information about the country that would enable the settlement to survive, but they shunned him. In desperation, he ordered the kidnapping of local Eora, whom he planned to make intermediaries between the British and the Aboriginal people. Two men did fall victim to his scheme; one died, the other escaped, and the Eora only became more distrustful of the interlopers.

Occasional contacts between Britons and Aboriginal peoples did occur, certainly, and increased over the next year, some of them positive and advantageous to both groups. Some of them set up camp on the periphery of the settlement, where the Eora learned to speak English; they began to use the metal tools the British brought with them, and to incorporate certain foods into their diets. But contacts also bred violence, which increased in frequency and intensity as freed convicts began to move inland from the coast to claim land. Along the Hawksbury River, for instance, about forty miles from Sydney, some 400 settlers established farms by the mid-1790s, blocking access to the river for the Dharug peoples who inhabited the area and cutting off their food supply. The Dharug resisted by crossing through the farmland or stealing corn; when they did so, settlers shot at them, setting off a campaign of Dharug raids on the farms and the destruction of crops. One of the raiders, a man named "Mosquito," was finally captured and exiled to Van Diemen's Land, where he headed an Oyster Bay group raiding settlers there. In 1823 authorities caught him and hanged him.

From the start, Australia held a unique position among Britain's imperial possessions, which would grow dramatically in size and number by the end of the Napoleonic Wars in 1815. British authorities had established New South Wales in order to relieve Britain of prisoners it could not handle at home, especially after the loss of the American colonies made it impossible to continue to ship convicts there. Officials determined who would settle there through a variety of mechanisms designed to ensure a homogenous white population steeped in British traditions. Indeed, Australians came to be regarded as more British than the British. Even the first settlers, the convicts themselves, had been chosen with certain qualities in mind, characteristics that would enable the penal colony to survive and expand. They were not a random cross-section of the overall prison population. They were laborers chosen for the work they could do in agriculture or manufacturing; the Scottish and Irish political prisoners of rank would serve the colony in an administrative capacity; and women would make up the wives and mothers of the colonists. Even when free citizens sought to emigrate to Australia, their selection depended upon the basis of need. Those allowed to go provided necessary experience in particular trades the colony required, or possessed enough money to make the kinds of capital improvements on the land they were granted to enable their enterprises to flourish. British authorities could exercise this kind of control because ordinary people wishing to emigrate to the southern hemisphere found it too expensive to do so; they tended to go west across the Atlantic to America or Canada. This kind of selection process created a particularly pronounced social division of haves and have-nots among Australian settlers.

Australia might have begun as a penal dumping ground, but other motives for colonizing the great southern continent existed as well. Above all, it was believed to be cheap. British officials expected convict labor to produce such agricultural products as wheat and maize, exports of which to the mother country would ultimately pay the costs of settlement. Australia's environment made it difficult to grow foodstuffs reliably, however, and wool turned out to be the more dependable export to Britain. Sheep proved to be the main driver of Australia's economy, promoting expansion into the interior of the country as settlers and freed convicts sought to gain the means to a prosperous life. Escaped prisoners, too, headed inland from the coast, seeking freedom in areas where the imperial state had little control. Whether as settlers granted territory by colonial authorities or squatters who simply took what they could find and defend, British colonists wasted little time in establishing themselves on the land.

This was land that the original inhabitants of Australia knew to be theirs. Having themselves arrived on the continent some 45,000 years earlier, the First Nations peoples of Australia numbered perhaps a million souls in 1788. Cook and Banks had reported that the country they "discovered" in 1770 enjoyed little habitation; certainly the land they observed was not cultivated by the Aboriginal people, at least not as they understood the concept. And so the British arrived in 1788 convinced that Australia constituted *terra nullius*, a Latin legal term for "land belonging to no one." If it belonged to no one, then it was Britain's for the taking, requiring neither purchase from nor treaty with the Indigenous peoples who lived on it.

Aboriginal peoples saw things differently. They did not live on or cultivate land the way Europeans did, occupying well-ordered plots carved out of the countryside, but they did observe complex rules about land ownership and how the land was to be utilized and cared for. Land held a central and crucial place in their cosmologies and social and legal systems; they had grave responsibilities for tending to and protecting sacred sites that dotted the landscape. And, of course, they lived on the land, hunting, fishing, and foraging for vegetables and fruits. When Britons first arrived, Indigenous peoples tolerated their presence, expecting that they would not stay for very long. As white people lingered, however, and began to expand their settlements and to seize as their own land that Aborigines roamed or inhabited, misunderstandings turned to tragedies. "The wild black fellows do not understand your laws," a Nyoongar man from Swan River explained to British officials, "every living animal that roams the country, and every edible root that grows in the ground are common property. A black man claims nothing as his own but his cloak, his weapons, and his name ... He does not understand that animals or plants can belong to one person more than to another."[3] When authorities arrested them for theft or settlers shot them outright, Aboriginal people struck back, defending their homes, their food sources, their very way of life. They attacked officers, settlers, and convicts who encroached on their land, assaults that British authorities regarded not as acts of defense of property but as crimes that had to be punished. As violence increased across the continent, settlers and soldiers formed bands and set out on what authorities called "punitive expeditions" against Indigenous peoples, carrying out horrific reprisals. When in 1803 a second colony was established on Van Diemen's Land, the island just to the southeast of New South Wales that would later be called Tasmania, the depredations against the Indigenous Tasmanians reached unprecedented levels, resulting in their near extermination.

The settlers and convicts arrived in Tasmania at a time when the Napoleonic Wars monopolized the attention of the British government; it paid little attention to the needs of its transplanted population, who nearly starved in the early years. Subsisting on as little as 450 calories a day until the first successful harvest came in in 1808, colonists hunted the local kangaroo, emu, and swan population to the brink of extinction, robbing Aboriginal people of their traditional sources of food. Desperate, many Aborigines turned to looting houses and killing livestock in order to keep their families alive. Violence, often extreme, characterized relationships between whites and Aboriginal Tasmanians. Convicts and settlers inured to brutality by the actions of officials in what amounted to a penal colony gave no quarter in retaliation against Aboriginal attacks on their homes; before long, they required no excuse to simply go out and kill them. "We shoot them whenever we find them," one settler told a missionary in 1819.[4] The extreme gender imbalance of the colony, moreover, made the rape and abduction of Aboriginal women and children by white men commonplace, infuriating the Indigenous community.

By 1826, they had had enough, and in defense of their very existence began a campaign of guerrilla warfare that came to be called the Black War. They killed a few settler and convict stockmen in the interior of the Settled Districts; in response Governor George Arthur empowered magistrates to send out police and soldiers to deal with them by raiding their camps during the night. In two years, over 400 Aborigines were killed in these ambushes, but they did not stop the Tasmanian attacks. Indeed, Aboriginal men began to kill white women and children in retaliation. Arthur declared martial law in August 1830, in effect legalizing the killing of all First Nations Tasmanians, but even that did not end the killing. More than 115 settlers or convicts had been killed and over 450 wounded when in September the governor called for the able-bodied white male population of the colony to come together to form the Black Line. Its intent was to rid Tasmania of the Aboriginal threat, and in that, it proved mightily effective, as we saw at the beginning of the chapter.

Starting in the 1820s, following the British government's reduction of import duties on Australian wool, 250,000 colonists flooded into Australia. Settlers and squatters moved west across the Blue Mountains into territories that would become the separate colonies of Victoria and Queensland. They brought 20 million sheep with them, occupying and grazing more than 400 million hectares of Aboriginal land. This was a profoundly gendered society based on an economy dependent upon itinerant seasonal labor, almost exclusively male. The absence of white women—in 1840, white men outnumbered white women thirty-eight to one—put Aboriginal women and girls in grave danger of sexual assault and kidnapping by settlers, who regarded them as fair game. In 1825, a missionary told of the anguish he experienced "at night [by] the shrieks of girls, about 8 or 9 years of age, taken by force by the vile men of Newcastle," referring to convicts. "One man," he recalled, "came to see me with his head broken by the butt-end of a musket because he would not give up his wife."[5] Sexual abuse and the seizure of women enraged Aboriginal peoples and constituted two of their greatest grievances against white settlers.

The presence of colonists' livestock on the lands held by Indigenous peoples changed the land dramatically, impinging on local water supplies, depleting the supply of root crops the Aboriginal people depended upon, and driving out the native animals that provided food for the local people. Unable now to hunt enough wallabies, kangaroos, and emus to feed themselves, Indigenous peoples began to hunt the sheep and cattle of the settlers instead, often attacking the shepherds who tended them. Punitive expeditions against the perpetrators inevitably followed these attacks, escalating the violence on the frontier to even greater heights. All-out warfare broke out at Swan River, Bathurst, and Van Diemen's Land. As white expansion and settlement intensified in the late 1820s, resulting in the creation of yet another colony, Western Australia, in 1829, Indigenous peoples lost out more and more, till it seemed that they would not survive. This possibility alarmed a number of people back in Britain, a story we will take up in the next chapter.

***

The Americans' war for independence had a profound impact on settlers in another land far distant from them. The politically active Irish— almost exclusively the Anglo-Protestant ascendancy—took advantage of the American revolution to push their own agenda of obtaining for the Irish parliament the right to legislate for Ireland. Ireland enjoyed its own parliament, but executive power rested in the hands of the lord lieutenant, who answered not to the Irish parliament but to the Westminster one. Throughout the course of the eighteenth century, Irish MPs had sought to change that, though never did they seek separation from Great Britain, knowing full well that their survival in the midst of an overwhelmingly Catholic country depended on British arms. When the American revolution broke out, Britain embargoed food and supplies to the colonists, a move that harmed Ireland, whose prosperity rested in large part on trade with North America. Irish MPs protested loudly against the provision, to no avail.

When in 1778 France entered the war in support of the American colonists, Britain felt compelled to transfer the massive number of troops stationed in Ireland to more pressing locales. Fearing a possible French invasion, Irish Protestants formed themselves into military units of Volunteers drawn from the gentry, merchants, and tenant farmers, sometimes enrolling Presbyterians to their ranks and even, in some places, Catholics as well. Without any connection to the local militias or to the government, the Volunteers were free to act at will. Amounting in some estimates to 40,000 men, they paraded, fully armed, through Dublin in support of such political measures as ending the British embargo of their products, threatening to withhold the payment of tax revenues to Britain until they had achieved their goals. Hamstrung by the need for funds to prosecute the American war, the prime minister, Lord North, had little recourse but to give in to their demands, granting "equality in trading rights" to Ireland in 1779. In 1782, in an even bolder move, the Volunteers in effect blackmailed the British government into changing the centuries-old Poynings' Law and repealing the Declaratory Act of 1720, thus granting the Irish parliament what it had been calling for for decades—autonomy from Westminster and the concomitant power to rule for Ireland. This victory was, of course, precisely what the American colonists had been seeking in the early days of their resistance, and it would not have been granted to the Irish in 1782 had Britain not found itself mired in crisis.

These reforms benefited the Anglo-Irish Ascendancy, but did little to address the needs and desires of Ireland's Catholic majority. When the French Revolution broke out in 1789, it reverberated loudly across the world, igniting the imaginations of many men and women with its cry of "Liberty, Equality, Fraternity." In Ireland, Protestants and Catholics established the Society of United Irishmen (UI) in 1791 to seek political reform and relief from legal disabilities suffered by Catholics. When in 1793 Great Britain went to war with France to halt the spread of revolution, Ireland became a source of real vulnerability for the UK, offering a staging ground from which the enemy could attack. To deal with the threat, Prime Minister William Pitt established a large Irish militia made up of both Protestant and Catholic recruits and officered by the gentry in each locality. He then pressured the Irish parliament to grant the vote for representatives to the Irish House of Commons to Catholics who owned the requisite amount of landed property. Designed to placate resentful and potentially rebellious reformers, the measure stunned the Protestant Ascendancy. It did not go far enough for the reformers, however. They sought the right of Catholics to sit in parliament and hold high office, and for the power of parliament to control the executive body—referred to as "the Castle" after the Dublin edifice in which it was housed—controlled by the British government. Angered by the refusal of the Castle to pursue further reform, the United Irishmen began to demand separation from Britain, a position the authorities condemned and determined to stamp out by imposing a number of repressive measures. By the spring of 1794, the United Irishmen, under the leadership of Theobald Wolfe Tone, had moved from a position advocating constitutional reform to one embracing revolutionary republicanism. Wolfe Tone initiated talks with the French for a possible invasion, which found a warm reception in Paris.

The United Irishmen also turned to a decidedly more radical group, the secret society known as the Defenders, for support. Drawn largely from the Catholic peasantry, Defenders sought an end to the tithes they were required to pay to the established church in Ireland and relief from high rents and taxes, an agenda that necessitated that the targets of their activism were Protestants, given the character of land-owning in most of the country. They terrorized the Protestants in the countryside through campaigns of arson, destruction of property, the maiming of cattle, assault, and even murder. But they also appealed to rural and urban people involved in manufacturing, and as the ideology of the French revolution infiltrated their ranks, they took on a kind of diffuse republican tone as well, adding a measure of political revolution to their economic demands. Their anti-Protestant actions disturbed many United Irishmen, but they persuaded themselves that they could control their new allies and quell the sectarian elements within the Defenders.

The UI–Defender alliance provoked the appearance of another secret society, this one made up of Protestants. Organized in response to Defender activity, and convinced that the Defenders existed only in order to exterminate all Protestants, they carried out attacks on Catholics, seeking to drive them off their lands and out of their counties altogether. After a particularly brutal fight in County Armagh in September 1795 known as the Battle of the Diamond, lower-class Protestants formed themselves into the Orange Order, so-named for William of Orange, the king who had been victorious at the Battle of the Boyne in 1691 and forced the Treaty of Limerick on James' Catholic followers. Orangemen escalated their attacks on Catholics; the Defenders responded in turn; and from that point on, sectarian hatreds could not be separated out from political demands. Religious conflict between Catholics and Protestants, however much or often condemned by the non-sectarian United Irishmen, would always inform the political differences between rebels and loyalists in Ireland. Religious hatred would make civil war, when it came, all the more vicious.

The Irish government, with substantial British encouragement, moved to stamp out the threat posed by the Defenders and the United Irishmen. An Indemnity Act of 1795 allowed local magistrates—all of them Protestants—to inflict harsh punishments on offending UI and Defenders. In 1796, anxious because the militia formed in 1793 contained significant numbers of Catholics who might easily be recruited to the UI ranks, Castle authorities established a new armed force called the Yeomanry, officered by conservative Protestant landlords and manned by their mostly Protestant tenants. The Insurrection Act of that year imposed curfews and bans on assembly, and gave extraordinary powers to the magistracy to ignore basic legal rights as they prosecuted criminal and political acts. People could be arrested and tried without juries or the presentation of conventional evidence; if found guilty, they could be sentenced to transportation to Australia for long periods. The taking of oaths—long a staple of secret society culture—could be punished by death. In October, habeas corpus was formally suspended throughout Ireland.

In December 1796, a fleet of ships carrying 15,000 French soldiers almost landed in West Cork. Bad weather prevented most of them from coming ashore, though some 400 soldiers did so, only to be killed or captured by the local Yeomanry. The British ordered General Gerald Lake, a member of the Protestant Ascendancy, to do whatever it took to quell revolt. Lake declared martial law in the province of Ulster and cracked down murderously on suspected rebels. He ordered the firing of houses; he billeted his troops in the homes of civilians; he tortured prisoners; and he executed men in the militia he suspected of having been converted to the revolutionary cause. His brutality alienated ever greater numbers of Irish men and women, but it had the effect of weakening the rebels in the north. Much of the Ulster leadership among the UI ended up in jail.

In Dublin, the UI established a secret Directory, modeled after France's government. Headed by Thomas Emmet, a barrister, and two MPs, Arthur O'Connor and Lord Edward Fitzgerald, it began to plan for a rebellion. In March 1798, working from a tip from within the ranks of the United Irishmen, Castle officials arrested a number of UI leaders who were meeting in Dublin. Lord Fitzgerald and a few others who had not been present escaped the dragnet. Their plans for insurrection continued, with local rebel commanders drilling their forces and awaiting the signal to act. The remaining members of the UI Directory named May 23 as the start of their rising. Once again, however, betrayal from within the UI ranks enabled Castle officials to arrest Lord Fitzgerald on his way to meet his troops on May 18 (wounded during his capture, he languished in prison and died of his injuries in July). Nevertheless, despite a disastrous lack of coordination from a now leaderless organization, thousands of rebels took up arms in Dublin and points south and west on the designated day, the cry of "Death or Liberty" on their lips.

Castle forces regained control within a week, taking advantage of the chaos surrounding the situation in Dublin. A different story unfolded in County Wexford, where a local rebel army took on and handily defeated a small force of loyalists on May 27. The insurgents had been galvanized by a particularly gruesome series of atrocities committed by the North Cork militia, which was commanded by the Earl of Kingsborough. His troops had carried out a campaign of half-hangings, floggings, house-burning, and pitch-capping against the local population. This last entailed pouring hot tar into a paper cone placed over one's head, resulting in severe burning of the scalp and face. Kingsborough and his army had long enjoyed a fearsome reputation for the viciousness of their repression of suspected Defenders over the past year, and now, in the midst of open rebellion, Wexford and Wicklow insurgents took their revenge at Oulart, County Wexford. Buoyed by their success, they moved on to take Enniscorthy on May 29, thence to Wexford town, whose defenders learned of the approach of the 15,000-strong rebel force and abandoned their positions. On May 31, the rebels declared a republic and established a government made up of four Protestants and four Catholics. Celebrations of victory mingled with fear of what might come. The insurgents set up camp at the base of Carrickbyrne Hill, from which they carried out "sweeps" of the surrounding countryside to round up those loyalists they deemed a threat. By June 4, they had gathered up about 124 captives: thirteen of the prisoners were women, eight were children; fifteen were Catholics, and the remaining 109 were Protestants. They held them in the village of Scullabogue.

Their victory was short-lived. On June 5, 1798, at New Ross, the Wexford rebels engaged with units from Lord Kingsborough's North Cork militia and suffered a grievous defeat. The fighting that day proved to be particularly brutal. Once the loyalist army overwhelmed the rebels, its soldiers began killing the wounded and prisoners in the streets indiscriminately. They set on fire a house where seventy rebels lay wounded, killing all of them. Insurgents retreating from New Ross brought tales of loyalist atrocities to Scullabogue and urged their fellows there to execute the prisoners they had captured earlier in the week. Rebel soldiers shot some forty prisoners on the lawn of the farmhouse, and then turned their attention to those they had locked up in the barn on the property. They set it ablaze, killing all of those inside.

The Scullabogue massacre haunts the memory of the Irish Rebellion of 1798. Men, women, and children suffered hideously at the hands of incensed rebel soldiers who ordered that the barn holding prisoners be put to the torch. The men in charge of the prisoners had initially refused the command, but after receiving a third set of orders, acceded to the demands of the rebels, who had just returned from a battle at New Ross. There, only a few hours earlier, loyalist militiamen had perpetrated their own incineration of some seventy wounded insurgents in a house on Mary Street.

Ulster province had remained quiet while first the counties around Dublin and then Wexford rose. But on June 7, Ulster United Irishmen, virtually all of them Presbyterians, took up arms in County Antrim. They held the town of Antrim for a few hours, but then were ousted by volleys of artillery fire from government troops. A few days later at Ballynahinch, twelve miles outside Belfast, rebel forces gathered, where they were met by loyalist troops and decisively defeated. The rising in the north, which had never really ever gotten going, collapsed. Freed up now to turn south, General Lake laid siege to the rebel camp at Vinegar Hill in County Wexford on June 21, using heavy artillery to drive out the insurgents. This proved to be the last real battle of the rebellion, though follow-up operations continued, generating significant casualties. As they ran down the rebels of Wexford, government forces made no distinction between combatants and non-combatants, raping women en masse and sometimes killing everyone in sight. In October, the British navy seized the French ship carrying Wolfe Tone to Donegal, where he hoped to organize another rising. Tried and sentenced to death, he foiled government efforts to showcase his execution by committing suicide. The Castle executed many of the rebel commanders on the spot and tried others trial in military tribunals. Some 600 Defenders and United Irishmen received sentences of transportation to Australia in the years between 1795 and 1806.

The Irish Revolution of 1798 serves to illustrate a complicated variation of that triangular relationship between settler colonists, Indigenous peoples, and the metropole we saw operating in Bacon's Rebellion and the American Revolution. It proved to be a momentous event with significant long-term consequences. Both sides in the conflict committed horrific atrocities and inflicted terrible losses on the country as a whole. Some 30,000 Catholic and Protestant antagonists perished in what turned out to be the bloodiest fighting in Ireland's history. Though, as we have seen, the United Irishmen consisted of both Catholics and Protestants who sought religious tolerance for all, religious hatreds at the level of the common people could never be overcome. Catholic members of the Defenders and Protestant affiliates of the Orange Order often let their sectarian prejudices rule their actions and the memories of atrocities on both sides would linger for decades, contaminating relationships and contributing to mistrust and misunderstanding.

Pitt's government feared that a rebellious Ireland might again provide a staging ground for French forces to invade Great Britain, and distrusted the capability of the Anglo-Irish to contain the situation. Seeking to find ways to contain the dangers that Ireland posed, Pitt weighed the option of establishing a permanent occupation force in Ireland, a possibility he realized could not be sustained either politically or materially. He decided instead on a proposal that he hoped would reconcile both Catholic and Protestant factions: political association with Great Britain. He put forward a plan for Ireland to be joined with England, Wales, and Scotland in the United Kingdom of Great Britain. In such a union Ireland's parliament would be abolished and its representation in the parliament in Westminster determined by proportional representation. Protestants liked the idea, seeing in the parliament at Westminster far greater protection of their interests than the parliament in Dublin, susceptible to Catholic pressure, could afford them. The Catholics of Ireland welcomed Pitt's promise of what is referred to as "Catholic emancipation," the right of Catholics to sit in the parliament in Westminster. In 1801, the Act of Union brought Ireland into union with Great Britain. To his dismay, however, Pitt could not honor his promise of Catholic emancipation because of hostility to it from members of his cabinet and, more importantly, from the king. As a result of the prime minister's failure to deliver on his promise, a mass movement of nationalists grew up in Ireland in the 1820s over the issue of Catholic emancipation, forecasting and in some instances igniting a vast array of liberal reforms in the Anglo settler communities across the globe.

***

South Africa proved to be the most complex of the settlement colonies, involving numerous African peoples, British settlers, and Boer (Afrikaner) farmers—descendants of seventeenth-century Dutch settlers who had worked the land of the Cape Colony for generations (see Dutch Counterpoint in Chapter 3). A fundamentalist people who took their direction from the tenets of the Old Testament, the Dutch had enslaved the pastoral Khoikhoi people and nearly exterminated the hunter-gatherer San.

By the time the British gained the territory from the Dutch in 1795 in the course of the Napoleonic Wars, the San were hard pressed to reproduce themselves as a society or a culture, nor could they continue to survive through their age-old practices of foraging. They continued to experience violence at the hands of the Afrikaner settlers, incidents of which the British were determined to end, if only because trying to maintain social order drew incessantly upon scarce resources. Authorities hoped to assimilate and "civilize" the San in order to impose peace on the Boer–San conflict; they hoped that by encouraging the San to become pastoralists they could be induced to settle down and become available to work as household servants and farm hands. The London Missionary Society sent out preachers to establish missions, hoping to attract San and Khoi converts to Christianity. Some did join the missions, but largely in order to find refuge from continued depredations and violence or to gain access to food. The missions themselves suffered from a lack of resources and were not able to last very long, a turn of events welcomed by white settlers who regarded them as competitors for San labor and as places that challenged settler control by educating Africans and leading them to think they were equal to whites. By 1806, when the British retook South Africa after a short hiatus, the San people had been reduced to servant status. They had no other option if they wanted to find food and shelter to survive. North of Cape Town, where British jurisdiction was scanty, Boers continued to harass and attack the San. One "boasted that only a few years ago they used to lie in wait for the Bushmen and shoot them like baboons."[6]

Conflict with the Xhosa in the eastern regions of the Cape occurred regularly, as Boer and Xhosa struggled regularly over the rich pasturelands of the Zuurveld, just west of the Fish River, in a series of "Frontier Wars" in the years after 1760. The British tried to bring them to an end in 1811 and 1812 by driving the Xhosa from their lands, burning their crops and settlements, and seizing thousands of cattle. In 1817, the governor asked the British government to send colonists to the Cape Colony; he planned to settle them on the Zuurveld as a means of keeping the Xhosa at bay. That had not been the only reason for the settling of Britons in South Africa: authorities at home feared that the severe economic downturn following the end of the Napoleonic Wars in 1815 would create a radical protest movement among impoverished working people and hoped that emigration would dampen such a possibility. Eighty-thousand people applied to go, but the scheme could only accommodate 4,000, 1,440 of whom were men, 800 women, and 1,760 children. Colonial authorities divided the new arrivals up into sixty-eight groups, segregating them by ethnicity (English, Scottish, Welsh, and Irish), and settling them on the land, where officials hoped they would create farms and ranches. Fewer than 40 per cent of them, however, had any experience farming, and the land proved less than ideal for extensive agriculture and settlement. Within a year or so, half of the settlers left their granted parcels and made their way to the cities of the eastern Cape, where they took up jobs as artisans and merchants. Some who stayed began trading with African groups further east beyond the colony boundary, while others turned to grazing sheep. Wool exports to Britain became a lucrative mainstay in the Zuurveld, which the colonial authorities renamed Albany. But the settlers had not been told that the lands they grazed their sheep and cattle on was claimed by the Xhosa for pasturing their cattle. They had been forcibly and violently dispossessed in 1811–12 and again in 1817–19, and were in no mood to let the British settlers simply take over what had long been theirs. Xhosa bands raided the settlements and seized settler animals, infuriating the colonists and ratcheting up tensions (see Figure 4.1).

Many of the settler farmers and those who had moved to urban areas to ply their trade or establish businesses had brought with them to South Africa a worldview informed by the humanitarian impulses that characterized a good deal of British thinking in the early part of the nineteenth century. Anti-slavery sentiment stood front and center in the minds of those who embraced humanitarian thought; indeed, it had compelled British lawmakers to outlaw the trade in enslaved persons in 1807 and would lead them to abolish slavery itself in 1833. Anti-slavery attitudes stood side by side with, and were, for many, informed by, liberal philosophies of free trade and the free movement of labor. The two strands came together momentously for the subsequent history of South Africa when the 1820 settlers found that they could not

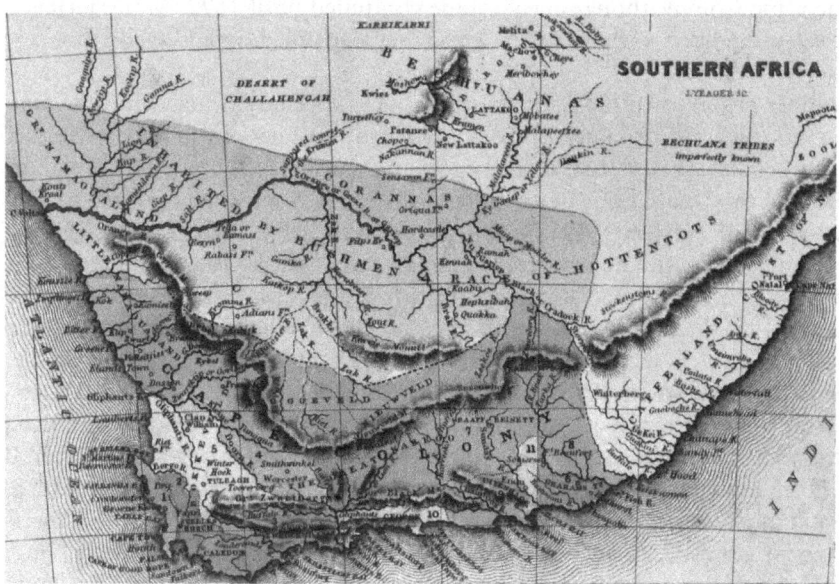

FIGURE 4.1 *1834 Carey Map of South Africa Cape of Good Hope Capetown Colony.*

obtain sufficient labor to conduct their enterprises effectively. Many of them tried to hire Khoikhoi and San who worked for Afrikaner households, in violation of the contracts the laborers had entered into that strictly limited their freedom and which LMS missionary John Philip had described as constituting near-slavery. Accounts of the harsh treatment of the Khoikhoi and San at the hands of the Afrikaners were picked up by the London press, leading the British government to feel that it must act. In Ordinance 50 of 1828, the government declared that Black and white men in the Cape Colony were, "in the most full and ample manner," equal before the law. This meant that Africans could possess land, travel freely, and appeal to local magistrates for redress if injured by whites. In practice, Cape Africans had lost their land already and had few resources with which to purchase any, but Ordinance 50 ensured that they could abrogate the coercive contracts imposed on them by Afrikaners and go to work for Britons.

Ordinance 50 infuriated Boers, who saw it as yet another example of Britain's deplorable treatment of them. The 1820 settlers, for instance, enjoyed rights denied the Afrikaners, who soon found it increasingly difficult to establish legal title to land. In 1826, the British made English the official language of the Cape Colony, further disadvantaging the Afrikaners and making them second-class citizens in the place they had lived for almost two centuries. But most galling was the British insistence on telling them how they could treat their African servants and the many Khoikhoi and San men, women, and children they had enslaved. The abolition of the slave trade in 1807 meant that no more enslaved men and women might be imported into the Cape Colony, though illegal trade continued until 1822. Many farmers greeted the news with horror because they depended on enslaved labor for their livelihoods.

Boer enslavement of Africans contributed to many British officials' and settlers' view of Afrikaners as backward, primitive people. In the eyes of the 1820 settlers, they were lazy and degenerate, dependent upon African labor because they would not bestir themselves to do what was necessary to live a "civilized" existence. As one British observer put it, "even when gain was evidently the ultimate reward, the indolence of these degenerate colonists pre-vailed ... over their avarice."[7] British settlers established their identity as freedom-loving virtuous citizens against the image of the Boers as brutish and brutal idlers who had devolved to near-beastly status. Except among the elites in Cape Town, British settlers generally did not mix with Afrikaners socially or politically, and did not intermarry with them, creating an ethnic division among the white population that recalled that of the French and British settlers in Canada. The difference was that in Canada the British outnumbered the French significantly, while in southern Africa, Afrikaners always had a 55 per cent numerical advantage over English settlers. And unlike settler colonialism in North America, Australia, and New Zealand, where Indigenous populations were dramatically diminished by the practices and presence of white settlers till they comprised only a tiny minority of the overall population, the African population always outnumbered the white population by at least four to one. Like Ireland, South Africa constituted a settler colony in which the exploitation of Indigenous labor was as crucial a factor as the acquisition of Indigenous land.

Counterpoint: Mexican Independence, 1810–21

The settler colony of New Spain obtained its independence from Spain in 1821, declaring itself the Republic of Mexico. The struggle lasted for more than a decade, and came about as a consequence of Napoleon's invasion of Spain, a movement among New Spain creoles (those born in New Spain to Spanish settler parents) to sever ties with the metropole, and a years-long popular insurrection undertaken largely by Indian people. Unlike the revolt of the American colonists against Britain, the rebellion constituted, in the words of one of its most prominent historians, "arguably the first great war of national liberation ... in which the ethnic difference between colonizers and colonized became a major political issue."[8]

Discussions and plans among creoles for separation from Spanish rule were underway in September 1810 when authorities got wind of a meeting in the Bajio region. One of the conspiracy's participants, a parish priest by the name of Miguel Hidalgo y Costilla, determined to prevent Spanish officials from disrupting their scheme for national liberation by unleashing a popular revolt. On September 16, he issued the Cry of Dolores, after the town where he lived and worked, calling for rebellion against Spanish rule. Peopled largely by Indian and mestizo men and women armed with staves, machetes, and farm tools, a crowd of several thousand marched to San Miguel el Grande under the banner of the Virgin of Guadalupe, taking the town without incident. There, despite the attempts of Hidalgo and other creole leaders to stop them, the insurgents looted the place. From San Miguel el Grande, where large numbers of recruits joined them, the rebels moved to take the town of Celaya, and marched back north to Guanajuato, now numbering some 20,000. They attacked the granary where the Spanish intendant had holed up with other wealthy locals, killing more than 300 Spanish men, women, and children and seizing the jewelry, gold, and other valuables their victims had brought with them.

Hidalgo kept attracting more and more workers and peasants to his force, issuing decrees to abolish tributes owed by Indian people and rescinding contracts for the rental of Indian land, agreements that often enabled the lease-holder to appropriate that land. The priest never had the opportunity to actually implement such decrees, but they appealed to Indian and mestizo communities that had long suffered under the regime of Spanish settlers. On the other side of the equation, the looting and killing and what was becoming a race- and class-based war alienated any creoles who might have joined the rebellion at that point. They sought to simply replace Spanish authority with their own, not to overturn the social or economic order in which they prospered.

In October, the rebels, now some 70,000 strong, entered Valladolid without any resistance, and, yelling "Death to the Spaniards," looted the city. Two weeks later, now numbering 80,000, they took Toluca on their way to Mexico City. At Monte de Las Cruces, they ran into a royalist army of 2,500 soldiers who almost fended them off, but had to retreat after a long and costly battle. For three days, the insurgents stayed outside Mexico City, awaiting Hidalgo's orders to attack the city. Those orders never came; instead, the priest, probably fearful that his undisciplined and unruly army could not prevail over well-armed royalist troops in Mexico City, commanded his followers to fall back to the west, sparing the capital what would surely have been a bloody and catastrophic battle.

In November, at Guadalajara, Hidalgo set up a rebel government and recruited new insurgents to his army from the Indian and mestizo villages surrounding the city. The rural population had fared badly over the last sixty years, losing their lands to Spanish settler elites who took advantage of the growing population of the city to increase their wealth. Despite its size, however, the rebel force proved no match for the royalist army that marched on Guadalajara in January 1811. Without sufficient weaponry, lacking in discipline and leadership, the insurgents could not hold off a much smaller contingent of trained and well-equipped soldiers under the command of Brigadier Félix Calleja. At Calderón Bridge, after a battle that lasted an entire day, the royalist army sent Hidalgo's rebels fleeing for their lives. In March, crown forces captured what was left of his army, taking Hidalgo and other leaders to Chihuahua and executing them there.

The rebellion continued, becoming more guerrilla in nature as it moved to the south and west under the leadership of Father José María Morelos. Over the next four years, rebels carried out attacks on haciendas, towns, and farms of those supporting the crown, hitting hard and fast and slipping away back to their strongholds, while royal forces burned villages and fields full of crops. Unlike Hidalgo, Morelos would not tolerate looting or racial attacks; he preached a racial equality that included all Mexicans, Spanish, Black, mestizo, mulatto, and Indian alike. His insistence that Indians and others had rights to land made him popular among the masses but kept creoles from supporting his movement. Morelos established a congress in September 1813 in the state of Guerrero, opening its first session by invoking Montezuma and other Indigenous leaders who resisted the conquistadors as agents of independence. In November, the congress declared independence from Spain, and the following year issued a constitution, all the while keeping on the move to prevent its capture by royalist forces. In the fall of 1815, Spanish authorities caught up with the rebels, imprisoning, trying, and executing Morelos at year's end.

Still the insurgency persisted, neither guerrillas nor royalist forces able to gain the upper hand. The conflict ground on for the next five years, till events in Spain compelled a solution. The restored king of Spain, Ferdinand VII, attempted to establish absolute rule there, provoking resistance both on the peninsula itself and in New Spain. Formerly loyal royalist creoles joined with those seeking independence, and under the leadership of Agustín de Iturbide, formed an alliance that brought about the collapse of the Spanish government. In 1821, following more than a decade of struggle, a new, independent Mexico was born, but one whose class- and race-based system of privilege would last for another one hundred years.

Primary Source Document

Settlement of South Australia, 1836

Privy Council (United Kingdom) — "Letters Patent under the Great Seal of the United Kingdom Erecting and Establishing the Province of South Australia and Fixing the Boundaries thereof, February 19, 1836" [1836] IndigLRes 1

Letters Patent under the Great Seal of the United Kingdom erecting and establishing the Province of South Australia and fixing the boundaries thereof, February 19, 1836

William the Fourth by the Grace of God of the United Kingdom of Great Britain and Ireland King Defender of the Faith **To all to Whom** these Presents shall come Greeting **Whereas** by an Act of Parliament passed in the fifth year of our Reign entitled "An Act to empower His Majesty to erect South Australia into a British Province or Provinces and to provide for the Colonization and Government thereof" After writing that, that part of Australia which lies between the Meridians of the one hundred and thirty second and one hundred and forty first Degrees of East Longitude and between the Southern Ocean and twenty six Degrees of South Latitude together with the Islands adjacent thereto consists of Waste and unoccupied Lands which are supposed to be fit for the purposes of Colonization And that divers of our Subjects possessing amongst them considerable Property are desirous to embark for the said part of Australia And that it is highly expedient that our said Subjects should be enabled to carry their said laudable purpose into effect It is Enacted that it shall and may be lawful for Us with the advice of our Privy Council to erect within that part of Australia which lies between the Meridians of the one hundred and thirty second and one hundred and forty first Degrees of East Longitude and between the Southern Ocean and the twenty-six Degrees of South Latitude together with all and every the Islands adjacent thereto and the Bays and Gulfs thereof with the advice of our Privy Council to Establish one or more Provinces and to fix the respective Boundaries of such Provinces **Now Know Ye** that with the advice of Our Privy Council and in pursuance and exercise of the powers in Us in that behalf vested by the said recited Act of Parliament We do hereby Erect and Establish one Province to be called the Province of **South Australia**—And we do hereby fix the Boundaries of the said Province in manner following (that is to say) On the North the twenty sixth Degree of South Latitude On the South the Southern Ocean—On the West the one hundred and thirty second Degree of East Longitude— And on the East the one hundred and forty first Degree of East Longitude including therein all and every the Bays and Gulfs thereof together with the Island called Kangaroo Island and all and every the Islands adjacent to the said last mentioned Island or to that part of the main

Land of the said Province **Provided Always** that nothing in those our Letters Patent contained shall affect or be construed to affect the rights of any Aboriginal Natives of the said Province to the actual occupation or enjoyment in their own Persons or in the Persons of their Descendants of any Lands therein now actually occupied or enjoyed by such Natives **In Witness** whereof We have caused these our Letters to be made Patent **Witness** Ourself at Westminster the Nineteenth day of February in the sixth year of our Reign.

By Writ of Privy Seal
Edmunds

Notes

1 Quoted in Lyndall Ryan, "The Black Line in Van Diemen's Land: Success or Failure?," *Journal of Australian Studies*, Vol. 37, No. 1 (2013), pp. 3–18, p. 9; quoted in Nicholas Clements, *The Black Line: Fear, Sex and Resistance in Tasmania* (Brisbane: University of Queensland Press, 2014), p. 128.
2 James Belich, *Replenishing the Earth. The Settler Revolution and the Rise of the Anglo-World, 1783–1939* (Oxford: Oxford University Press, 2009), p. 179.
3 Quoted in Richard Broome, *Aboriginal Australians, A History Since 1788* (Sydney: Allen & Unwin, 2010), p. 40.
4 Benjamin Madley, "From Terror to Genocide: Britain's Tasmanian Penal Colony and Australia's History Wars," *Journal of British Studies*, Vol. 47, No. 1 (2008), pp. 77–106, p. 88.
5 Quoted in Broome, *Aboriginal Australians*, p. 42.
6 Quoted in Mohamed Adhikari, *The Anatomy of a South African Genocide: The Extermination of the Cape San Peoples* (Athens: Ohio University Press, 2011), p. 75.
7 Quoted in Alan Lester, *Imperial Networks: Creating Identities in Nineteenth-Century South Africa and Britain* (London: Routledge, 2002), p. 15.
8 See Eric Van Young, *The Other Rebellion: Popular Violence, Ideology, and the Mexican Struggle for Independence, 1810–1821* (Stanford: Stanford University Press, 2001), p. 7

Further Reading

Mohamed Adhikari, *The Anatomy of a South African Genocide: The Extermination of the Cape San Peoples* (Athens: Ohio University Press, 2011).
James Belich, *Replenishing the Earth. The Settler Revolution and the Rise of the Anglo-World, 1783–1939* (Oxford: Oxford University Press, 2009).
Richard Broome, *Aboriginal Australians, A History Since 1788* (Sydney: Allen & Unwin, 2010).
Jim Smyth, *Revolution, Counter-Revolution, and Union: Ireland in the 1790s* (New York: Cambridge University Press, 2000).

5

Liberal Empire, 1830s–70s

In 1836, Gerritt Maritz loaded his family and possessions into seven wagons, drove out of the Cape Colony district of Graaff-Reinet, and, with 700 other Boer settlers, headed eastward on what came to be called the Great Trek. These Voortrekkers (or pioneers) sought new lands on which to settle and to escape what they regarded as the oppressive and wrong-headed governance of Britain, which had introduced laws and policies that struck at the heart of Boer economic and cultural life. They particularly objected to Ordinance 50, which gave Africans the same rights Boers enjoyed; the abolition of slavery in 1833, which cut deeply into their ability to obtain the labor they needed to keep their farms afloat, proved to be the last straw for them. As Piet Retief, the leader of another group of Voortrekkers, put it in a manifesto published in 1837, "We complain of the severe losses which we have been forced to sustain by the emancipation of our slaves, and the vexatious laws which have been enacted respecting them." Retief listed a number of other grievances, concluding with the declaration that "We are now quitting the fruitful land of our birth, in which we have suffered enormous losses and continual vexation, and are entering a wild and dangerous territory; but we go with a firm reliance on an all-seeing, just, and merciful Being, whom it will be our endeavour to fear and humbly to obey."[1]

The lands into which the Voortrekkers ventured proved wild and dangerous indeed. Physical hardships abounded on the long journey eastward. Where roads existed, they were often steep and rocky; the lack of wood on the wide open Karoo prevented families from building fires to cook food or even brew coffee. They forded the broad Orange River by building rafts for the women and children and drove their thousands of cattle, oxen, and sheep across southern Africa's largest waterway. Most perilous of all, they encountered African peoples like the Ndebele and the Zulu who, fearing the invasion of their lands by white settlers, sought to kill them. Many Voortrekkers lost their lives to the attacks of Africans protecting their lands and livelihoods; far many more Africans lost theirs to the trekking Boers.

The Great Trek, a foundational moment in Afrikaner history and tradition, constituted an act of rebellion against British rule. As Retief phrased it, "We quit this colony under the full assurance that the English Government has nothing more to require of us, and will allow us to govern ourselves without its interference in future."[2] It took place in the context of reform movements, the liberalizing of governments, and settler and Indigenous rebellions that had been occurring across Britain and in the white colonies of settlement since the 1820s.

***

During the years between 1815 and 1870, Britain's social, economic, and political structures became transformed. Once a system characterized by ranks and orders, in which landed and commercial elites whose wealth derived from agriculture and commerce monopolized political power, it gave way to one in which frequently antagonistic classes vied with one another for political power within an economic system dominated by industry. After 1832, with the passage of the Reform Act of that year, a classical liberal political system derived from a franchise restricted by property and gender qualifications came into being. It championed principles of meritocracy, individualism, property ownership, free trade, and respectability.

A number of core principles underpinned the liberal order and formed the backdrop against which British settlers and officials perceived Indigenous and Native peoples, chief among them the sanctity of property ownership and the notion of individualism. Together, they constituted a signal element of liberal thinking, called possessive individualism—the conviction that pursuing one's individual self-interest by acquiring and owning things enhanced the prosperity of society as a whole. Most Native peoples lived by a different ethos, one based on the well-being of the community rather than that of the individual. Working together to provide for the survival of the whole, most Indigenous groups could not fathom the idea that one person could own a piece of the earth. It belonged to all, to benefit all. This clash of worldviews manifested itself in all kinds of dealings between settlers and Native peoples and would lead to profound misunderstandings about such things ranging from the nature of treaty agreements to the morality of those who did not accept the lifeways of the other.

Debate about the status of white colonies of settlement had roiled Britons for some time by the 1830s. With the stench of the American revolt still strong in their nostrils, some Britons in the metropole believed that the white colonies should be let go before they caused trouble. Evangelicals and humanitarians, however, especially those in the Aborigines' Protection Society, dedicated to "protecting the defenseless and promoting the advancement of uncivilized tribes," feared that white colonists would not treat Indigenous peoples or descendants of enslaved Africans with the respect and dignity they deserved; they insisted that rule from Britain was required to protect them from oppression. Colonial reformers such as Edward Gibbon Wakefield looked to further colonization of the white territories to ease the social problems Britain faced as industrialization displaced thousands of people. "No pains should be spared to teach the labouring classes to regard the colonies as the land of promise" he wrote in 1839.[3] For the settlers themselves in Canada, southerm Africa, Australia, and New Zealand, colonial rule had begun to rankle, and sometimes vociferous demands for self-government could be heard regularly. And if the colonies remained part of Britain, just how were Britons overseas to be governed? Did they, should they, possess the same rights and responsibilities at Britons at home? If so, what kind of relationship between colony and metropole should prevail? These questions became more pointed and more relevant in the aftermath of the Reform Act of 1832.

The British government turned to the man who had helped pass the Reform Act, Radical Jack Durham, to fashion a policy that would settle the question. The Durham Report, issued in 1839, proved to be a momentous document, though it wasn't accepted as official policy until 1846, when Prime Minister Lord John Russell finally put it into practice. The report recommended that the white colonies of settlement be regarded as extensions of British society and of the British state, and, as such, urged that they be seen as comprised of people entirely capable of governing themselves. White settlers, as merely displaced Britons, could be counted on to remain loyal to their queen and country and therefore need not be ruled by coercion from the metropole. As responsible members of the British empire, they should be permitted to form their own governments, the governor-general—formerly appointed by and answerable to the queen's government—now answerable to the elected legislatures of the white colonies. The acceptance of the Durham Report meant that far-reaching self-government—leaving only the power to conduct foreign relations, make constitutions, carry on overseas trade, and dispose of public lands in the hands of the British government—would, over the next twenty years, come to Canada, Australia, and New Zealand. Ireland, southern Africa, and the United States produced a different set of liberalization measures, each with their own momentous outcomes for Indigenous peoples and settlers alike. In almost every instance, the concerns expressed by evangelicals and humanitarians for the plight of Indigenous peoples proved prescient: settlers given the right to rule themselves wreaked havoc on the Native peoples whose land and labor they coveted.

***

Efforts to reform the political system of Great Britain appeared first in Ireland, where Daniel O'Connell, a devout Catholic of radical principles, organized thousands of people in his Catholic Association, and turned a network of priests into an electoral machine that was able to challenge the political monopoly of Protestant landlords. Against the backdrop of terrible depression in the agricultural sector, which produced regular famines throughout the 1820s, O'Connell rallied peasants, small landholders, larger landowners, and urban working and middling sorts into an organization that emphasized their Gaelic-Catholic identity and their sense of exclusion from political life under Protestant rule. He aimed to replace Protestants as the rulers of Ireland by reforming the British parliament, the institution that governed Ireland. O'Connell did not seek revolution or independence from Great Britain; he sought instead to make it possible for Irish Catholics to sit in parliament so that their majority interests and concerns would be represented. So disparate a group of Catholics—from landless peasants to landed gentry to urban workers and artisans to shopkeepers and professionals—certainly did not share common economic interests. What welded them together, what made them a formidable and finally unignorable interest group, was their Gaelicness and their Catholicism. Cultural identity served as the adhesive, the glue, that held these different folks together. "Catholic Ireland" ranged itself against the Protestant Ascendancy in a series of "monster meetings;" and in the elections of 1826 and 1828, won a few seats in County Wexford and County Clare.

O'Connell opposed violence in all parts of his campaign, a stance that earned him the support of the Catholic clergy and its hierarchy. But he showed no reluctant to use the endemic violence of the countryside to press his point about the need to reform the political structures under which Ireland was governed. Playing up both the virtues of the Irish Catholic nation and the threats of violence emanating from the countryside in the form of the Whiteboy movement, O'Connell exploited English fears of Irish civil war to wrest emancipation from the die-hard Tory government of the Duke of Wellington in 1829. Though it came some twenty-eight years after William Pitt had promised it as part of the Act of Union with Great Britain in 1801, the Roman Catholic Relief Act of 1829 gave wealthy Irish Catholics the right to sit in parliament.

With Catholic Emancipation, property-owning Irish Catholics could now take seats in the House of Commons in Westminster, but the act did nothing to change the situation in the cities and port towns of Ireland, where the Protestant Ascendancy maintained control over the corporations that ruled and administered the urban areas. Breaking their power would require more thorough-going reform of the political system, which allowed only landed men to vote and gave representation to old "rotten" boroughs with few to no people living there and refused it to the fast-growing cities. The Great Reform Act of 1832 accomplished this change, expanding eligibility for voting and making it uniform in the boroughs. Where before 1832 one had to *own* property worth 40s. in order to vote, largely restricting the franchise to the landed interests of the country, now any man owning £10 worth of land or buildings or paying rent of £10 a year qualified, opening up direct political representation to the middling classes of the nation. The size of the electorate skyrocketed overnight: the Irish county electorate rose from about 37,000 to 60,000 or so. Borough voters increased, especially among Catholics, but overall Irish representation per capita fell far behind that of England and Wales. Across the United Kingdom as a whole, the electorate more than doubled. Had the actual size of Ireland's population been taken into account, it would have gained 100 seats. Its MPs asked for twenty-five, but no English minister was prepared to swamp the Commons with representatives elected by a majority of Catholics; it received only five new seats.

The Whig government, brought into power through the changes established by the Reform Act, set about implementing its colonial agenda immediately, passing legislation in 1833 that diminished the extent and power of the Anglican Church in Ireland and reduced the tithes owed by Irish peasants. These carrots accompanied a particularly sharp stick, however, in the Coercion Act of 1833, which suspended habeas corpus and imposed severe penalties on those involved in the agrarian unrest that plagued the countryside.

In 1845, Ireland suffered a potato blight, which worsened in 1846 and again in 1847–8. By the 1840s, the potato had become the staple crop for millions of Irish peasants, and when it failed, those peasants had very little else to turn to. In the years 1845 to 1851, the country lost some 2.25 million people, perhaps half of them to death by starvation or disease, the other half to emigration to England, Australia and New Zealand, and the US. Robert Peel, Tory prime minister, responded robustly to the crisis in 1845, purchasing 20,000 tons of Indian corn and meal from the US and exporting it to Ireland. The Indian corn soon proved sufficient to feed most of the Irish who needed it. Peel also pushed through the government the repeal of the Corn Laws, which had artificially raised prices on imported grains so that English landlords could sell their crops at good prices. Now grain could come into Ireland from other countries at lower prices.

The action of Peel's government in 1845 and 1846 prevented disaster. But when the harvest failed again in 1846, the new Whig government fell far short of what was needed to relieve the hunger of so vast a population. Imbued with the ideology of *laissez-faire*, which preached non-intervention by the government in the workings of the economy, the Whig minister in charge of the situation, Charles Trevelyan, refused to ban the exportation of grain from Ireland. This led to increased deprivation and then starvation, which in turn made the population vulnerable to infectious diseases. The government tried to address the problem by putting Irish peasants to work on public works projects, by establishing soup kitchens, and then by increasing the eligibility for assistance under the poor laws by making it possible for people not entering the poor house to receive aid. This last effort, however, included a provision put forward by a large landholding Irish MP that no one could receive relief without surrendering their land holdings to their landlords. This meant, in effect, that Irish peasants either lost access to the land or that they starved because they would not give up their land. This provision proved to be the strongest evidence to later Irish nationalists that the British had intentionally starved the Irish, committing, in essence, genocide. They had not, but it was not hard to believe the charge, given the lack of information about what the government was doing and the callous statements in the press regarding the famine.

The famine changed everything. Socially, economically, religiously, culturally, and politically, Ireland emerged from the disaster of the 1840s and early 1850s an entirely different country. Fully 20 percent of the population had vanished, having either died or emigrated, and the numbers still have not recovered. Irish farming and the rural society it sustained—or, more accurately, failed to sustain—were transformed: tilling the land for food production gave way to grazing animals on it, and the cottagers who had done the potato farming earlier vanished. Smallholdings and the laborers who worked them gave way to larger farms tenanted by families with fewer children. The appearance of railways in Ireland's interior made it possible to communicate with and transport products to and from formerly isolated people, and the improvement of England's economy following the "hungry forties" allowed wage earners there to purchase increasing volumes of Irish meat and dairy products. The standard of living among virtually all classes of Ireland rose and the amenities of life—housing, public health facilities, and the like—improved concomitantly. These benefits, it must be said, were a brutal consequence of the massive loss of population: those who were left fared better in the absence of the dead and the departed. The material "equilibrium" achieved in the post-famine years, moreover, depended upon the continuing emigration of some of the most productive members of society to brighter futures in Canada, the US, South Africa, Australia, and New Zealand. Each year some 65,000 Irish men and women left the land of their birth, only 30,000 of whom were replaced by natural increase, yielding a net loss in Ireland's population of about 35,000 annually.

The famine had made it crystal clear that the system of land tenure in Ireland was deeply problematic and needed to be reformed. Those who stood in the way of land reform belonged overwhelmingly to the Protestant Anglican landlord class, whose influence in the British parliament gave them power disproportionate to their numbers and even wealth. If the land question was to be effectively addressed, it became apparent to more and more people, the national question of Ireland's relationship to England would have to be resolved in Ireland's favor. Nationalists used the famine to tie the land question to the national question, and in so doing set the path of Irish politics for more than sixty years to come.

Farmers organized in a Tenant League seeking land reform joined in the early 1850s with a number of Irish MPs in the Liberal party to establish an independent Irish parliamentary party. The MPs, Catholics themselves or representing Catholic constituencies, had been sickened by the anti-Catholic initiatives undertaken by their party leader, Lord John Russell, and they determined to do something about it. Styling themselves the "Irish Brigade," they began in March of 1851 to act in opposition to their own party's actions in parliament. For the election of 1852 they fielded their own slate of candidates; with the full-throated support of a resurgent Catholic clergy, the Irish Brigade returned some forty-eight MPs who shared their determination to act independently of the Liberals. Their success was short-lived, however, and by 1859 the fledgling Irish parliamentary party, lacking a sustainable organization, a coherent platform, and a credible set of practices—which, after all meant supporting the Tories, the party of Irish Protestants and Irish landlords—collapsed.

In the absence of any constitutional means by which the land and national questions could be redressed, an organization pledged to the overthrow of British rule and the creation of an Irish republic emerged. The Fenians, or the Irish Republican Brotherhood, as they were sometimes called, formed in Dublin in 1858 under the leadership of James Stephen, who enjoyed the emotional and financial support of the large Irish population in America. Within six years, the group could boast a membership of 54,000 adherents recruited largely from the farmer and artisan classes. Unable to either socially or politically advance themselves, owing to their status and level of income, they found in the Fenians an association of like-minded rebels. It became a powerful and influential political movement in the 1860s.

***

The numbers and welfare of Indigenous peoples in northeastern Canada had been reduced significantly over the past century and a half, as contact with Europeans brought devastating disease, depleted hunting and farming lands, and exacerbated warfare, leaving fewer than 25,000 Aboriginal people in the eastern lands by the middle of the nineteenth century. In Nova Scotia and New Brunswick, perhaps 3,000 Mi'kmaq people lived on reserves created for them, which had been shrunk by about a sixth between 1840 and 1860. In the northern regions of Quebec, about 3,600 Cree, Montagnais, and Innu peoples lived relatively unchanged lives, but in the southern part of the province, around 5,000 Mohawk, Abenaki, Algonquin, and Nipissing people inhabited reserves. Ontario contained the greatest number of Indigenous people in the eastern part of the continent, where 12,000 or so First Nations people lived on reserves established through treaties made with the British government. Indigenous populations lived on marginal lands in the eastern reserves, barely getting by on the sale of agricultural products and manufactured goods.

On the prairies to the west of Ontario, 45,000 Cree, Assiniboine, western Ojibwe, Dakota, and Blackfoot peoples lived as they had for centuries, though now the source of their vibrant economies, the massive buffalo herds that roamed the plains, were falling into decline. Farther west still, beyond the Rocky Mountains, dozens of Native communities inhabited the inland and coastal areas of what would become British Columbia. Their numbers declined dramatically as diseases brought by Europeans began to decimate their ranks. White miners and settlers further eroded their societies; in the fifty years following 1835 the Aboriginal population in British Columbia dropped from 70,000 to 28,000.

Most of the white population lived in the northeastern regions of the continent. About one-quarter of the 2.5 million Britons living in British North America in 1850 or so hailed originally from Ireland; 16 percent of them came from Scotland, and 20 percent from England and Wales. Scottish Protestants constituted by far the majority of whites living in the lands held by the Hudson's Bay Company in the far north and west of the country. Some 750,000 descendants of early French settlers lived mainly in Lower Canada, while people of mixed Indigenous and French or Scottish background—the Métis—populated the area around what is today Manitoba in the Red River settlement. Further to the west, 100,000 or so Aborigines lived lives mostly undisturbed by Europeans, but that situation would change dramatically after 1850. The presence of French and Irish Catholics fueled religious hatreds among Scottish and English Protestants, which only increased after the 1846 famine propelled 300,000 more Irish emigrants to settle in Canada. The same Orange Orders we saw springing up in Ireland to counter what Protestants regarded as a Catholic threat appeared in the North American colonies as well in the 1830s.

In 1837 and 1838, rebellions against established political authority broke out in Lower and Upper Canada. Informed both by British liberal thought that emphasized notions of free trade and *laissez-faire* and American ideas about agrarian independence and democracy, some reformers demanded that the political rights enjoyed by Britons at home be extended to the North American colonies; others sought a reform of land-holding policies that benefited the upper classes. In Lower Canada, French-Canadian nationalism played an important part in the rebellion as well. British forces easily put down the uprisings, executing some of the leaders and transporting hundreds of participants to Australia. These revolts led to the Durham Report referenced earlier, though the government would not implement its recommendations for a decade, when Nova Scotia and the two Canadas—having been joined in the United Province of Canada containing Ontario and Quebec in 1841—won responsible government in 1848. Prince Edward Island followed in 1851, New Brunswick in 1854, and Newfoundland in 1855.

In 1846, Britain and the US agreed upon a boundary between the two nations of North America running all the way to the Pacific. Britain ceded Oregon to the US and established the island of Vancouver as a crown colony in 1849. When, eight years later, gold was found on the mainland, hundreds of miners from the US flooded north across the border to seek their fortune. Fearful of an American effort to annex these lands, Britain in 1859 quickly, if reluctantly, declared them to be the new colony of British Columbia. Within two years, the white population had reached 50,000. In 1866, Vancouver and British Columbia joined together to form a single administrative unit.

In 1867, the four colonies of Quebec, Ontario, Nova Scotia, and New Brunswick joined together to form the Dominion of Canada, with its capital at Ottawa. This new, self-governing possession of the crown expanded dramatically in 1869 when the Hudson's Bay Company ceded its huge tracts of territory across the continental land mass to the new Canadian government; British Columbia joined it in 1871, as did Prince Edward Island in 1873, creating an enormous nation stretching from the Atlantic to the Pacific oceans. (Newfoundland remained apart from the Dominion of Canada until 1909.) The planned transcontinental railroad, everyone agreed enthusiastically, would enable the British to settle the "empty" lands of the west, exploit its resources and civilize its spaces, and keep the expansionist-minded Americans at bay.

Well, not quite everyone. The Canadian government decided that westward expansion would take place from the site of the Red River settlement, which, it believed, needed more Anglo-Saxons sent out from Ontario who would serve as a counterweight to the Métis, the Americans, and the French Canadian Catholic missionaries who lived in the area. When they learned in 1869 that the Red River colony was now to be governed by a new authority based in Ottawa, the Métis feared for their livelihoods. Ottawa sent out military surveyors to determine the best possible locations for new settlers, an act the Métis seized upon to signal their refusal to go along with any such plan. Fully aware that new settlement would mean an end of the openness of the prairie and the hunting, fishing, and trapping that undergirded the Métis lifestyle, a number of them accosted the surveying party outside of Fort Garry in the late fall of 1869. A fiery young man named Louis Riel, the son of a half-French, half-Indian father and a French mother, stepped on the chain held by a soldier sent out by the new Canadian government to survey land near the Red River and announced, "you go no further."[4]

Shortly thereafter, Riel mustered a militia force to prevent the arrival of the newly appointed lieutenant-governor of the North-West Territories (as the area had come to be called), William MacDougall. MacDougall despised Catholics and half-breeds, as he styled the Métis, and determined that they would come under the rule of the new Canadian government. When he arrived at the boundary of the new province, Riel's people handed him a paper that decreed, "The National Committee of the Red River Métis notifies Mr. McDougall [sic] of the order that he is not to enter the North-West Territories without special permission from the Committee."[5] In the meantime, Riel and a hundred followers had ridden to Fort Garry and seized authority, assuring people there that they were not rebelling against Canadian or British rule but simply seeking to negotiate the terms by which the area would be incorporated into the new confederation of Canada. To that end, Riel called a convention made up of both English-speaking and

French-speaking representatives; when some of the Anglo-Saxon settlers protested, he threw seventy of them in the stockade. The Métis having successfully established their control over Red River, at least for the time being, MacDougall slunk back to Ottawa.

From London, colonial authorities urged restraint upon Canadian officials. For the time being the Canadian government chose a moderate course, trying to cajole the Métis into submission. If they followed the orders of the government and gave up the province, the governor-general declared, they would be allowed to go free without punishment. In the meantime, in the convention at Fort Garry, a significant portion of both Métis and Anglo-Saxons were being won over by the argument of an emissary from the Hudson's Bay Company that confederation with Canada would respect all of their civil and religious rights, confirm them in their property-ownership, and confer upon them the same rights that all British subjects of the dominion, no matter their race or religion, enjoyed. They were invited to send their own representatives to Ottawa in order to "explain the wants and wishes of the Red River people, as well as to discuss and arrange for the representation of the country in Parliament," a prospect that was met with approbation.[6] Just when it seemed that the rebellion had been forestalled, violence broke out when settlers attacked Fort Garry and freed the prisoners Riel had captured when he took over the fort. A local Scotsman and a Métis were killed in the melee; when the would-be liberators tried to return to their farms, they were stopped and thrown into the brig. One of them, Thomas Scott, an Orangeman who was known for his hatred of the Métis, was charged with taking up arms against the Red River government, found guilty in an ad hoc trial, and executed by a drunken firing squad. Public opinion in Ottawa was outraged.

Despite heightened feelings against the Métis, the delegation that had made its way to Ottawa to "arrange for the representation of the country in Parliament" received assurances that their rights would be protected. By the Manitoba Act of 1870, a new province by that name would be established, 1.4 million acres of which were to be given over to the Métis in perpetuity. The act recognized the French language, provided separate schools, and guaranteed existing land titles and occupancies. The government confided to the delegates that an imperial army would have to be sent to Fort Garry, but only to placate those who had been so outraged by Scott's murder, as they saw it; Riel would remain in control until a new governor arrived, and his militia could maintain its presence until relieved by the new force. Importantly, the act did not refer to anything like amnesty, though the delegates were told repeatedly that one was forthcoming and that all would be well. The Métis, it appeared, had won the day, preserving their heritage and way of life, and claiming their rightful place in the new confederation of Canada.

But the death of Thomas Scott had not been forgotten, and the presence of a half-caste Catholic rebel at the head of the new province was never going to stand. The amnesty promised initially by the governor-general and reiterated by officials to the Red River delegates never materialized. Nor did the armed force envisioned to be a "benevolent constabulary" ever consider itself to be formed for that purpose. Instead, under the command of Colonel Garnet Joseph Wolseley, the army that rode out from Ottawa took as its charge the punishment of a rebel force. Wolseley, an Anglo-Irish Protestant with a profound dislike of Catholics, regarded Riel's rebellion as part of a Catholic conspiracy to block westward expansion of the empire. His mission, as he and his officers and men saw it, was to defeat these subversive Catholic elements and humiliate Riel and his followers. Many of them ardent Orangemen, they looked forward to waging "war" on the rebel Métis.

They were never given the chance. Realizing, finally, just what kind of armed force they were dealing with, Riel and his men abandoned Fort Garry, leaving open the south gate for Wolseley's charging cavalry officers. Disheartened by such a denouement, Wolseley ordered that the Union Jack be raised above the fort and a royal salute be fired from the cannons he had brought along on his misguided adventure. The troops headed back east, and Fort Garry grew into the bustling city of Winnipeg, from which, as many had envisaged, the expansion of Canada westward went on apace. But authorities had learned an important lesson: they could not simply ignore Indigenous or Métis groups as they sought to extend white settlement. When the lands that became Manitoba Province entered confederated Canada they did so under legislation—the Manitoba Act—that put aside 1.4 million acres for the children of Métis families, acknowledging that they, like the Indigenous peoples, had a long-standing claim to territory in the region.

***

The end of the War of 1812 saw the emergence of a strong anti-Indian bloc in the US government, men who held views about the need to eradicate Indian people entirely from their new nation that resonated powerfully with a significant portion of the American public. Anti-Indian sentiment would fuel successful runs for the presidency by notorious Indian fighters Andrew Jackson and William Henry Harrison, the former carrying his campaigns against Native Americans in the 1812 war further into Florida territory in the First Seminole War of 1816–18. When he got to the White House in 1829, he supported efforts by states like Georgia to extend their jurisdiction over Native communities and spearheaded the Indian Removal Act of 1830, which targeted the 48,000 Indian people north of the Ohio River (the Northwest Territory) and the 75,000 people of the five so-called "civilized tribes" of the southeast—Creeks, Choctaws, Cherokees, Chickasaws, and Seminoles—for deportation to territory west of the Mississippi River.

The plan to remove Indian communities from the eastern portion of the US had been in place long before 1830: Thomas Jefferson had identified the lands obtained in the Louisiana Purchase of 1803 as the site for their relocation. What he seems to have ignored, however, was that white Americans would soon seek those lands for themselves, so any location identified as part of what came to be called "Indian Country"—modern-day Oklahoma—would only be temporary. Indigenous Americans moved there through deportation inevitably displaced Indian people who had lived in the area for generations. And as whites continued to move west they dislodged recent arrivals from land they had just inhabited, forcing them to move again. Indian removal, in other words, was not a simple one-and-done policy; it necessarily involved multiple relocations of peoples whose lives were constantly disrupted.

We tend to associate Indian removal exclusively with the southern states, but it had a powerful impact on Native Americans in Ohio, southern Michigan and Wisconsin, Indiana, Illinois, and New York as well. Northeastern politicians and commercial elites sought the lands of those regions for white settlers and, as cities in the east grew larger and larger each year, for workers who might otherwise disrupt the social and political order. In the end, only about half of the Native population in the north moved westward, and in New York the Haudenosaunee people resisted fiercely. Their opposition led New York's political leaders to back off their plans for deportation in return for Haudenosaunee land concessions and agreement to be taxed.

The deportation of Native peoples from the southern states of America was inextricably linked to the creation and expansion of an enslaved labor empire. In 1830, Cherokees still held more than 10 percent of the land in Georgia; Creeks held almost 17 percent of Alabama; and Chickasaws and Choctaws held 50 percent of Mississippi. White planters sought to expel the tribes that inhabited the territory in order to settle enslaved Africans on them who would grow cotton to feed the global demand for the commodity. Indian people in the north and the south did not want to move from their homelands, and fought tenaciously to stay. Their refusal to go turned what had been couched as a benevolent plan to relocate Indigenous Americans out of harm's way into an open campaign for forcible removal and then out-and-out extinction.

The Choctaws were expelled first, agreeing under threat of military invasion in the 1830 Treaty of Dancing Rabbit Creek to leave their cherished homelands and go to the "Land of Death," as they referred to the west. Over a three-year period, as many as 18,000 men, women, and children followed the "Trail of Tears" to southeastern Oklahoma, enduring horrific winter weather, flooding, and disease without adequate food, clothing, or shelter. Some 2,500 died en route. Those who survived suffered an enormous loss of wealth. In 1829, for instance, the Choctaw herd of roughly 15,000 ponies had been estimated to be worth almost half a million dollars. The agent in charge of removal, William Armstrong, had urged the secretary for war to build a special ferry boat for the ponies, but it never materialized. Within three years of removal, Armstrong estimated, some 2,000 ponies had died or had been stolen. The removal treaty had not provided for compensation for lost horses, but hundreds of Choctaws made claims totaling nearly $8,000. The loss of even a single horse often meant destitution for its owner and dependence upon family, other tribal members, or the agent in charge of the removed Indians. The treaty did make provisions for losses of cattle left behind, but agents offered "almost nothing" for each head.[7] A staggering 95 percent of deported Choctaws got nothing at all in compensation for the land and the personal property they were compelled to leave behind.

Subsequent efforts to deport Native peoples led to warfare against US troops. In the Black Hawk War of 1832, the Sauk people fought against General Winfield Scott's army. The Americans prevailed, though cholera decimated the troops. The Seminoles, led by Osceola, conducted raids on the US troops sent to remove them from their Florida villages in a war that lasted from late 1835 until 1842, killing some 20 percent of the Seminole people. The Creek War in Georgia, which began in May 1836, saw intense violence on the part of citizen militias that tracked down Native families with the cry, "Removal or death."[8] Even under the putative protection of federal troops, Creeks suffered grievously at the hands of vigilante citizens, who claimed the authority of "the people" in their pursuit, rape, and murder of Creek families. Massacres occurred regularly, sometimes compelling Creek women to smother their infants to keep them from revealing their hiding places with their crying. When capture appeared imminent, many women killed their children and then themselves.

Still the Cherokees refused to leave, despite a rump faction led by John Ridge having signed the Treaty of New Echota agreeing to do so in 1835. The vast majority of Cherokees followed John Ross in his insistence that they remain in their homeland. By 1838, the federal government had determined on a military invasion of the Cherokee nation, sending down the Engineering Corps to plan for the building of roads. On May 28, the eight-year anniversary of the passage of the Removal Act of 1830, 3,500 soldiers under the command of General Winfield Scott swept through Georgia, rounding up some 18,000 Indian men, women, and children and marching them off to internment camps. Within weeks, they had succeeded in capturing all but a few score of Cherokees who fled to North Carolina. "Georgia has been entirely cleared of red population," Scott declared in late June.[9] Four months later, agents began to move the Cherokee prisoners west to Indian Country. At least 4,000 and perhaps as many as 8,000 of them died along the way, marched to their deaths on the 700-mile journey through rain, mud, ice, and snow. When those who made it arrived in Oklahoma, half-starved, the agent in charge gave them corn and meat that was inedible.

Deporting 80,000 Native Americans from their homelands across the Mississippi River cost the US government around $1 trillion in today's currency—about $12.5 million for each person expelled. These were not dollars spent compensating Indian people for their losses of land, livestock, and personal property, but on soldiers, armaments, steamboat captains, and provisioners of all sorts. The government earned all of it back and more by selling the lands it confiscated from Indian people to settlers and planters who, in turn, profited handsomely from their windfall. Forty percent of the value of agricultural products of Mississippi and Alabama in 1850, for example, derived from lands formerly held by Chickasaw, Choctaw, and Cherokee peoples; 16 percent of all the ginned cotton in the US came from Native lands. The Chickasaws alone lost land worth around $7 million in 1850 dollars. The compounded generational wealth lost beggars the imagination, but of course it pales in comparison to the losses of people, homes, communities, and cultures. As one prominent historian of Indian removal put it, "the dispossessed lost the accumulated place-based knowledge of a thousand years."[10]

Following the Civil War, American settlers moved westward in enormous numbers, setting off a conflict that pitted nomadic Arapahos, Assiniboines, Atsinas, Blackfeet, Cheyennes, Comanches, Crows, Kiowas, and Sioux seeking to preserve their lands for bison hunting against white settlers seeking access to and through those lands for purposes of ranching and mining. Fighting had gone on throughout the early 1860s in the Colorado, Wyoming, and Montana territories, culminating in the Sand Creek massacre in Colorado in 1864, when volunteer troops under Colonel John Chivington set upon and killed 150 Cheyennes, 100 of whom were women and children; and in a series of wars fought along the Bozeman Trail in 1866. In the last of these 1866 conflicts, a group of Sioux warriors had wiped out an entire unit of eighty cavalrymen near Fort Phil Kearney, in Wyoming territory.

Congress sent a peace commission to adjudicate these conflicts, and in 1867 and 1868, the treaties of Medicine Lodge and Fort Laramie, respectively, claimed to have done so. The first of them, Medicine Lodge, established the Arkansas river as a border land, north of which Americans could build roads and put down rails to the gold mines in Colorado and create settlements. The treaty gave the land south of the Arkansas to Indian people for purposes of hunting bison, "so long as the buffalo may range thereon in such numbers as to justify the chase." The treaty also banned whites from settling there, though it did not forbid them from hunting bison south of the Arkansas. The treaty of Fort Laramie likewise established a boundary, ceding land south of the Platte River to settlers in return for the abandonment of forts in the Powder River valley and the closure of the Bozeman trail. It also affirmed that the Native American hunting lands west of the Missouri River, north of the Platte River, and east of the Bighorn mountains would not be encroached upon—either through settlement or mere traveling through—"so long as the buffalo may range thereon in such numbers as to justify the chase." By this treaty, the government created the Great Sioux Reservation, which included the Black Hills of South Dakota. Nine years later, after gold was discovered in the Black Hills, the government forced the Sioux to give them up by threatening renewed warfare and the cutting of rations. Although only 10 percent of the tribes' membership signed on to the "agreement," the Black Hills were ceded to the federal government. The Sioux would spend the next century trying to get them back.[11] In the meantime, in 1871, Congress passed a law ending all treaty-making with Indian tribes.

The treaties of Medicine Lodge and Fort Laramie gave the appearance of guaranteeing Indian hunting rights on the great plains. But not only were loopholes built into them, they also were contingent upon the continuing presence of the bison. At the time the treaties were signed, both parties to them recognized that bison numbers had fallen into steep decline, owing to a variety of pressures. Over-hunting by nomadic Indian hunters since the 1840s; the introduction of cattle and sheep in large numbers by white settlers, severe drought, the building of the transcontinental railroad, and newly introduced bovine disease all combined to reduce the bison herds. But, above all, it was commercial hunting carried out by whites in the 1870s that rendered them nearly extinct by 1883. Despite the treaties of 1867 and 1868, federal authorities permitted the slaughter of bison to go forward, for they regarded their elimination as the way to force Indian groups on to reservations.

General William Sherman noted that the elimination of the bison would spell the end of free-roaming plains Indians. The army demurred when it came to enforcing the treaties that were supposed to keep white hunters out of Indian lands, and often supplied them with the guns and ammunition they needed to conduct their slaughter. For the hunters did what the army and US officials wanted done—the elimination of the bison and the forcing of Indian people on to reservations. By 1883 the animals had been almost entirely eradicated from the plains. In the two-year period between 1872 and 1874, for example, the Santa Fe railroad shipped 460,000 hides east. The Kansas Pacific and the Union Pacific railroads sent at least as many, respectively. In order to obtain that number of skins, they had to have killed three times as many animals, so a conservative estimate of the number of bison killed each year came to about 1 million. The southern plains held perhaps 15 million bison in the late 1860s; it wouldn't take very long for a thousand hunters—also a conservative estimate of those who filled the plains in the 1870s—to reduce those numbers almost to zero. By the end of the 1870s, a few hundred bison remained on the southern plains. In 1889, when naturalist William Hornaday conducted a survey of bison in the US, he found twenty-five in Texas, twenty in Colorado, ten in Montana between the Missouri and Yellowstone rivers, twenty-six near the Bighorn mountains in Wyoming, and 200 in Yellowstone National Park.

The destruction of the bison complemented another campaign against Indian peoples' animals that drove them onto reservations, the seizure or killing of their horses. On a strictly functional level, taking horses eliminated a mode of transportation and hunting for Indian people. But it did far more than that, as the army and government officials well knew: it struck at the very heart of Indian culture and lifeways, in which horses played a crucial central role. The introduction of horses among Native groups in the late seventeenth century had dramatically transformed hunting, allowing men to range widely in pursuit of buffalo and enabling women to transport large caches of buffalo meat and hides back to their villages miles and miles away. Men counted their wealth in horses and secured their positions and those of their relatives by gifting horses to various individuals. Horses became central to warrior culture among many Indian peoples, facilitating their success against enemies while also serving as the focal point of military prowess. Among the Crow and other plains Indians, for example, raiding enemy camps for horses became a recognized marker of warrior status. A good war horse surpassed all other attributes of successful fighting. Equally if not more important than the material value they represented, horses stood at the heart of spiritual and social life. Many Indian people regarded horses as sacred, imbuing them with supernatural powers given by the Great Spirit or Creator. Horses (and other animals) conveyed spiritual power to human beings. Medicine men among the Crow, Lakota, Blackfeet, and other Indian peoples believed that their powers derived from "horse medicine" that conferred upon them strength, speed, stamina, and agility. Women might possess "horse medicine" as well, as did Lozan, a Chiricahua Apache who helped her brother and his warriors anticipate the arrival of US troops.

Over the course of the nineteenth century, the US government came to recognize that seizing and slaughtering horses was one of the most effective ways of pacifying and then subjugating Indigenous Americans; the policy would inform its tactics against Indian people till the end of the century. In 1868, for example, cavalry under the command of Colonel George Custer swept down into the camp of Cheyennes and Arapahos on the Washita River in present-day Oklahoma, and after a heated battle, killed over 100 warriors. Custer immediately proceeded to round up and kill their horse herds. In 1870, Major Eugene Baker attacked a Piegan Blackfeet village, killing 173 people and taking 314 ponies. Colonel Ranald MacKenzie based his 1874 campaign against Comanches who had broken out of reservations on seizing and destroying their horses. "It was the surest method of crippling the Indians and compelling them to go into and stay upon their reservations which they had fled from," declared one of MacKenzie's officers. At Palo Duro Canyon, in West Texas, MacKenzie's troops captured as many as 2,200 Comanche horses and after driving them to the base camp, shot them. The Comanches and their allies among the Kiowas, Southern Cheyennes, and Arapahos, asserted his lieutenant,

> never recovered from the blow which Mackenzie [sic] and the 4th Cavalry struck them in the Palo Duro Canon [sic] on September 28, 1874, when their various camps were destroyed and about 2200 ponies were captured and killed, which was the greatest blow of all, as the Indians without their ponies were comparatively helpless. They began going in a few families at

a time, until by the last of April 1875 only one band ... [was] remaining out of the Fort Sill and Fort Reno Reservations.[12]

After the defeat of General Custer at the battle of Little Big Horn in June 1876 at the hands of Lakota, Northern Cheyenne, and Arapaho warriors who had refused to be confined to reservations, General Philip Sheridan, commander of the division of the Missouri, took control of the Indian agencies on the northern plains. He instituted a policy of dismounting the tribes under his jurisdiction, certainly in order to hamper Indian mobility but also as a means of punishing Indian people and crushing their spirit. As he explained his plan to General Sherman, "Our duty will be to occupy the game country and make it dangerous and when they are obliged from constant harassing and hunger to come in and surrender we can then dismount, disarm and punish them at the Agencies as was done with the Southern Indians in the last campaign," referring to MacKenzie's fight against the Comanche.[13] Sheridan believed dismounting would bring about "a final settlement of all further difficulties with the Sioux."[14]

Hunkpapa Sioux member Josephine Waggoner, who was five at the time, climbed a hill and watched with her mother and sister as "the horses belonging to all the friendly Indians were being taken by the military ... [U]nderneath the great clouds of dust on this stifling-hot day in August, the great herds of horses were being driven. The hillsides were a black mass of moving horses," she recalled, "thousands of them were being driven in from every direction."[15] In October, Sheridan directed Generals Terry and Crook to round up horses at the Standing Rock, Cheyenne River, Spotted Tail, and Red Cloud agencies. By May 1877, troops had brought in more than 7,000 horses.

As a tool of empire, dismounting Indians worked. Certainly it made it difficult for any resisting groups to continue the fight against encroachments on their lands. As Captain William Wood put it, "A Sioux without his horse is, comparatively, a very harmless being."[16] Sheridan and others regarded the policy of dismounting as going well beyond keeping Indians from conducting warfare or refusing to come in to various agencies. After all, the vast majority of Sioux horses seized were taken from those people classified as "friendly." The army refused to distinguish friendly from hostile, determined to treat all Indian people the same way. Unable to pursue the remaining buffalo and other game they relied on to feed themselves and their families, Indians across the west had to enter or return to reservations in order to survive, dependent upon inadequate rations and capricious and often corrupt officials. As one missionary described the Lakota horse seizures,

> It was worse than the ordinary seizure of property without color of law. It was not merely robbery of our friends. It was cruel. The Indians are compelled to camp from 10 to 40 miles away from the agency to find

fuel. They have to cross this distance in the coldest weather to obtain their rations, and without ponies they must cross on foot, and some of them may perish.[17]

Dismounting Indians and slaughtering horses struck directly at Native American identity. On the material level, taking a source and sign of wealth meant physical and social impoverishment. On the emotional, spiritual, and cultural planes, it tore at the hearts of Native people and reduced them to subjects of the colonial state. As Josephine Waggoner put it following the 1876 Sioux horse seizures, "so the horses were all gone. The life, the hope, the pride of the Indian was gone with them. The sole dependence on them. It was like losing your father and mother to them ... It was like the love of a beloved child, only a man is dependent on a horse." She and her sister, along with other tribal children, used to look out over the plains from the hill behind Fort Yates on the Standing Rock reservation in North Dakota. "We could see the wind-whipped tipis in the dust-beclouded prairies for miles away without a horse moving around," she recalled.

> Here and there we could see men and women laboriously dragging wood home or carrying small quantities on their backs. Every tent seemed to be silent except where children were crying for food. Silence, because there was no enjoyment in talking, no enjoyment in singing, only a wailing song at times came with the wind, a song of grief and regret.[18]

Sheridan knew exactly what he was doing in seizing Indian ponies, observing succinctly, "A Sioux on foot is a Sioux no longer."[19]

***

In 1833, as we've seen, the British parliament outlawed slavery and extended the ban to its colonies the following year, striking a massive blow to the Boer way of life in South Africa.[20] In the late 1830s, some 6,000 Afrikaners headed out on their Great Trek from the eastern Cape inland to the high veld of southern Africa, where they could settle where they wished and act according to their own lights. The Voortrekkers, as they called themselves, journeyed to the Orange River, which formed the boundary of the eastern Cape, settling in 1837 at the foot of the Drakensberg mountains. They then expanded their territory, which they were beginning to think of as a state, into Natal, which the British had decided not to annex to its holdings, despite the fact that a small group of Britons had settled on the coast in a town they named Port Natal (now Durban).

The Afrikaner expansion into Natal took place with the consent of the Zulu king, Dingane, who claimed suzerainty over the territory. He permitted the Boers to settle there in return for their promise to kill his enemies, the Basuto. They did so, in a gruesome spectacle of slaughter. Dingane, seeing the Boers now as a threat, reneged on his bargain and killed a number of Boers. In response, a small Boer contingent fell upon the Zulus and killed 3,000 of them in what the Boers called the Battle of Blood River. Disturbed by the reports of depredations against the Basutos and the Zulus, the British government ordered the governor of the Cape Colony, Sir George Napier, to annex Port Natal. At the end of November 1838, a contingent of British soldiers landed in the port and took over a fort that had been built for their occupation.

The British sought to establish peace between the Afrikaners and the Zulus, which they did by imposing harsh terms on Dingane. They required Dingane to remove himself far to the north, giving to the Boers not just the entire territory of Natal but half of Zululand as well. Dominant now in what they called the Republic of Natal, the Afrikaners did not wish to see British control extended into the state. In this they were thwarted, however, when in 1842 the British claimed suzerainty over and ended the Republic of Natal. In response, the Boers embarked on another trek, this time over the Drakensberg mountains and across the Vaal River into Matabeleland. There they set up the Republic of the Transvaal. In 1843, Britain formally annexed Natal to its possessions, and in the years 1849–52 settled 5,000 Britons to replace the Boers who had left.

At the time of annexation, the British proclaimed "that there shall not be in the eye of the law any distinction of colour, origin, race, or creed; but that the protection of the law, in letter and in substance, shall be extended impartially to all alike."[21] This declaration, so near and dear to the hearts of evangelicals and humanitarians at home and in South Africa, proved not to be very effective in practice, especially as it pertained to landholding. Ninety-three percent of Natal's population of roughly 300,000 consisted of Africans; Europeans, both British and Afrikaner, comprised about 6 percent of the population; and South Asians brought into the colony to provide labor made up the remainder. But a commission appointed by British officials to address the issue of land determined that of the 12.5 million acres contained within the colony, 2 million should be given over to "reservations" on which Africans were to live. The remaining 10.5 million acres fell into the hands of Europeans as private property or of the government as "crown lands." Over 90 percent of the population—Africans—in other words, obtained only 16 percent of the land; the other 84 percent of it rested in the hands of the 6 percent of the population that was white.

Following the principles of the Durham Report, the Cape Colony obtained responsible government in 1853. Three years later, Natal established its own legislature, in which a majority of the electorate was white. Not surprisingly, voters returned a white membership to the legislature. Just as evangelicals had feared, self-government in the white settlement colony of Natal proved to be a very bad deal for Indigenous peoples. As early as 1854, a commission reporting on "native policy" had described Africans as "savages," "superstitious," "crafty," "indolent," "bloodthirsty and cruel," and "debased and sensual"; it had declared that Africans had no right to the land of Natal, and asserted that as "Natal is a white settlement," the 1843 proclamation announcing racial equality in the colony was "utterly inapplicable."[22] Over the next number of years, the rights of Africans were increasingly whittled away as Britons took advantage of the divisions among African chiefs to introduce policies that encroached further on their way of life and their lands. It didn't always go well for the British, as we'll see in the next chapter. The Zulu people resisted British expansion with stunning success at times.

In the Cape Colony, by contrast, a new constitution adopted in 1853 established a non-racial franchise. Cape Liberalism, as it came to be called, looked good on paper, but because electoral eligibility required men—and it was only men—to own property worth at least £25, Africans who could actually exercise the right to vote were limited in number. Those who did tended to be people who had accrued businesses and property through their relationship with Christian missions, which had arrived in southern Africa in the early nineteenth century. African chiefs happily granted land to the missionaries, for they brought such benefits as schooling and medical care. Those who arrived at the stations were usually poor and destitute. In some cases, they had lost their families in the upheavals of the *mfecane*, a period of interethnic violence and upheaval that marked the 1810s and 1820s; others had been ostracized because they were accused of witchcraft. Some parents dropped their children at the mission stations because they could no longer afford to feed them, or because a woman had borne twins; many peoples in southern Africa considered this unlucky, and left one child with the missionaries to raise. The missions gave these outcasts and impoverished refugees religious and material sustenance.

As the nineteenth century progressed, the position of those Africans who aligned themselves with the mission stations became secure. The numbers of early African Christians were small, but over the next several decades, they would amass an inordinate amount of power and wealth. Communities of up to as many as 1,000 grew up in and around the mission stations, whose residents came to adopt an entirely different lifestyle from the majority of those living around them. In Zulu areas, for instance, mission-raised Africans rejected cultural practices including polygyny—the taking of multiple wives—the drinking of alcohol, and *lobola*, a long-standing institution involving the payment of bridewealth in cattle from a man's family to that of his prospective wife. Converts learned to read and write in English under missionary supervision, becoming fluent as they listened to sermons from the pulpit and read passages from the Bible. They organized their daily duties around the ringing of church bells, sounds that reflected a European sense of time and discipline. And they dressed like Europeans, the men in long trousers, waistcoats, and even top hats, and the women in long dresses, invoking much amusement among their neighbors who continued to wear skins.

Missionaries in Africa sought to develop a class and gender system much like that of England's, in which they occupied the role of the prosperous professional middle class and Black Africans became part of a free labor force comprised of industrious workers. For Black men they sought "a fair day's work for a fair day's wage." For Black women who had to earn, domestic service appeared to missionaries to be the most appropriate kind of work for them, for it did not appreciably subvert the emphasis on domesticity for women in that way that work in the fields of a plantation might. The degree to which an African family resembled the ideal family of white, middle-class Britons denoted exactly the degree to which they had become civilized in the eyes of Britons.[23] Under Cape Liberalism these educated, wealthy, and western-conforming elites won the same legal rights colonial settlers possessed.

***

By 1820, white settlers had established themselves on lands in Australia's New South Wales, Van Diemen's Land, Victoria, and Queensland, displacing and sometimes destroying outright the First Nations peoples who had lived there. The numbers of whites remained relatively small up till the end of the 1820s, when, starting in 1828, a dramatic in-migration of Britons began. A total of about 180,000 people made their way to Australia and New Zealand in the years 1828–42, establishing new settlements at Perth (1829) and Adelaide (1836) in Australia, and Auckland, Wellington, New Plymouth, and Nelson in New Zealand in the years 1840–2. The Australian governors offered large grants of free land to people of substance who could develop it, and they provided convict labor to work it. Those settlers, in turn, wrote home to extol the virtues of their new country, attracting more Britons and more capital with which to further improve the colony. All this expansion required that Aboriginal peoples be removed forcibly from their ancient territories, resulting in a drawn-out and bloody "Black War" that—along with the presence of a significant number of convicts—necessitated the constant presence of British troops right up until the 1860s. First Nation clans fought hard and effectively, but they could not overcome the weaponry of their European enemies, nor could they spend all of their time fighting, as professional soldiers could do.

Australia's beginnings as a penal colony and the government's grants of free land to wealthy men created a problematic social order that the descendants of convicts and new arrivals to the colony chafed against. In the 1830s, a campaign to render the colonial society more equitable and less class-oriented arose; in part as a consequence of the movement, the government stopped granting land to men who would become oligarchs using unfree labor and instead put land up for sale by auction. With the revenue it earned, it sponsored more migration to Australia from Britain, dramatically changing the patterns of British emigration to that time. At the start of the 1830s, fully 98 percent of British emigrants made their new homes in the US or Canada. By the end of the decade, 25 percent of them opted for Australia instead. During the 1840s—the Hungry '40s as they were known in Europe—80,000 settlers arrived in New South Wales.

White settlement received an even greater boost after 1851, when significant deposits of gold were found in Victoria, attracting people to the territory to seek their fortune. Thousands and thousands of men and women from all over the world traveled to Australia, tripling the non-Aboriginal population in the space of ten years. Victoria's population alone grew from 77,000 in 1851 to 540,000 in 1861; the continents as a whole grew from 430,000 to 1.15 million in the same period. Railroads and telegraph systems began to crisscross the continent, and steamships crammed with people and commodities tramped from Europe to Australia, rapidly developing the infrastructure necessary to sustain the mining boom, which provided a third of the gold output for the entire world in the 1850s.

In 1855 and 1856, the British government conferred constitutions and self-government on the colonies of New South Wales, Tasmania, Victoria, and South Australia; when Queensland established itself out of New South Wales in 1859, it won its own constitution as well. Unlike the case of Canada, the Australian settler governments possessed the authority to determine Indigenous policy, a state of affairs that alarmed humanitarians at home in Britain but which settlers deemed crucial to their self-identification as manly and independent colonists. They would use that power to enact discriminatory laws against Aboriginal people.

Australian settlers moved inland from the coastal areas into the "outback" over the course of the next four decades. The climate and geography of northern Australia, in particular, offered enormous challenges to a people used to a moderate climate and a gentle topography. Families pasturing sheep and cattle on the grasslands of the continent didn't require much in the way of labor, but other enterprises, such as the sugar plantations of Queensland, depended on significant numbers of laborers, far more than the population of whites could supply. Workers from the Pacific islands were brought in, sometimes at the point of a gun, to work the plantations as indentured servants. They received harsh treatment from recruiters and planters alike, suffered high mortality rates, and earned little pay. In Western Australia, the government resumed the use of convict labor from Britain to build roads and other infrastructure projects that would encourage pastoralism.

Grazing sheep and cattle in northern Australia offered profound challenges. First and foremost, it entailed moving Aboriginal peoples off their lands, a process that involved even greater violence and death than in earlier conflicts. First Nations people fought tenaciously to protect their livelihoods, killing white men, women, and children in a number of encounters in the late 1850s and early 1860s. Bloody confrontations continued into the 1880s, as when some 600 Aboriginal fighters met settlers and police in 1884 at Battle Mountain in west Queensland, and later in the decade, when some

1,000 Aboriginal warriors died in fighting in Alice Springs in the Northern Territory. But ultimately they would be defeated by white force of arms and drafted into the pastoral industry as drovers, shepherds, and servants. They had not voluntarily chosen their employment in this sector of the economy, but their participation in it enabled them to fare better than First Nations people in the southern part of the continent, where they became, essentially, wards of the state and confined to the equivalent of reservations.

***

The Aboriginal peoples of New Zealand, the Māori, organized into a number of warrior clans in fortified villages across the two islands, managed better and for a longer period of time after coming into contact with Europeans than did the Aboriginal Australians. They had been trading with Europeans for a number of decades in the second half of the eighteenth century, and some had even traveled on whaling ships to Sydney, where they came to the attention of the governor of New South Wales around 1800. Māori saw opportunities in establishing links with Sydney and a brisk commerce commenced. One Māori trader, Ruatara, invited evangelicals from the Church of England to set up a mission station in the Bay of Islands in 1814, thereby securing a monopoly on supplying it with the goods and services it needed to do its work. Some of these missionaries complained to the governor about the abuse the Māori suffered at the hands of many Europeans; he responded by declaring that the Indigenous peoples of New Zealand fell "under the protection of His Majesty." His proclamation imposed British law upon those who interacted with Māori and Pacific Islanders, making them accountable for their actions and liable to punishment if they transgressed British standards of behavior.

In the years after 1815, inter-tribal warfare among the Māori clans increased in frequency and intensity, owing largely to the pressure population growth exerted on resources on the two islands. In the past, warfare to settle disputes had been rule-bound and even ritualistic, ensuring that few warriors died in the fighting. Now, however, with the guns made available through contact with Europeans, clashes turned more deadly and destructive. Over the next twenty-five years, the so-called "musket wars" among the Māori killed thousands of people, displaced huge numbers of others from their lands, and left some areas around what would come to be called Auckland and Wellington completely depopulated, thus opening up space where Europeans would later settle. But the wars also created a large number of Māoris who were familiar with guns, knew how to strategize effectively using guns, and could build forts, *pa*, able to withstand rifle fire. This knowledge would serve them well in their conflicts with Europeans in later years.

In 1833, in response to a petition from a number of chiefs in the Bay of Islands to the British king for protection against both French and British intruders, the government in Sydney sent a British "resident," James Busby, to New Zealand. Lacking any kind of power to enforce his pronouncements for the "maintenance of tranquility," this "watchdog without teeth," as the Māoris called him, could do little to ameliorate the violence among Māoris and between them and Europeans. He did, however, issue a Declaration of Independence in 1835 that proclaimed New Zealand an independent state under the protection of the British government. Thirty-five chiefs designating themselves "The United Tribes of New Zealand" signed it, as did seventeen more chiefs a little later. The chiefs believed they were asserting their sovereignty by putting their names to the document; Busby, for his part, was seeking to ward off French intrusion in New Zealand affairs.

At home, the Colonial Office still pursued a policy of "minimum intervention" in New Zealand, a stance they would alter over the next few years as more petitions from Māori chiefs requested British protection from their enemies. Busby and Captain William Hobson, who would become lieutenant-governor of the colony, circulated a treaty to Māori chiefs that recognized British authority on the islands of New Zealand, asserted that the dissemination of land titles would be the prerogative of the British government, and guaranteed the Māoris possession of their lands and property. Importantly, the Treaty of Waitangi, named after the location in the Bay of Islands where it was signed, granted Māori people the rights and privileges of British subjects, a clause that enabled Māori leaders to win some claims against the selling of their land in subsequent decades (see Figure 5.1). The treaty as a whole recognized Māori sovereignty, a status that few Indigenous peoples in the other Anglo settler colonies could enjoy. More than 500 chiefs signed the documents, which had been translated into their language by missionaries. In the meantime, private interests in Britain that had established the New Zealand Company, a joint stock operation that sought to buy up Māori land and settle it with emigrants from Britain, moved quickly to make their purchases and claims before the government could establish its control. Their settlers arrived in Wellington in early 1840, prompting Hobson to declare in May of that year British sovereignty over the entirety of New Zealand as an offshoot of New South Wales. The following year, New Zealand became a crown colony in its own right.

At this point, Māoris still enjoyed significant control over their societies, culture, lands, and livelihoods. That would change, however, over the course of the next three decades, as successive waves of British emigrants made their way to the new colony. The first, in the 1840s, saw the arrival of some 10,000 settlers sponsored by the New Zealand Company. The second occurred with the discovery of gold in Australia in the 1850s; some of those who had not found their fortune crossed the Tasman Sea to New Zealand. When gold was discovered on New Zealand's south island in 1861 a huge

FIGURE 5.1 *Signing the Treaty of Waitangi, 1840.*

influx of gold diggers followed, increasing the white population by nearly 200,000 people. Not all of them stayed, but the more than 100,000 who did transformed New Zealand's social and political landscape. The vast increase in Europeans—and the relatively high infant and child death rates among the Indigenous population—altered the demographic balance considerably. In the late 1850s, a roughly equal proportion of Māoris to whites prevailed. By the end of the 1870s, whites outnumbered Māoris by a ratio of ten to one.

The history of New Zealand from 1840 through the 1890s centered on a series of land wars fought between Māoris and European settlers. Despite the terms of the Treaty of Waitangi and the intention of the colonial government to protect the interests of the Māori people, illegal land purchases and confiscations resulted in significant losses of Māori territory. Māoris tried to resist land grabs by settlers and by the colonial government, and succeeded in preventing some of them in the 1840s and 1850s. But New Zealand won substantial self-government in 1852 with the passage of the New Zealand Constitution Act. One element of the act delegated power over Indigenous affairs to the legislature, ensuring that the white settler government would determine the fate of Māori lands and thus the Indigenous peoples who inhabited them. By 1860, the colonial government had bought two-thirds of the land in New Zealand, most of it on the south island. The governor wished to add the north island—where most of the Māori lived—to his territories; the New Zealand Settlements Act of 1863 enabled parliament to take land and gave the governor the authority to establish settlements there. Through the Settlements Act and with the creation of the Native

Land Court, white settlers obtained through confiscation or purchase the vast majority of lands on the two islands. The governor also instigated a new round of warfare in the 1860s. Again, Māoris resisted, but time and numbers were not on their side. In 1867, parliament set aside four seats for Māori representation, a proportion that fell far short of the fourteen or fifteen seats their population size warranted. Over the next decade, Māori people suffered massive population decline, a deterioration caused and accompanied by the loss of their lands.

Counterpoint: Americoes in Liberia

Following the American Revolution, the number of free African Americans grew significantly, some having escaped their bondage during the war itself, others having been manumitted upon the deaths of their former owners. The increase in the size of the free Black population, which continued into the early nineteenth century, alarmed many whites, a number of whom joined together to form the American Colonization Society (ACS) in 1816. They aimed to remove free and newly emancipated African Americans from the US to West Africa, where they would be unable to "mix" with whites.

The overwhelming majority of free Blacks had no interest in uprooting themselves from the only home they had known and believed they had every right to live in, but some, tired of the racist abuse and discrimination they faced every day, and others, eager to take advantage of what might turn out to be a lucrative economic opportunity, chose to make the leap. In 1820, eighty-eight settlers—most of them mixed-race—sailed out of New York harbor, bound for Sierra Leone on board the *Elizabeth*. When they arrived at their destination, they found that earlier Black British settlers had had a very tough go of it, falling prey to disease in disastrous numbers. They continued on along the coast of West Africa some 200 miles southeast to Cape Mesurado, where in 1822 ACS and US navy agents used a combination of political suasion, bribery, and the threat of arms to secure a land concession from local Africans.

The newcomers thought they had gained ownership of the land; the native Africans—Mel-, Mande-, and Kwa-speakers—believed they had merely given visitors permission to use land they regarded as still theirs. The disagreement provoked two bloody battles, which the settlers won using superior military technology over the Africans, who outnumbered the African Americans by about 100 to one. Soon the Americoes, as they began to refer to themselves in the new settler colony of Liberia, established dominion over the cape and immediately-adjacent inland territory. Over the next twenty years or so, some 20,000 free African Americans joined them there. In search of land to call their own, they expanded the area settled by Americoes some 150 to

250 miles into the hinterland by a combination of treaty concessions and military force.

As was the case in virtually all of the Anglo-American settler colonies, Liberian settlers resisted what we might regard as metropolitan control. In this instance, the ACS constituted that element of the triangular relationship we saw playing out in North America, Ireland, Australasia, and southern Africa. Between their arrival in 1822 and 1841, the African American settlers lived under the administrations of white American governors, who themselves answered to the ACS Board of Managers in Washington, DC Chafing under their power, Americoes began to demand greater autonomy for themselves through their elected legislative council. Besieged by money difficulties at home, and increasingly frustrated by Americo insistence on real self-government, the ACS appointed an Americo to the governorship in 1841, in effect turning over the colony to the settlers themselves. In 1847, the Americoes declared Liberia an independent country.

The settlers, while descended from Africans, did not see themselves as such and were regarded by the Native inhabitants as foreigners. Indeed, Native Liberians often referred to the Americos as "black white men."[24] The settlers dressed differently, in full-blown Western attire despite the discomforts caused by the heat, the men sporting suits and ties, the women wearing long Victorian gowns; they built houses reminiscent of their abodes back in their "native land," as they called the US; they spoke in what they considered their "mother tongue"; and they embraced the ideal of individual landholding, in contrast to Indigenous customs of holding land in common. Possession of land entitled Americoes to vote and hold office in political institutions modeled after those of the US; Africans, however, had no such rights and were ruled as subjects of the settler state. The Liberian government claimed sovereignty over African groups and insisted that its laws superseded those of Indigenes. And it required Africans to eschew customary practices the Americoes regarded as "uncivilized," such as plural marriage, trial by ordeal, and, above all, slavery.

The African American settlers established a system of segregation based upon a racial hierarchy. Regarding themselves as occupying the top rungs of the ladder and placing Indigenous Liberians at the bottom, they in many ways replicated the very social system they had left when they crossed the ocean from the US to the west coast of Africa. Americos believed themselves superior to Indigenous Africans, and sought to bring "light," "knowledge," and true religion to them in order to stamp out what they deemed the "barbarism" and "paganism" of Africa.[25] Their success in doing so, and in imposing their rule over Indigenous Africans, proved frustrating to the founders of Liberia, limited as it was to the areas in which the Americoes actually settled. The lands beyond the settlements, while strictly-speaking Liberian, according to the settler government, remained beyond the influence and control of settler values, institutions, and laws for decades.

Primary Source Document

The Treaty of Waitangi, 1840

THE TREATY OF WAITANGI

Her Majesty Victoria Queen of the United Kingdom of Great Britain and Ireland regarding with Her Royal Favor the Native Chiefs and Tribes of New Zealand and anxious to protect their just Rights and Property and to secure to them the enjoyment of Peace and Good Order has deemed it necessary in consequence of the great number of Her Majesty's Subjects who have already settled in New Zealand and the rapid extension of Emigration both from Europe and Australia which is still in progress to constitute and appoint a functionary properly authorized to treat with the Aborigines of New Zealand for the recognition of Her Majesty's sovereign authority over the whole or any part of those islands - Her Majesty therefore being desirous to establish a settled form of Civil Government with a view to avert the evil consequences which must result from the absence of the necessary Laws and Institutions alike to the native population and to Her subjects has been graciously pleased to empower and to authorize me William Hobson a Captain in Her Majesty's Royal Navy Consul and Lieutenant Governor of such parts of New Zealand as may be or hereafter shall be ceded to Her Majesty to invite the confederated and independent Chiefs of New Zealand to concur in the following Articles and Conditions.

Article the first

The Chiefs of the Confederation of the United Tribes of New Zealand and the separate and independent Chiefs who have not become members of the Confederation cede to Her Majesty the Queen of England absolutely and without reservation all the rights and powers of Sovereignty which the said Confederation or Individual Chiefs respectively exercise or possess, or may be supposed to exercise or to possess over their respective Territories as the sole sovereigns thereof.

Article the second

Her Majesty the Queen of England confirms and guarantees to the Chiefs and Tribes of New Zealand and to the respective families and individuals thereof the full exclusive and undisturbed possession of their Lands and Estates Forests Fisheries and other properties which they may collectively or individually possess so long as it is their wish and desire to retain the same in their possession; but the Chiefs of the United Tribes and the individual Chiefs, yield to Her Majesty the exclusive right of Preemption over such lands as the proprietors thereof may be disposed to alienate at such prices as may be agreed upon between the respective Proprietors and persons appointed by Her Majesty to treat with them in that behalf.

Article the third

In consideration thereof Her Majesty the Queen of England extends to the Natives of New Zealand Her royal protection and imparts to them all the Rights and Privileges of British Subjects.

[signed] W. Hobson Lieutenant Governor

Now therefore We the Chiefs of the Confederation of the United Tribes of New Zealand being assembled in Congress at Victoria in Waitangi and We the Separate and Independent Chiefs of New Zealand claiming authority over the Tribes and Territories which are specified after our respective names, having been made fully to understand the Provisions of the foregoing Treaty, accept and enter into the same in the full spirit and meaning thereof in witness of which we have attached our signatures or marks at the places and the dates respectively specified.

Done at Waitangi this Sixth day of February in the year of Our Lord one thousand eight hundred and forty.

The Chiefs of the Confederation

Notes

1 Piet Retief, "Manifesto," quoted in Clifton Crais and Thomas V. McClendon, eds., *The South Africa Reader: History, Culture, Politics* (Durham: Duke University Press, 2013), pp. 76, 77.

2 Retief, "Manifesto," p. 77.

3 Edward Gibbon Wakefield, *A Letter from Sydney, The Principle Town of Australasia* (London: Joseph Cross, 1829), p. i.

4 Quoted in James Morris, *Heaven's Command: An Imperial Progress* (New York: Faber Paperbacks, 1973), p. 342.

5 Quoted in Morris, *Heaven's Command*, p. 343.

6 Quoted in Morris, *Heaven's Command*, p. 348.

7 Quoted in Claudio Saunt, *Unworthy Republic. The Dispossession of Native Americans and the Road to Indian Territory* (New York: W.W. Norton, 2021), p. 128.

8 Quoted in Saunt, *Unworthy Republic*, p. 251.

9 Quoted in Saunt, *Unworthy Republic*, p. 278.

10 Quoted in Saunt, *Unworthy Republic*, p. 315.

11 See Martin J. LaLonde, "Review of *Black Hills/White Justice: The Sioux Nation Versus the United States*," *Michigan Law Review*, Vol. 90, No. 6 (1992), pp. 1433–43.

12 Robert G. Carter, *On the Border with Mackenzie, or Winning West Texas from the Comanches* (Texas State Historical Association, 2007) (orig. pub'd 1935), pp. 495, 523.

13 Quoted in Francis Fuller Victor, *Our Centennial Indian War and the Life of General Custer* (Norman: University of Oklahoma Press, 2011), pp. 92–3.

14 Quoted in George W. Manypenny, *Our Indian Wards* (London: Forgotten Books, 2018), p. 312.

15 Josephine Waggoner, *Witness: A Húnkpapha Historian's Strong-Heart Song of the Lakotas* (Lincoln: University of Nebraska Press, 2013), p. 132.

16 Quoted in Richmond L. Clow, "General Philip Sheridan's Legacy: The Sioux Pony Campaign of 1876," *Nebraska History*, Vol. 54, No. 4 (1976), pp. 461–77, p. 468.
17 Quoted in Victor, *Our Centennial Indian War*, pp. 92–3.
18 Waggoner, *Witness*, p. 134.
19 Quoted in John W. Bailey, *Pacifying the Plains. General Alfred Terry and the Decline of the Sioux, 1866–1890* (Westport: Greenwood Press, 1979), p. 167.
20 Quoted in Morris, *Heaven's Command*, p. 54.
21 Quoted in Philip Curtin, Steven Feierman, Leonard Thompson, and Jan Vansina, *African History* (Boston: Little Brown, 1978), p. 323.
22 Quoted in Curtin et al., *African History*, p. 325.
23 Quoted in Curtin et al., *African History*, p. 325.
24 Quoted in James Ciment, "Americo Liberia as a Settler Society," in Edward Cavanagh and Lorenzo Veracini, eds., *The Routledge Handbook of the History of Settler Colonialism* (New York: Routledge, 2017), p. 219.
25 Quoted in M.B. Akpan, "Black Imperialism: Americo-Liberian Rule Over the African Peoples of Liberia, 1841–1964," *Canadian Journal of African Studies/Revue Canadienne des Etudes Africaines*, Vol. 7, No. 2 (1973), pp. 217–36, p. 220.

Further Reading

James Rodger Miller, "From Riel to Métis," *Reflections on Native-Newcomer Relations: Selected Essays* (Toronto: University of Toronto Press, 2017), pp. 37–60.

Cormac Ó Gráda, *Ireland before and after the Famine: Explorations in Economic History 1800–1925* (Manchester: Manchester University Press, 1993).

Claudio Saunt, *Unworthy Republic. The Dispossession of Native Americans and the Road to Indian Territory* (New York: W.W. Norton, 2021).

Leonard Thompson, *The History of South Africa* (New Haven: Yale University Press, 2014).

6

Expansion, Intensification, and Resistance, 1860s–1914

In June of 1911, 10,000 Maa-speaking men, women, and children began to move out of the Rift Valley in the highlands of Kenya, headed for land designated for them on a reserve lacking sufficient water and grass for the 175 million cattle and 1 million sheep they drove ahead of them. Although chiefs had purportedly agreed to the relocation, the Maasai people did not want to go. "We were pushed by force," recalled Thomas Ole Mootian, who as a young child helped to move his family's livestock.

> A white man called Bilownee [E. D. Browne]... accompanied by askaris [police] ... were pushing us by force—it was not a joke. The askaris were holding guns. They were beating the people. When you stopped, they hit you with the butt of the gun. And if women made a joke or became lazy, they were caned. And when the sheep or cows became weak, they were killed.

The forced march took a heavy toll on everyone, human and animal alike, but women often bore the brunt of hardship, expected as they were to provide temporary shelter and food for their families and care for the sick. "Women were the ones who took care of the children during the move," recounted Kirapusho Ene Gilisho, whose mother told her stories of her experiences on the trip.

> They had medicine in case a child became sick on the way. And when a woman gave birth on the move, they had to spend two or three days in one particular place in order for her to recover her strength. She would be given sheep's oil, blood and meat and after a few days she would be ready to move with the others ... There was not enough food, many people died of hunger on the way.[1]

In August three-quarters of the Maasai arrived at the summit of the Mau escarpment (the rest of them had gone around it), where heavy cold rains, muddy pathways, insufficient grazing land, and lack of shelter compelled them to halt their journey. Despite strenuous efforts by British officials to move them along, the Maasai refused to budge, knowing that ahead of them they faced certain death. Many of them died of starvation and exposure atop the Mau, as did a good number of their animals. Henry Boedecker, a British doctor later sent by authorities to investigate the debacle, reported that by his calculations, perhaps as many as 4 percent of the Maasai population perished on the Mau, along with an "enormous" number of cattle and sheep.[2]

Moving the Maasai—in the words of one historian of Kenya—from their homelands in the highlands of Kenya occurred as a consequence of white settlers' insistence that the land be given to them. Considered "white man's country" by the British and South African settlers who coveted it, the Kenyan highlands became monopolized by Britons and South African whites, turning into a settler "playground carved by the colonial state from the dry-season pasturage of the former lords of East Africa, the Maasai," in the words of two Kenyan historians.[3] The forced removal of the Maasai onto reserves typified the dynamics of settler colonialism across the Anglo world in the late nineteenth and early twentieth centuries. Everywhere in the countries treated by this book, land—seeking it, seizing it, losing it, trying to retain it, regaining it—stood at the heart of Indigenous/settler interactions, characterized by expansion, intensification, and resistance.

***

In the last quarter of the nineteenth century, most Native American people lived on some 300 reservations that had earlier been established on lands located far from settler communities. As white settlers moved westward in massive numbers, they coveted the lands where reservations existed, creating tensions that often resulted in conflict and bloodshed. In response, the US government shifted its policies, determining now to demolish reservations and assimilate Indian people into white society. It adopted the policy of allotment, established by the Dawes Act of 1887, which worked alongside unhorsing in an overarching campaign to assimilate Native people out of existence. As the US Supreme Court later acknowledged, the framers of the Dawes Act (formally known as the General Allotment Act) sought "to extinguish tribal sovereignty, erase reservation boundaries, and force the assimilation of Indians into the society at large."[4] They looked to undermine the collective land-owning practices of Native American tribes by issuing each member a specific plot of land—an allotment of 160 acres—to be farmed or ranched individually. Proponents of the Dawes Act sought to break down tribal customs and practices of collectivism and to inculcate notions of possessive individualism—private property—that would purportedly enable Indian people to prosper. It didn't work, both because the allotted plots proved unsuitable for farming and ranching and because Indian people simply did not wish to live the way whites wanted them to. But allotment had another aim that proved far more successful: the alienation of more Indian-owned land to non-Indians. For once tribal land had been parceled out to individuals, the remaining acreage was then sold to settlers. In the half-century following 1887, more than two-thirds of the 150 million acres held by Indian tribes was sold to non-Indian people.

Allotment and unhorsing American Indians were only two elements of a wide-ranging campaign by the US government to take Indian land and to eliminate Native peoples by destroying their cultures and societies. The Indian wars had proved mightily expensive and time-consuming; authorities sought another, more cost-effective way to eliminate Indianness through education. In 1877, Congress legislated monies for the establishment of residential boarding schools for Indian children, where, as one historian has put it, a new phase of warfare against Native peoples would be conducted. "The next Indian war would be ideological and psychological, and it would be waged against children," noted David Wallace Adams. At institutions like Carlisle Indian Industrial School, founded in 1879 to "kill the Indian in him, and save the man," as its founder, Richard Henry Pratt put it, Indian boys and girls would be disabused of the values their traditions placed on communal well-being and the dissemination of wealth and instructed in the principles undergirding a liberal society: the sacredness of private property, the virtues of self-reliance, the morality of amassing personal wealth. Customary familial relationships among Indian people, which might include polygamy, women owning property, and vast kinship networks, must be rooted out and replaced by the ideals of domesticity and the patriarchal nuclear family. Boarding schools, Adams points out, were "the institutional manifestation of the government's determination to completely restructure Indigenous minds and identities."[5]

Many Indian people welcomed the opportunity for their children to be educated in the ways of white people. If schooling was offered to them on their reservations they readily accepted it. Taking children from their families to be educated in schools far from their homes, however, was a different matter altogether, and it devastated parents who grieved the loss of their sons and daughters. Lieutenant R.H. Pratt witnessed the seizure and transporting of Indian children to the Carlisle School in 1879. "The fathers of these children are chiefs or leading men in their tribes," he wrote to the Commissioner of Indian Affairs.

> They have great affection for their children. Thousands gathered at each Agency to see them off and more affecting tears, grief and mourning could not be imagined. Chiefs whose names are known all over the Country exhibited all the emotions of the kindest natures. Many expressed their sorrow by acts of benevolence. Parents and relatives gave many horses

and other valuable property to the old and infirm of their tribe. Horses which must have been the pride of the owner were given freely to some old and shriveled woman. One man gave 17 horses away because his daughter was going.[6]

Gifting horses served as a measure of profound emotional expression. Many Indian people marked the death or loss of a tribal member with a generous giving away of possessions, among which horses were the most valuable. No other action could have more aptly articulated the immense hurt felt at the loss of their children.

Indian children suffered badly at the residential schools far from their homes, to which many of them had been forcibly removed. Some, like Luther Standing Bear (Lakota) and Zitkala-Ša (Dakota), chose to leave their families to venture east to gain an education, but their initial enthusiasm quickly gave way to distress as the enormity of their decisions set in. Bewildered by their unfamiliar surroundings and the strangers who received them, children were immediately stripped of their traditional clothing, scrubbed down, and outfitted in stiff uniforms and unforgiving shoes. Bewilderment gave way to dismay when they realized that their hair would be cut off (see Figure 6.1). Zitkala-Ša tried to hide under a bed to escape the humiliation, but was easily discovered and "dragged out, though I resisted by kicking and scratching wildly. In spite of myself, I was carried downstairs and tied

FIGURE 6.1 *Native Americans at Carlisle Indian School.*

to a chair. I cried aloud, shaking my head all the while until I felt the cold blades of the scissors against my neck, and heard them gnaw off one of my thick braids. Then I lost my spirit," she recalled.[7]

Personal indignities, regimented routines, insufficient and tasteless food, cold dormitories, and lonely nights characterized the lives of Indian children in the residential boarding schools. They were punished physically for speaking their language or failing to obey arcane rules. Substandard living conditions provided a perfect breeding ground for aggressive viruses and bacteria. Lacking adequate medical care, many fell ill to a variety of diseases, especially tuberculosis, and they died in very large numbers. Hundreds died at Carlisle alone, a death rate matched by numerous other residential schools for which Carlisle served as a model.

When they returned to their homes, boarding school Indians found themselves utterly adrift; they could not or would not join the white world but they had lost the traditions, customs, and ties that had bound them to their tribes and families. Education had estranged them from their very identities. As Zitkala-Ša attested,

> for the white man's papers I had given up my faith in the Great Spirit. For these same papers I had forgotten the healing in trees and brooks. On account of my mother's simple view of life, and my lack of any, I gave her up, also. I made no friends among the race of people I loathed. Like a slender tree, I had been uprooted from my mother, nature, and God.[8]

In the late 1880s, Native peoples responded to the depredations against their lands, their livelihoods, and their lifeways by embracing a spiritual movement known as the Ghost Dance. Appearing first among the Northern Paiutes of the Nevada Territory, it spread rapidly across the west, drawing in a great number of adherents with a message of cultural renewal, autonomy, the departure of the white man, and the return of the buffalo. The message of hope and resurgence led to a kind of civil disobedience among Indian people against the rules of the reservation. Families kept their children away from government schools and taught them traditional customs instead; they eschewed Christianity for their own spiritual practices. And they danced, often for days at a time.

On the Lakota reservations in South Dakota, where starvation had set in as a consequence of the Bureau of Indian Affairs cutting rations in half, the Ghost Dance envisioned a "renewed Earth" in which "all evil is washed away," as Lame Deer recounted.

> They told the people they could dance a new world into being. ... The earth would roll up like a carpet with all the white man's ugly things—the stinking new animals, sheep and pigs, the fences, the telegraph poles, the mines and factories. Underneath would be the wonderful old-new world as it had been before the white fat-takers came ... The white men will be rolled up, disappear, go back to their own continent.[9]

White settlers in the area and local Bureau of Indian Affairs (BIA) agents panicked, believing that the dancing presaged an armed attack. No such plan existed but in early December 1890 the government sent a large contingent of soldiers to the Pine Ridge reservation, driving up tensions between settlers and Indian communities ever further. The army launched a campaign to disarm the Lakota. On December 29, the inadvertent firing of an Indian rifle into the air caused soldiers to panic, setting off a massacre of a small Lakota band camped along the shores of Wounded Knee Creek. Firing off a Hotchkiss gun, soldiers killed more than 150 Lakotas, most of them women and children, as well as about twenty-five of their own men; over the next couple of days, the army ran down and killed an additional hundred Indian men. The massacre at Wounded Knee has conventionally marked the moment when American Indians were fully pacified.

***

For Indigenous peoples and the Métis of Canada, representative and responsible government for white colonists had spelled disaster, as humanitarians and abolitionists back in Britain had feared. White settlement and expansion necessarily took place at the expense of Native peoples, as colonists and colonizers confiscated land and interrupted the migration patterns of bison and other animals that provided the food eaten by First Nations peoples. Following the Red River debacle, the government in Ottawa sought to avoid conflict with the bands of Aboriginal peoples on the plains by signing a series of so-called "Numbered Treaties" with them that created land reserves and promised the seeds, tools, and instruction that would enable them to farm the land. The treaties also guaranteed hunting and fishing rights. Facing the depletion of bison stocks, their lives and way of life endangered by encroaching white settlement, the 34,000 First Nations people of the plains had little choice but to accede to the terms, which, in any event, proved largely illusory. White expansion continued unabated. In 1872, the Dominion Lands Act provided free plots of 160 acres to settlers, further intruding upon Indigenous people's livelihoods.

The British North America Act of 1867, which made Canada a dominion and granted it internal self-government, had charged the new government with the responsibility for protecting all "Indians and lands reserved for Indians." This principle derived and carried over from the long-standing policy of British recognition that bands of Native peoples constituted "nations," which was officially set down in the Proclamation Act of 1763. The proclamation asserted that Indian people had rights to the lands they held and it explicitly acknowledged that First Nations people had the standing, within an overarching imperial sovereignty, to govern themselves. Within a very few years of Canada achieving dominion status, however, some of the most fundamental tenets of the proclamation were gutted as the federal government asserted its own priorities for Aboriginal people.

At the heart of those priorities stood assimilation. As Canada's first prime minister, John A. Macdonald put it, parliament must "do away with the tribal system and assimilate the Indian peoples in all respects to the inhabitants of the Dominion."[10]

Macdonald and virtually all subsequent governments right up until the latter part of the twentieth century sought to end the tribal system through "enfranchisement," the incorporation of individual First Nations people into Canadian citizenship, with all the rights and responsibilities therein. Enfranchisement required the individual Indian man—and only a man—to renounce his tribal membership and give up his rights to Indian status, becoming, in effect, a non-Indian. An 1857 attempt to sell enfranchisement in Ontario and Quebec had attracted exactly one applicant, a failure that convinced government officials agents that First Nations leaders could not be trusted to bring their people into the light of "civilization." So far from constituting responsible nations, Macdonald and others insisted, they were like "persons underage, incapable of the management of their own affairs."[11] The situation demanded, they claimed, the removal of "petty chieftainships"—the abolition of long-standing customs of governance through councils and the imposition of a system largely controlled by an agent of the new Department of Indian Affairs. The Act for the Gradual Enfranchisement of Indians, the Better Management of Indian Affairs became law in 1869, beginning the process of ending First Nations self-governance that subsequent Indian Acts would refine and enhance.

In 1876, the Canadian parliament passed the Indian Act, legislation that consolidated previous laws pertaining to Indian people and giving authority to determine policies for the reserves and for individual Aboriginal people exclusively to the federal government. The act enabled the Department of Indian Affairs to reach into virtually every aspect of Native life, from codifying who could be defined as Indians and what rights and responsibilities they enjoyed, to land use, to how people were to live their lives, to determining how and by whom Aboriginal communities would be governed. The Indian Act defined so-called "status Indians"—those who lived on reserves and held the right of "protection" by the federal government—on the basis of property ownership, creating a profoundly gendered system. "Any male person of Indian blood reputed to belong to a particular band"; "any child of such person"; and "any woman who is or was married to such a person" qualified. Any Indian woman who married a non-Indian, or an Indian from a different band and reserve, lost her status vis-à-vis the terms of the act, as did her children and subsequent descendants, and could kicked off the reserve. Treaty benefits, health care, educational opportunities, her very personhood before the law would be lost. In the larger scheme of things, this portion of the act removed from First Nations the capacity to determine for themselves who belonged to their tribes and who did not. The 1876 Indian Act added to the 1869 Gradual Enfranchisement Act the power of the Department of Indian Affairs to remove chiefs for "dishonesty, intemperance, immorality, or incompetency."

These acts proved unable to assimilate First Nations people as quickly as government officials wished, particularly when it came to turning collectively owned land into individually owned land that could be sold to white settlers. Politicians, religious leaders, and bureaucrats, vexed by their inability to turn Native peoples into "civilized" citizens of the dominion, sought other means of making that happen. One such piece of legislation incorporated into the Indian Act in 1884—the "Potlatch Law"—banned the feasts held in the Pacific Northwest where gift-giving and the passing down of wealth to others took place. The potlatch held a critical place in the culture of many First Nation communities, as federal authorities well knew; they believed that this kind of community event of providing food and distributing wealth got in the way of individualizing Aboriginal peoples by promoting community bonds. Bans against the sun dance and other ceremonies followed in 1895 for the same reason.

Above all, Canadian authorities looked to education to assimilate Indian people of the plains and west. The numbered treaties had provided for schools on the reserves, but critics began to bewail their ineffectiveness in changing the cultures of First Nations children. As Macdonald told the House of Commons,

> when the school is on the reserve the child lives with its parents, who are savages; he is surrounded by savages, and though he may learn to read and write his habits, and training and mode of thought are Indian. He is simply a savage who can read and write ... Indian children should be withdrawn as much as possible from the parental influence, and the only way to do that would be to put them in central training industrial schools where they will acquire the habits and modes of thought of white men.[12]

In 1883, the government introduced just such a program of "industrial schools," schools located far from the reserves where Aboriginal children would be taken—often by force—to learn trades such as carpentry, blacksmithing, shoemaking, and farming for the boys, domestic training for the girls. These residential boarding schools, run largely by Christian clergy, proliferated over the next four decades. By 1923, eighty of them operated in northwestern Ontario, the plains provinces, British Columbia, and the Northwest Territories. Perhaps a third of First Nations children attended them; with Inuit and Métis students included in the count, the number reached about 150,000.

The residential schools, despite incorporating only a minority of Aboriginal children, had an outsized impact on First Nations communities. The academic and vocational skills they provided fell far short of the promises made by the schools and the expectations of the children's parents. It could hardly have been otherwise, as the whole purpose of the schools was to destroy First Nations cultures and to instill European ways of looking, acting, and thinking. To that end, teachers and principals denigrated and demeaned Indian ways. They cut students' hair immediately upon their arrival at the unfamiliar institutions; they took their clothing away and dressed them in ill-fitting and uncomfortable uniforms; they forbade students to speak their own languages and punished them severely if they did. "Sister Marie Baptiste had a supply of sticks as long and thick as pool cues," recalled George Guerin, a former chief of the Musqueam Nation. "When she heard me speak my language, she lift up her hands and bring the stick down on me. I've still got bumps and scars on my hands. I have to wear special gloves because the cold weather really hurts my hands. I tried very hard not to cry when I was being beaten."[13]

Other infractions brought down the wrath of the whip or the terror of isolation. Physical, psychological, and sexual abuse on the part of both teachers and fellow students went unpunished and therefore flourished. Students suffered terrible cold in the unheated dormitories and classrooms; the superintendents failed to feed them sufficiently to keep them satisfied or healthy. Without enough warmth and proper nutrition, students died in droves when diseases struck. Tuberculosis proved a frequent visitor and caused widespread death. A government inspector estimated in 1907 that nearly a quarter of all Native students were dying in the residential schools, a figure that did not include those children already sent home because they were sick. That same inspector believed that a half to three-quarters of students sent home from Alberta and Saskatchewan boarding schools died upon their arrival.

The efforts to destroy Indigenous cultures and control Aboriginal people intensified in the aftermath of protests against the federal government's failure to provide the resources enumerated in the numbered treaties. In the spring of 1885, two risings occurred in the Northwest Territories, one on the part of young Cree and Assiniboine men and the other on the part of a Métis community led by Louis Riel. Though they were not coordinated, government agents claimed they constituted a single Northwest Rebellion, as it came to be called.

Many Métis had moved to the Northwest Territories in the aftermath of the Red River Rebellion of 1869–70. In 1883, they discovered that lands they believed to be theirs had been sold by the federal government to the Prince Albert Colonization Company to further white settlement on the prairie. In 1884, fearful that the decline of the buffalo and settler demand for their land would leave them destitute with no means of sustaining themselves, a group of Métis asked Louis Riel, who had fled to the US after the Red River incident, to return and help them petition the government for redress. When the government failed to respond with anything but vague statements, Riel and a number of his associates declared on March 18, 1885, the establishment of the Provisional Government of Saskatchewan to pressure Ottawa to act. The decline of the buffalo had had a terrible impact on First Nations people on the prairie as well, leaving them dependent upon food rations doled out by the Department of Indian Affairs. Since 1880, in violation of the numbered treaties, those rations had been made conditional upon work and were reduced in size, till by 1883 Aboriginal people faced starvation. The years 1884 and 1885 saw poor harvests, pushing First Nations people and Métis to the brink.

Desperation drove some to violence. For two months in the early spring of 1885, Métis and First Nations bands largely comprised of Cree warriors separately attacked a number of settler communities in Saskatchewan. At Batoche and Duck Lake, Métis forces defeated local militias, resulting in the deaths of more than forty people. Inspired by reports of the Métis successes, Cree warriors conducted their own assaults on settlers at Frog Lake and Battleford, killing eleven. Federal troops dispatched from Ottawa ultimately put down the two rebellions, which had led to the deaths of thirty-five Aboriginal and Métis warriors and fifty-three settlers and militia fighters, but it took more than six weeks before they prevailed.

The federal government acted quickly to punish those it regarded as traitors: it hanged Luis Riel and eight Cree warriors and imprisoned or exiled dozens of other Crees and Métis.

The Department of Indian Affairs used the resistance movements to justify further depredations against First Nations people by instituting a pass system, forbidding Aboriginal people to leave their reserves without obtaining permission of the local Indian agent. It banned a number of First Nations ceremonies and rituals, continuing its efforts to culturally exterminate Aboriginal peoples by destroying the practices and lifeways that helped give them their identities.

***

During the last decades of the nineteenth century, British immigration to Australia grew considerably, till by 1888 three million white settlers inhabited the colonies of New South Wales, Victoria, Queensland, South Australia, and Western Australia. White Australians enjoyed a level of economic well-being not matched in the other Anglo settler colonies, but despite their general prosperity, divisions of class, gender, and race impeded the instantiation of a sense of national belonging among them. Worker-employer conflicts, class resentment, deep antipathy against the presence of Chinese laborers, and a vibrant and vociferous feminist movement focused on what proponents regarded as the dangerous nature of masculinity imperiled the cohesion of the "new Britain" in the southern hemisphere. Internal discord, combined with external threats from the growth of Japanese power in the Pacific world, prompted the development of an increasingly compelling campaign to create an Australian federation that would unify the individual colonies. That desire became a reality on January 1, 1901, when the Commonwealth of Australia came into being.

The very idea of the commonwealth rested on and was inseparable from the notion of a White Australia. As Alfred Deakin, a leading proponent of federation put it, "the unity of Australia is nothing, if that does not imply a united race. A united race means ... a people possessing the same general cast of character, tone of thought ...." Support for federation, he acknowledged, derived from "the desire that we should be one people, and remain one people, without the admixture of other races." One of the federated parliament's first pieces of legislation, the Immigration Restriction Act, sought to enforce a whites-only immigration policy by instituting language tests that would prevent non-white people from entering the commonwealth. Deakin described the White Australia policy as one "by which the whole of our social, industrial and political organisation is governed."[14] The commonwealth constitution excluded non-Europeans from the vote. The individual states took steps to render Indigenous people wards of the state, placing them under the authority of protection boards that controlled their places of residence, the terms of their employment, their ability to marry and cohabit, and, as we'll treat below, the custody of their children.

The foundational belief in White Australia acted to efface the very existence of Aboriginal people, who played no part in the events that celebrated the establishment of the commonwealth and never appeared in the works of art and literature that represented and related the story of the new national identity. The new commonwealth constitution omitted them from the census counts that would determine parliamentary representation. Denial of Indigenous peoples reached an absurd height in the creation of the Australian Natives Association, membership in which was restricted to Australian-born whites. Australian leaders in politics and the professions believed that Aboriginal people were dying out, the consequence of a Darwinian struggle for survival that Indigenous groups would lose because they were unable to adapt to new circumstances. The 67,000 Aboriginal people enumerated in 1901 severely undercounted them: some states didn't bother to include them in their own censuses and those that did often excluded people of mixed race. These practices served to virtually define Indigenous people out of existence and thus confirm the belief in a "disappearing race."

Beginning in the 1890s, all of the individual states implemented policies designed to facilitate the disappearance of Indigenous people by empowering them to remove Aboriginal children from their families. What many Indigenous parents regarded as the theft of their children was directed at so-called "half-caste" youth, who, by virtue of their racial mixture with Europeans, were deemed redeemable for civilization in a way that "full-blood" Aboriginal people were not. Full-blood Aboriginal people, white opinion had it, could not support themselves in a modern society such as Australia; racially mixed people, the thinking went, possessed a sufficient amount of white virtue and capability to allow them to succeed. To provide them with that "opportunity," states established schools and other educational institutions to which Indigenous children were forcibly relocated. In New

South Wales, for example, the state government removed some 300 girls from their families between 1893 and 1909 and placed them in a training school where they were prepared for domestic service. Other states followed suit. In South Australia, Iris Burgoyne, a member of the Mirning-Kokatha clan, "saw countless children stolen from their mothers on the mission" where she lived. A matron from a residential school "would visit the mission every month or so in a shiny black car with two other officials," she recounted, "and always leave with one or two of the fairer-skinned children ... I shed tears when I remember how those children were ripped from their families, shoved into that car and driven away. The distraught mothers would be powerless and screaming, 'Don't take my baby!'"[15] Parents learned quickly to hide their children when officials and policemen showed up; some buried their children in the ground to keep them from the clutches of child-stealers.

The usually unspoken expectation behind removing mixed-race Aboriginal children from their parents and training them to enter the world of whites—indeed, into their very homes—was that they would intermarry with non-Aboriginal people. In this, Australia differed markedly from other settler colonies, where miscegenation was regarded as taboo (the reality was often at odds with the principle). Indeed, Australian policy rested on the assumption that racial mixing would eliminate Aboriginal people—would dilute them out of existence, in effect, by breeding them out. This way of thinking took assimilation to a whole other level, one in which cultural genocide would be accompanied, it was expected, by biological genocide through dilution of their racial composition. Aboriginal Australians did not die out. Their numbers, however, continued to decline owing to poor health and living conditions.

* * *

In New Zealand, the 1870s and 1880s witnessed a dramatic demographic transformation as the number of white settlers—whom Māori called Pakeha—increased, while that of Māori people declined. In 1873, the government offered free passage to the country in an effort to entice Britons to immigrate; more than 200,000, most of them farm laborers, took advantage of the offer to escape the agricultural depression ravaging Europe at the time. The settler population rose from 79,000 in 1860 to 624,000 in 1890; Māoris declined in number from about 100,000 in 1840 to 44,000 in 1890. Not incidentally, the amount of land held by Māori fell significantly from 27 million hectares in 1840 to some 4.5 million in 1890; the following decade saw continued decline in Māori landholding. This was a function of a deliberate government policy historians refer to as the "settler contract," a concerted effort to establish a secure polity based on a stable society of landholders. White landholders, that is: the settler contract did not apply to Māori people. Settlers received low-interest loans with which to purchase land at heavily discounted prices and grants to invest in working it. Through a series of land acts, the government made it far easier to alienate Māori land, thus dispossessing thousands of Indigenous families.

The impact of the late-nineteenth-century land grab hurt Māori communities badly, but they did not accept the depredations against their livelihoods without resistance. A pan-tribal movement called the Kotahitanga—meaning unity—along with the four Māori MPs sitting in parliament, led a campaign in the 1890s to stop the assaults against their people. In parliament, Māori MPs argued that the settler contract violated the 1840 Treaty of Waitangi; their oratory brought the issues of land loss and the deteriorating situation of Indigenous New Zealanders into public view. The newspaper published by Kotahitanga likewise publicized the government's failure to address the land loss and declining Māori population. The organization itself convened a separate Māori parliament in 1897 to deal with pressing problems and to call upon the government to return the land to Māori chiefs.

The efforts to separate themselves from the settler government did not go very far, but they did launch a new political force, the Young Māori Party, that looked to modernize Indigenous people. Led by Apirana Ngata and James Carroll, the group sought to halt the demographic decline of Māori people through health reform and to lift up Indigenous New Zealanders by demanding they be included in the settler contract. For a while Ngata's and Carroll's efforts bore fruit, producing a deal with the government in 1900 that set up Māori Land Councils to defend Māori landholding against Pakeha demands to settle on it. Some of the councils effectively blocked land loss, but before too long the government moved to hamstring their efficacy. It passed a Native Land Act in 1909 that made it even easier to alienate Māori land to settlers.

Ngata and other leaders of the modernizing movement hailed from schools set up to assimilate Māori boys and girls to Pakeha ways. In 1867, the government passed the Native Schools Act, by which it transferred the responsibility for educating Māori youth from Christian missions to the state. In doing so, it sought to locate schools in local Māori communities, a departure from the practices we've seen in Canada, Australia, and the US, where students were purposely removed from their families in order to inculcate them in European ways without interference from their Native environment. To be sure, New Zealand authorities also sought to assimilate Māori children, but unlike the situation in places like Canada, Australia, and the US, schools in Indigenous New Zealand communities were intended to actually serve the interests of their students. For one thing, the government required Māori communities to request a school and to provide the land upon which it would be built, thus demonstrating material buy-in to educational schemes. It directed educators to work assiduously to teach their charges the English language, but it recognized that students would need to continue to use their own languages in the process of learning the "mother tongue." Authorities also allowed Pakeha children to attend

Māori schools, and Māori children to attend Pakeha schools, a practice that excited comment among observers.

Compared to educational policies and practices in Australia, Canada, and the US, New Zealand's appear positively enlightened. We shouldn't overstate the case, but a number of differences between the settler colonies did exist, owing to factors related to their founding. The Treaty of Waitanga that marked the creation of New Zealand acknowledged the presence and authority of tribal chiefs who commanded long-standing and mature societies; the document served to constrain some settler efforts to totally override Māori interests. Māori had won representation in parliament on the basis of the treaty, and politicians recognized that if they were going to vote on national affairs, they would need to be adequately educated. Finally, although Indigenous New Zealanders were regarded by Pakeha as holding an inferior position on the evolutionary scale of civilization, relatively speaking they occupied a higher rung than Native Americans, Aboriginal Australians, or First Nations people. They might be perceived as lesser than Pakeha in a cultural sense, but not as biologically inferior, as was the case in the other settler colonies.

***

South Africa, by the early 1870s, consisted of two British colonies—the Cape Colony and Natal; two republics independent of Britain and controlled by Afrikaners—the Orange Free State and the Transvaal, the latter also known as the South African Republic; and a number of African chiefdoms—the Xhosa, the Zulu, the Pedi, the Tswana, the Sotho, the Swazi, and the Venda. Many of the African groups, though not all, retained control over their lands and the way they used them; the white colonies, by contrast, remained relatively insecure in the sense that they could not command effective control of much of the territory they claimed as theirs. By the end of the century, however, British, colonial, and Afrikaner military forces had reduced most Africans to subject status, having taken their lands, commanded their labor, and limited their ability to materially sustain themselves.

In 1871, diamonds were discovered in the area that became named Kimberley in Griqualand, which the Orange Free State and the Transvaal claimed for themselves. Faced with this competition from the independent republics, the British seized the territory and annexed it, engendering the enmity of Afrikaners across the entirety of southern Africa and helping to initiate the stirrings of an Afrikaner nationalism that would have profound consequences down the road. The rivalry between the British and Afrikaner settlers intensified as the Transvaal persisted in its efforts to expand its territory to the east and especially to secure access to the Indian Ocean with a port at Delagoa Bay. Should the republic succeed in gaining its own port, it would depend far less heavily on the Cape Colony, diminishing that entity's ascendancy in southern Africa. To prevent such a turn of events, Britain annexed Delagoa Bay for itself in 1875, and went on to formally annex the Transvaal to the Cape Colony in 1877.

The governor of the Cape Colony, Sir Bartle Frere, determined to expand British territory even further, this time against the Zulus, who lived in the lands north of Natal. Under the leadership of Cetshwayo, who had been crowned king by the representative of the Great White Queen over the seas, the Zulus were a powerful warrior society whose presence on the borderland of Natal unsettled many Britons. Frere convinced himself that they had to be pacified if British rule were to prevail; moreover, the defeat of the Zulus would force thousands of young men into the Kimberley mines that they had thus far avoided. Frere therefore cooked up an ultimatum demanding that the Zulus disband their armies, reform their system of justice, and permit the presence of a British resident at their capital, Ulundi. When Cetshwayo failed to reply, Frere, without the approval of his superiors in London, ordered an invasion of their lands. He sent 16,000 troops north to defeat this mighty enemy in January 1879 under the leadership of the commander-in-chief of the South African army, Lord Chelmsford, a distinctly incompetent officer who enjoyed the friendship and support of Queen Victoria.

Chelmsford figured on a quick and decisive victory. Instead, the army of 24,000 Zulus divided their forces, and drew out two-thirds of the 5,000 British troops that were encamped at Isandhlwana. Some 12,000 Zulus set upon the remaining 1,760 British and allied African soldiers on January 22. Some Zulus were armed with smooth-bore rifles—effective at a far shorter range than the British Martini–Henry breech-loaders—but their victory was derived from swamping the defenders with constant waves of *assegai*-wielding warriors, who braved efforts to shoot them down before they could reach the British lines. Thousands of Zulus died by rifle fire, but thousands more surrounded the British troops and cut them down. It proved an unmitigated disaster. Of the 1,760 British soldiers who had started out that day, only 55 escaped, and 858 Britons and 470 African auxiliaries died.

Determined to redeem himself, Chelmsford marched 5,000 troops onto the Ulundi plain in July with the intention of taking down his nemesis. This time, facing Gatling guns and soldiers with repeating rifles, the Zulus could not prevail. At the end of the day, all of them—some 1,500 warriors—were killed. Thirteen British soldiers died in the battle. With a British victory in hand, colonial officials imprisoned Cetshwayo, divided up Zululand into thirteen powerless chieftaincies, called "kinglets," and placed them under British suzerainty. They gave much of the Zulus' land to the Transvaal, relegating the Zulus to reserves. The British next turned on the Pedis, determined to crush Sekhukhune's state in the eastern Transvaal. In November 1879 a powerful force of British and African troops easily took the Pedi capital of Tsate. The chief surrendered and was put in prison in Pretoria; his people's lands were confiscated and they were sent to live in scattered and isolated new reserves that had few resources to support them. The confiscation of land had a lasting impact on Pedi autonomy, and the imposition of heavy taxes—payable in cash, not in kind—forced Pedi men into the diamond mines as laborers. A number of subsequent wars against African peoples culminated in the defeat of the Vendas in 1897.

The Zulus and the Pedis having been crushed by British troops, Afrikaners acted upon their rage at the Transvaal having been annexed in 1877: they revolted against British rule in 1880 and declared an independent republic. With an army of perhaps 7,000 mounted civilian soldiers, they prepared to defend their republic in what they called their war for independence. The British army fared badly against them, unable to lift the sieges to the garrisons that kept the troops captive inside them. British Prime Minister William Gladstone chose to settle with the Transvaal rather than continue to try to fight it. In 1881, the Transvaal—the South African Republic—regained its independence. Convinced that the British would not intervene to stop them, Transvaal settlers, called "freebooters," immediately set about expanding their borders to the east and west, grabbing up the land of the African chiefdoms there. One such seizure took place in the lands just north of the Cape Colony, in what would come to be called Bechuanaland, today's Botswana.

Facing what they considered a hostile government in the Transvaal, the British moved to shore up their position, sending some 4,000 troops north in 1884 to expel the freebooters and secure Bechuanaland. Britain commandeered other territory till all of the unannexed coastal and inland areas between the Cape of Good Hope and Delagoa Bay was in its hands. Anger against the annexation ranged well beyond the Transvaal. Afrikaners in the Orange Free State were already resentful of the Cape's grab of the diamond mines. Those in the Cape Colony (for not all Afrikaners had trekked off in the 1830s and 1840s, and others had migrated into the Cape from the east in later years) feared that their culture would soon be absorbed into that of the British.

The discovery of mineral wealth had monumental repercussions for the lives of Africans in southern Africa. By the 1890s, a migrant labor system drew Africans from all over the region to the diamond mines of Kimberley and the gold mines of the Witwatersrand ("The Rand") after 1886. The system created social pressures and the reordering of rural communities; it produced the urban sprawls of Kimberley and Johannesburg; and it spurred the formation of a modern sense of "tribe" that we still recognize today. Perhaps most importantly, the racialized legislation passed to control Black migrant laborers formed the basis for twentieth-century "segregation" and then apartheid in South Africa.

The situation for Africans across southern Africa deteriorated badly in the aftermath of the South Africa War (1899–1902), which broke out when Britain provoked a conflict with the Transvaal in order to secure its hold on the gold mines of the Rand. Confident of their success, politicians and the public were stunned when their armies suffered a series of humiliating and embarrassing defeats in the first months of the war. Despite being heavily outnumbered, the Afrikaners inflicted a series of losses on the British forces. The British performance in the first months of the war proved inept, but started to turn around in February 1900 with the relief of two towns, Kimberley and Ladysmith. The war continued on, the fighting bitter and ugly and seemingly endless. Britain carried out a scorched earth policy, torching farmhouses and fields. Both sides executed prisoners in the field, ignoring international rules governing warfare. Twenty-two thousand Britons died, two-thirds of them from disease. The British threw Afrikaner women and children into concentration camps, among the first the world had seen, whose terrible conditions left their inmates diseased and malnourished. Twenty-five thousand Afrikaners died, 20,000 of them women and children who had suffered in the camps. The number of Africans who perished in concentration camps ranged between 13,000 and 20,000.

As the ignominious war effort staggered towards its end in 1902, the question of the future of South Africa's Black population came to the fore. African intellectuals and chiefs hoped that the peace settlement would contain at least some protections of African rights. But on this score, Britons and Afrikaners agreed. As Sir Alfred Milner, the British high commissioner at the Cape, put it, "the white man must rule because he is elevated by many, many steps above the black man; steps which it will take the latter centuries to climb ... [if] at all."[16] Milner's disinterest in African rights determined the status of Africans under the Treaty of Vereeniging, signed in May 1902 to bring the conflict to a conclusion. He threw out any clauses protecting African rights if they stood in the way of bringing the two sides' positions closer. As Milner put it, "sacrifice 'the n—r' absolutely and the game is easy."[17]

The Peace of Vereeniging offered generous terms, designed as it was to reconcile the Afrikaners to membership in a union of the four colonies of South Africa. The treaty compensated the Transvaal for the devastation it had suffered, guaranteed full equality within the union, and formally recognized the Afrikaner language. The British hoped that their magnanimity would enable them to establish a secure Union of South Africa, dominated by British citizens who could control the gold fields and provide some degree of protection of Africans from Afrikaners. But they miscalculated voting patterns: in 1907 and 1908, Afrikaner parties won elections in the Orange Free State, Transvaal, and Cape Colony, with only Natal remaining British-dominated. Ultimately, the British left the decision of whether to grant Africans political representation and voting rights to the white populations of the Orange Free State and Transvaal, effectively guaranteeing that they would receive neither.

In 1910, the governments of each of the four colonies created a draft constitution for a union modeled on the British political system. It enacted formal color bars against voting in the Orange Free State and Transvaal, gave negligible voting rights to Africans in Natal, and maintained the nonracial franchise in the Cape Colony. The British government accepted the changes in the South African Act, and on May 31, 1910, the Union of South Africa came into existence under the leadership of South African War veterans Prime Minster Louis Botha and his deputy, Jan Smuts. South Africa became a self-governing "dominion" of the British empire, a status it shared with Canada, Australia, and New Zealand.

The creation of the Union of South Africa paved the way for segregation in the country for virtually the rest of the twentieth century. In 1913, the South African government passed the Native Lands Act, placing 7 percent of the country's land in reserve for its African population, who in 1910 comprised two-thirds of the South African population of nearly 6 million (4 million Africans, 500,000 coloureds, 150,000 Indians, and 1,275,000 whites). Africans could only buy or rent land in these "reserve" areas, which frequently contained only poor-quality land, and they were forbidden to take up occupations outside of the reserves. The legislation forced peasant farmers off of their land and onto the reserves, which were insufficient in size and quality to sustain them, transforming a huge group of peasant producers into farm laborers or mine workers. The Native Lands Act, the first in a long list of racialized legislation, also set the tone for the segregationist impulses that would define South Africa for much of the century (see Figure 6.2).

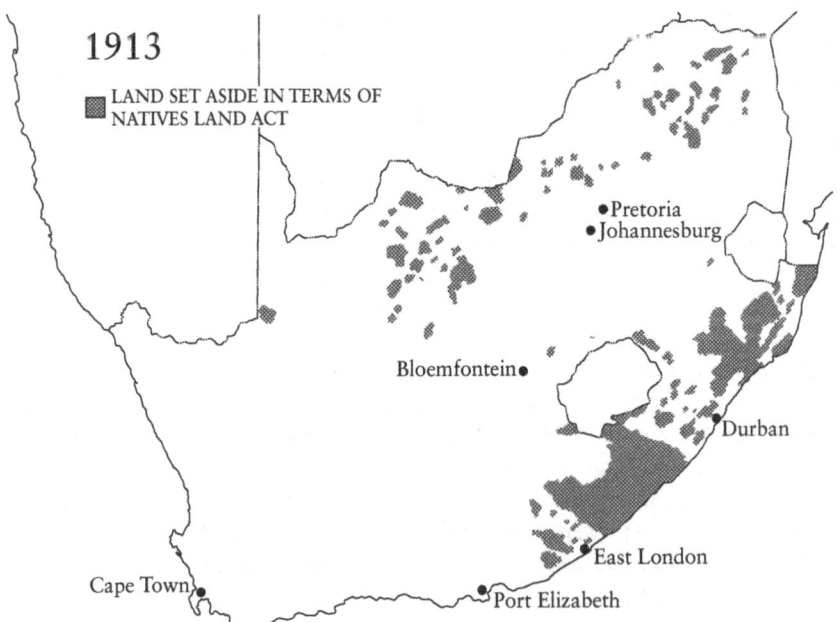

FIGURE 6.2 *Lands designated for African by Native Lands Act of 1913.*
Source: https://www.theheritageportal.co.za/article/1913-land-act

In response to the indignities and injuries suffered by Africans at the hands of the new South African government, a number of educated, Christian African elites—Sol Plaatje, Saul Msane, Thomas Mapike, and Walter Rubusana among them—formed in 1912 the South African Native National Congress, the forerunner of what would become the African National Congress (ANC). In one of its first acts it sent a delegation to London to petition King George V to overturn the 1913 Native Lands Act, reminding him that they had "loyally and cheerfully submitted to your Majesty's sway in the full belief that they would be allowed to possess their land as British subjects, and would be given the full benefits of British rule like all other British subjects."[18] Their petition failed. Over the next eighty years, Afrikaners would tighten their control over African land and African people under systems of segregation and apartheid while Africans struggled hard to resist their increasingly marginalized condition and create a world of dignity for themselves.

***

The discovery of gold on the Witswatersrand of the Transvaal in 1886 led many Britons and Afrikaners to believe that fantastic riches lay to the north in the area known as the Zambesi. Tales of vast treasures and great wealth in the region had circulated for decades in adventure stories and even serious publications, leading men like mine owner (and subsequent prime minister of the Cape Colony) Cecil Rhodes to dream of expanding their operations into the territory of what the British called Matabeleland (part of modern-day Zimbabwe). There, the Ndebele people held sway. Their chief, Lobengula, commanded a powerful army of warriors who had enabled the chief's influence to expand north and east into Mashonaland and south into parts of Bechuanaland. Lobengula exacted tribute from the Shona and the Tswana as well as a number of other groups in the Zambesia region. He guarded his lands carefully, establishing military posts along his borders to control the influx of whites and Africans from other areas. He permitted some missionaries to work in Matabeleland and occasionally allowed white hunters to pursue big game, but, for the most part, Lobengula only rarely let visitors venture into his jurisdiction.

In 1887, Rhodes dispatched a missionary named John Moffat—who was friendly with the chief—to open negotiations with Lobengula to allow the British access to his lands. Moffat persuaded him that granting a single mining concession to Rhodes would keep away all the other petitioners who sought his permission to set up shop on his lands, and the chief, hoping to rid himself of other Europeans demanding concessions, agreed to place Matabeleland—and much of Mashonaland, territory he did not possess—within Britain's sphere of influence. As "King of Matabeleland, Mashonaland and certain adjoining territories," Lobengula signed an agreement on October 30, 1888, to give Rhodes "the complete and exclusive charge over all metals and minerals situated and contained in my kingdoms, principalities and dominions together with full power to do all things that they may deem necessary to win and procure the same and to hold, collect and enjoy the profits and revenues ... from the said metals and minerals."[19] In return, Rhodes promised Lobengula a monthly cash payment and a one-time grant of 1,000 Martini–Henry breech-loading rifles, along with 100,000 rounds of ammunition. Rhodes's agents also promised—though the chief failed to get it in writing—that only ten white men would be allowed to dig in Matabeleland, and then only under the jurisdiction of Ndebele laws. The chief fell for the deception, and when he realized the fraud he disavowed the agreement.

But it was too late, for in October 1889, Queen Victoria had formally recognized Rhodes's British South Africa Company (BSAC) as the governing entity of the lands of Zambesia, authorizing it to build roads, railways, telegraph systems, banking services, and police, and charging it with the responsibility of establishing laws and awarding land grants to immigrants. Rhodes gathered up some 200 whites—"pioneers," he called them—to invade and occupy Mashonaland. Promising them mining claims and 3,000 acres of land each, he supplied the pioneers with uniforms and weapons, and primed them with tales of the untold wealth that could be found right near the surface. On June 27, 1890, escorted by 500 military police with artillery and machine guns, the pioneers set out to make good their claims on Lobengula's lands. They set up headquarters at Fort Salisbury, which would become the capital of what was starting to be called Rhodesia.

But gold was nowhere to be found, a calamity exacerbated by heavy rains that brought heavy flooding and outbreaks of malaria in its wake. The failure to find gold threatened the financial health of the BSAC, compelling the company to alter its course. Between 1891 and 1893, it carved out huge tracts of land to give out to syndicates and private investors on the condition that they put money into its development. Designated for white farms, little of the land was actually worked at the time, but the scramble for it was on. The Shona people knew that this land grab spelled disaster for them.

Thwarted in their efforts to get rich quick in Mashonaland, white settlers came to believe that Matabeleland to the west presented better chances for finding gold, and under the leadership of Rhodes's friend Leander Starr Jameson, they ventured south and west into Lobengula's kingdom. Rhodes had known for some time that war with the Ndebele must come, for not only did they constitute an independent power of considerable military might, they also stood in the way of the diamond magnate's ambitions to consolidate all the British territories in southern Africa. Lobengula well understood the threats he faced from company encroachments on his lands, and worked tirelessly to keep his warriors from engaging in raids that might instigate a military campaign. But he also had to protect his authority, and when he sent a party to punish a Shona chief for stealing his cattle, Rhodes and Jameson used the incident as an excuse to wage war against the Ndebele chief. The fighting did not last long, as Ndebele regiments, despite carrying breech-loading rifles received as part of the agreement granting Rhodes his mining concession, came up against BSAC forces armed with machine guns and artillery. They fell to those advanced weapons in the thousands.

Lobengula died shortly after his defeat in 1893. Rhodes and Jameson set up a "Loot Committee" to distribute cattle and land to whites, leaving only two "native reserves" in peripheral areas for the Ndebele. The following year, the British government recognized the BSAC's authority over Matabeleland, leaving Rhodes to administer the region as he chose. The Ndebele, whose anger and resentment over the theft of their cattle and land remained intense, suffered acutely from a drought, an invasion of locusts, and rinderpest, a disease that killed what few cattle they still owned. In March 1896, they rose up, left their native reserves, retrieved the arms they had hidden at the time of Lobengula's surrender in 1893, and attacked whites in outlying farms, mining camps, and trading posts. Within a week, they had killed some 200 settlers, wiping them out in the remote areas of the colonies. Whites in the towns called for help from police and soldiers from the Cape Colony and Natal. Rhodes arrived with a 150-man volunteer force. The combined forces pushed the Ndebele back from the main settler towns, but just when it looked as if the Ndebele could hold out no longer, the Shona joined the rebellion in June 1896. Shona people had long lived under the Ndebele yoke, but the depredations of white settlers overrode their traditional enmity toward the Ndebele. The Shona attacked the white settlers, killing more than 100 men, women, and children. The revolt continued into the fall, until Rhodes—whose company had the responsibility for paying for the campaign—cut a deal with the Ndebele chiefs in October. In return for ending their hostilities, the chiefs would not be punished; those who pledged their loyalty to Rhodes would receive appointments and salaries. The Ndebele would get their land back, Rhodes promised. The ploy worked: Rhodes saved his company, even if he enraged white settler and official imperial opinion with his leniency towards the chiefs. The Ndebele did not get back their land, however; in fact, they lost even more. When they returned to Matabeleland, two-thirds of them discovered that they now lived on "white" land. The Shona, less well-armed and organized, received no clemency at all. Company and imperial troops hunted them down, extracting vengeance until they had destroyed all resistance.

Having established military control, the BSAC moved to appropriate land for white settlers by establishing reserves for Africans, moving them to territory unsuitable for farming or grazing. With little water and located far from transportation routes and market towns, the reserves eliminated African competition for white farmers. By 1914, the African population of 836,000 occupied only 23 percent of the land, and marginal land at best. One such reserve was described by a land-settlement director as "practically a conglomeration of koppjes [hills] with very small cultivable valleys in between." "The area in question," he noted, "is infested with baboons and is only traversable by pack animals."[20] The 28,000 settlers, who comprised 3 percent of Rhodesia's total population, held 75 percent of the productive land.

* * *

Like Rhodesia, Kenya came late to settler colonialism. In 1886 and 1890, during what is called the European scramble for Africa, Britain and Germany divided East Africa between themselves, Britain taking what became Kenya and Uganda, and Germany annexing the lands to the south. The British government set up the Imperial British East Africa Company (IBEAC) to govern this vast tract of land extending westward from the Indian Ocean 600 miles inland to the lakes region of East Central Africa. Kenya became a settler colony when the British decided that the most cost-effective way to recoup the money they had spent to build a railway linking the protectorate of Uganda to the coast would be to establish white farmers and ranchers on the land to exploit the wealth of East Africa.

By the Crown Lands Ordinance of 1902, the British government took possession of all of the land in Kenya. Under the direction of Chief Commissioner Charles Eliot, it proceeded to forcibly remove the Maasai from lands that would become called the "White Highlands," as we saw at the start of this chapter; 7.5 million acres of the best farmland in Kenya would ultimately be placed in the hands of white settlers who paid virtually nothing for it. Land in the central highlands, where Kikuyu people predominated; in western Kenya, where the Kalenjin lived; and in the Konza and Athi River areas, inhabited by the Kamba people, was also seized and parceled out at fire sale prices to settlers from Britain and South Africa. Initially, the small number of settlers meant that they had a relatively minor impact on Africans: in 1907, the East Africa Protectorate could boast only 2,000 settlers. The Kenyan government formalized control over labor through the Native Authority Ordinance in 1912, a law permitting colonial authorities to compel Africans to perform "compulsory labor" without payment. Much of the colonial infrastructure was built by African men conscripted under the ordinance.

Though small in number, settlers procured vast farms and exerted pressure on the government to assist them in their dealings. The colonial government provided instruction, seeds, tools, and fertilizer to ensure their success; it built railway lines and roadways to get their products to market. Over time, Africans who had not lost their land to settlers adjusted their economies to the capitalist market; those who had been dispossessed, like the Kikuyu and the Kamba, made accommodations that enabled them to persist in their economic lives. The Maasai, along with other pastoral communities who lost the greatest amount of land, saw their economies destroyed. In the years following the Great War, which we will treat in the next chapter, dramatic influxes of white settlers and the policies the colonial government made to support them, would transform the lives of Kenyans.

***

The outcome of struggles over land turned out differently in Ireland than in South Africa, Kenya, Rhodesia, Australia, New Zealand, and the US. Here, uniquely for this particular historical moment, the Irish peasantry whose land had been taken and held by English conquerors won a good deal of it back in the years 1882–1913. The first of Britain's settler colonies became the first to claw back land taken by English settlers. In 1870, for example, 97 percent of Irish farmers did not own their land; they were tenants on the estates and farms of often absentee landlords, the vast majority of them Protestant. By 1929, by contrast, following a series of so-called "land wars," land acts designed to bring conflict to an end, and, most prominently, the achievement of Irish independence from Great Britain in 1922, more than 97 percent of Irish farmers owned their land.

A depression that began in 1873 devastated a populace still reeling from the famine of the 1840s. As prices for agricultural products dropped, so too did peasants' income, till they were no longer able to pay rent for the land they farmed. Their mostly Protestant landlords took harsh steps in response to their loss of income, evicting tenants by the thousands, many of whom then became violent. In 1879, the failure of the potato crop provoked even more distress; that year, an ex-Fenian by the name of Michael Davitt formed the bitter Catholic peasantry into the Land League, an organization that sought relief for farmers in the short run and the elimination of the landlord class in the long term by nationalizing the land and giving it over to the peasants. During what was called the Land War of 1879–82, an angry and resentful Catholic peasantry carried out a campaign of protest, destruction, and violence against the largely Protestant aristocracy and gentry who made up the landed class of Ireland.

Although the "three F's"—fair rent, fixity of tenancy, and free sale of land—constituted the initial demands put forward by the Land League, peasant proprietorship of the land stood at the heart of the agrarian movement. Radicals like Michael Davitt regarded it as "unwritten law" that the land belonged exclusively to the people of Ireland, whose claims to it had been violently usurped by conquering Englishmen who had seized the territory centuries ago and passed it down to their descendants in violation of God's law. The rural Irish believed virtually as one that the land should be possessed by those who worked it, not by an alien group of landlords who had no right to it beyond their capacity to impose their will by force. As James Fintan Lalor had put in 1848 in terms that resonated even more powerfully in 1879, the absolute... ownership of the lands of Ireland is vested of right in the people of Ireland ... they, and none but they, are the first landowners and lords paramount as well as the lawmakers of this island ... no man has a right to hold one foot of Irish soil otherwise than by grant of tenancy and fee from them. [21]

The misery, humiliation, ill-usage, and injustices they suffered at the hands of English landlords derived from the theft of their lands, the members of the Land League believed, and the only remedy was to rid the island of the English landlords and the British government. At a meeting of the Killala Land Meeting in County Mayo, in late 1879, a parish priest named Peter Nolan charged that England "exulted in the destruction of our race," accusing the government of "deliberately and effectually putting the people to death." "For all the miseries of our country," he concluded, "there is one unfailing remedy—that Ireland should be permitted to manage her own affairs in her own Parliament."[22]

In conjunction with a newly formed Irish Party under the leadership of the aristocratic Protestant Charles Parnell, whose MPs pledged themselves to obstruct the workings of parliament until that body took up the issue of home rule for Ireland, the Land League forced politicians to pay attention to the needs and desires of the Irish people. Through an island-wide campaign of regular and frequent mass meetings, a no-rent movement, physical intimidation of landlords or their representatives, resistance to evictions by local groups wielding farm implements and assaulting constables trying to serve eviction notices, the Land League posed a formidable challenge to British government. In one of the most effective weapons of the land wars, Davitt and Parnell initiated a campaign to ostracize anyone who took over a farm from which a tenant had been evicted. These boycotts—so named after its first target, Captain Boycott—proved successful in reducing the number of tenant evictions by Protestant landlords who could no longer find tenants to work their land. The government headed by Prime Minister William Gladstone reacted to the violence with a coercion bill suspending habeas corpus and permitting police to arrest and detain Land Leaguers without cause. Parnell was arrested under its provisions on October 13, 1880, and the Land League was outlawed a week later. Parliament knew it had to do something to prevent further violence against Irish landlords and their agents; it passed the Land Law (Ireland) Act in 1881, giving some tenants the opportunity to purchase land. More importantly for the future, it established the Irish Land Commission and a Land Court, to which tenants could appeal for reductions in rent.

By the terms of the so-called Kilmainham Treaty of May 2, 1882, Parnell pledged to bring his influence to bear to stop the agrarian "outrages" in return for the government's promise to release the Land League prisoners and substantially address the question of rents and land tenure. Davitt and Parnell formed the Irish National League to replace the outlawed Land

League; for his part, Gladstone persuaded parliament to pass the Arrears of Rent (Ireland) Act of 1882, giving the Land Commission formed in 1881 the power to cancel back rent owed to landlords. The Purchase of Land (Ireland) Act of 1885 provided loans of up to 100 percent of the purchase price to qualifying tenants, enabling, by 1888, more than 25,000 farmers to purchase the land they worked.

In 1886, Gladstone brought forward a home rule bill, seeking to give Ireland its own legislature for consideration of most domestic Irish concerns. He had little support from his own party—which soon split into two irreconcilable factions—and the bill failed. The National League responded with a Plan of Campaign, as it was called, a renewal of the land wars of the early 1880s. Once again, rent strikes, mass meetings, boycotts, and attacks on process servers convulsed the countryside, leading the British government to crack down hard. A new coercion act came into force, under which hundreds of Irish men and women were imprisoned. The law abolished trial by jury, banned the National League, and allowed the government to engage in violence in the enforcement of evictions. At one point, the chief secretary for Ireland, Arthur Balfour, dispatched the army to lay siege against cottages and use a battering ram to force resisting tenants to leave their farms. Balfour tried to balance his iron-handed law enforcement with a new land law of 1887, which made £33 million available to help tenants purchase their land, but with all kinds of hoops to jump through. The act proved ineffective until it was amended in 1896, when far more generous terms made it possible for Irish farmers to take advantage of it. The Land Purchase (Ireland) Act of 1903, perhaps the most far-reaching piece of land legislation until Ireland became independent in 1921, came into effect as a consequence of continued and persistent pressure on the part of Irish MPs sitting in parliament. It made it easier for tenants to purchase their holdings, and effectively ended the ability of absentee landlords to control their tenants. By 1914, some 316,000 tenant farmers owned 11.5 million out of a total of 20 million acres. Two other acts, the Labourers (Ireland) Acts of 1906 and 1911, provided the funds to build cottages that could be purchased by laborers on manageable terms, dramatically altering the landscape of rural Ireland by replacing primitive hovels with state-funded housing for more than 250,000 farm workers and their families.

These seemingly generous actions on the part of the British parliament were a consequence of the political power wielded by the Irish Parliamentary Party and the United Irish League. When the Liberal party returned to office in 1905, following nearly twenty years in the wilderness, they relied on the Irish Parliamentary Party for their majority. In 1912, the Liberals enacted a bill that would create an Irish parliament in Dublin through which legislation affecting local Irish concerns could be created. The House of Lords objected but the law could not be delayed beyond 1914; home rule would come to Ireland, it was clear. Immediately, six counties of Ulster announced their intention to oppose home rule by any and all means, and under the leadership of Sir Edward Carson, built up a mass movement of resistance. In 1913, Ulstermen began to arm themselves and formed the Ulster Volunteer Force, promising to defend union with the United Kingdom through violence if necessary. In April they obtained 24,000 guns from Germany.

The south of Ireland responded on November 25, 1913, with the establishment of the Irish Volunteers at a meeting in Dublin. Operating behind the scenes as much as possible, the Irish Republican Brotherhood formed a significant core of the Irish Volunteers, and used the specter of the armed Protestant north to try to persuade the Irish people that independence would come not from parliamentary manoevering but from armed conflict. In March of 1914, as home rule for Ireland was just about to be passed into law, the government ordered troops in Ireland to march north to cut off an anticipated rising by the Ulster Volunteers. In what became known as the Mutiny at the Curragh, a significant number of army officers threatened to resign their commissions rather than carry out their orders. They did so at the secret urging of Conservative leader Andrew Bonar Law and Sir Henry Wilson, chief of military operations at the War Office. By the end of July 1914, Ireland—and England, too, if the actions of Carson, Bonar Law, and the highest echelons of the military command are taken into account—teetered on the precipice of civil war. The Great War came just in time to prevent it, dousing the flames of insurrection with a bracing blast of cold water. As we will see in the next chapter, the Great War had a powerful impact on Indigenous communities in all of the settler colonies under review here.

Counterpoint: Japanese Settler Colonialism

In Asia, Japan proved the equal of British and American settlers on Indigenous lands. In 1868, as a consequence of the inability of the Tokugawa shogunate to prevent an intrusion of an American fleet to "open" Japanese ports to trade with the Western powers and its willingness to sign what many regarded as a humiliating treaty with the US, a force of disgruntled samurai elites and supporters of the emperor overthrew the shogunate and established imperial court rule. The Meiji restoration, as it was called, disrupted the Japanese social, economic, and political order as reformers sought to transform the country from a feudal society into a liberal capitalist one. The upheaval left many samurai high and dry, stripped of the ability to sustain themselves as part of a warrior class and deeply resentful of their decline in social status. Almost immediately, the government sought a way to placate these newly impoverished samurai, hitting upon the colonization of Ainu Mosir, an island just to the north of Japan that it renamed Hokkaido. Just a year after the overthrow of the shogunate, the government seized the island and declared it *terra nullius*, uprooting the hunter-gathering Ainu people who had inhabited it for over 600 years. The new Hokkaido Development Agency offered land grants to samurai who would settle there, luring some 2,000 of them within the next four years. Subsequent tax and land reform measures on the Japanese mainland spurred the migration of thousands and thousands of peasants to Hokkaido, further displacing the Indigenous Ainu and, within two decades, nearly wiping them out.

Government officials believed that their best route to preserving Japanese power in the face of Western expansion lay in imitating the West, in adopting the economic system, technologies, values, and lifestyles of Europeans and Americans. Their mimicry often took gendered forms: Japanese gentlemen, for instance, took to wearing the costume of Western men, including the high-collared shirts that became a caricature of westernization. "High-collar" gentlemen garnered derision and scorn from those, mainly samurai, who saw in such attire the mark of effeminacy. These critics adopted an oppositional style of dress and conduct, fashioning themselves as tough, primitive, foul-mouth "barbarians." One university student spoke for many, many others when he decried his fellow students' desire to emulate the West. "They have lost their interest in barbarism," he lamented, "and their tastes have become like those of schoolgirls."[23]

For many in Japan, imperialism offered the antidote to what was perceived to be a debasing of the warrior tradition exemplified by the decline of the samurai. As they moved on and colonized Okinawa, Taiwan, Korea, and later Manchuria, Japanese began to contrast themselves against their Asian subjects, peoples they identified as weak and inferior, by casting the Chinese, for instance, as pig-tailed, effeminate, ridiculous creatures and themselves as manly guides who would show the way to recovering their self-respect. As a top government official put it in regard to Korea, the Japanese had an obligation to uplift that benighted nation. "A poor, effeminate people, with no political instinct, with no economic 'gumption,' with no intellectual ambition, is become the Brown Japanese Man's burden," wrote Nitobe Inazō, a politician and diplomat who served as the administrator of Taiwan in the early twentieth century, recalling Rudyard Kipling's "White Man's Burden." "Something must be done to resurrect a dead nation."[24]

At the same time that government officials promoted an imperial masculinity as the means by which Japan could hold itself up against the West, they looked to women to play a central role in Japan's settler colonies. The role of women in the Japanese empire was markedly different from that of women in most European settler colonies. While men made up the overwhelming majority of settlers in the latter for decades, if not longer, there were roughly equal numbers of Japanese men and women in the colonies in Korea and Manchuria. Japanese officials viewed empire as "women's business" because they believed women were better suited to the key tasks of colonization, including "languages, business, and the management."[25] This led to high numbers of middle-class women business-owners and managers as well as women in positions of authority within the local administration, which contrasted with more conservative gender roles in metropolitan Japan. Such liberal advances for women raised concerns among certain officials at home, leading to the extension of the ideology of "good wives, wise mothers" to Korea. In 1912, for instance, the Girls' Public Higher School Ordinance of Korea declared that

> attention should be put on the following matters. 1) It should have students cultivate the virtues of modesty and thrift, and keep gentleness in languages and behaviors. 2) It should have students acquire a lot of knowledge and practical skills. Attention should be made so that they would not become unfaithful to family matters, and in particular, learn things necessary for becoming good housewives. 3) Students should be educated to cultivate virtues as well as knowledge.[26]

Other women were forced to become sex workers by an official policy that authorized the use of Indigenous women in Taiwan, Korea, and Manchuria to service the sexual needs of soldiers. The indenture of "comfort women," as they were called, would characterize Japanese settler colonialism in Asia, and become the source of some of the most indelible shame experienced by Indigenous women at the hands of colonizers.

Primary Source

Native Lands Act, Union of South Africa, 1913

The Natives' Land Act

[No. 27, 1913]

ACT TO Make further provision as to the purchase and leasing of Land by Natives and other Persons in the several parts of the Union and for other purposes in connection with the ownership and occupation of Land by Natives and other Persons.

Be it enacted by the King's Most Excellent Majesty, the Senate and the House of Assembly of the Union of South Africa, as follows:

1. (1) From and after the commencement of this Act, land outside the scheduled native areas shall, until Parliament, acting upon the report of the commission appointed under this Act, shall have made other provision, be subjected to the following provisions, that is to say: –

    Except with the approval of the Governor-General –

    a. a native shall not enter into any agreement or transaction for the purchase, hire, or other acquisition from a person other than a native, of any such land or of any right thereto, interest therein, or servitude thereover; and

b. a person other than a native shall not enter into any agreement or transaction for the purchase, hire, or other acquisition from a native of any such land or of any right thereto, interest therein, or servitude thereover.

(2) From and after the commencement of this Act, no person other than a native shall purchase, hire or in any other manner whatever acquire any land in a scheduled native area or enter into any agreement or transaction for the purchase, hire or other acquisition, direct or indirect, of any such land or of any right thereto or interest therein or servitude thereover, except with the approval of the Governor-General.

(3) A statement showing the number of approvals granted by the Governor-General under sub-sections (1) and (2) of this section and giving the names and addresses of the persons to whom such approvals were granted, the reasons for granting the same, and the situation of the lands in respect of which they were granted, shall, within six weeks after the commencement of each ordinary session of Parliament, be laid upon the Tables of both Houses of Parliament.

(4) Every agreement or any other transaction whatever entered into in contravention of this section shall be null and void ab initio.

2. (1) As soon as may be after the commencement of this Act the Governor-General shall appoint a commission whose functions shall be to inquire and report –
   a. what areas should be set apart as areas within which natives shall not be permitted to acquire or hire land or interests in land;
   b. what areas should be set apart as areas within which persons other than natives shall not be permitted to acquire or hire land or interests in land.
   c. The commission shall submit with any such report –
      i. descriptions of the boundaries of any area which it proposes should be so set apart; and
      ii. a map or maps showing every such area.
   ....

4. (1) For the purposes of establishing any such area as is described in section two, the Governor-General may, out of moneys which Parliament may vote for the purpose, acquire any land or interest in land.
   ....

5. (1) Any person who is a party to any attempted purchase, sale, hire or lease, or to any agreement or transaction which is in contravention of this Act or any regulation made thereunder shall be guilty of an offence and liable on conviction to a fine not exceeding one hundred pounds or, in default of payment, to imprisonment with or without hard labour for a period not exceeding six months, and if the act constituting the offence be a continuing one, the offender shall be liable to a further fine not exceeding five pounds for every day which that act continues.
   ....

6. In so far as the occupation by natives of land outside the scheduled native areas may be affected by this Act, the provisions thereof shall be construed as being in addition to and not in substitution for any law in force at the commencement thereof relating to such occupation; but in the event of a conflict between the provisions of this Act and the provisions of any such law, the provisions of this Act shall, save as is specially provided therein, prevail:

Provided that –

a. nothing in any such law or in this Act shall be construed as restricting the number of natives who, as farm labourers, may reside on any farm in the Transvaal;

b. in any proceedings for a contravention of this Act the burden of proving that a native is a farm labourer shall be upon the accused;

c. until Parliament, acting upon the report of the said commission, has made other provision, no native resident on any farm in the Transvaal or Natal shall be liable to penalties or to be removed from such farm under any law, if at the commencement of this Act he or the head of his family is registered for taxation or other purposes in the department of Native Affairs as being resident on such farm, nor shall the owner of any such farm be liable to the penalties imposed by section five in respect of the occupation of the land by such native; but nothing herein contained shall affect any right possessed by law by an owner or lessee of a farm to remove any native therefrom. ....

8. (1) Nothing in this Act contained shall be construed as, –

....

b. invalidating or affecting in any manner whatever any agreement or any other transaction for the purchase of land lawfully entered into prior to the commencement of this Act, or as prohibiting any person from purchasing at any sale held by order of a competent court any land which was hypothecated by a mortgage bond passed before the commencement of this Act; or

c. prohibiting the acquisition at any time of land or interests in land by devolution or succession on death, whether under a will or on intestacy; or

....

f. in any way altering the law in force at the commencement of this Act relating to the acquisition of rights to minerals, precious or base metals or precious stones; or

g. applying to land within the limits in which a municipal council, town council, town board, village management board, or health committee or other local authority exercises jurisdiction; or

h. applying to land held at the commencement of the Act by any society carrying on, with the approval of the Governor-General, educational or missionary work amongst natives; or

i. prohibiting the acquisition by natives from any person whatever of land or interests in land in any township lawfully established prior to the commencement of this Act, provided it is a condition of the acquisition that no land or interest in land in such township has at any time been or shall in future be, transferred except to a native or coloured person; or

j. permitting the alienation of land or its diversion from the purposes for which it was set apart if, under section one hundred and forty-seven of the South African Act, 1909, or any other law, such land could not be alienated or so diverted except under the authority of an Act of Parliament; ...

9. The Governor-General may make regulations for preventing the overcrowding of huts and other dwellings in the stadts, native villages and settlements and other places in which natives are congregated in areas not under the jurisdiction of any local authority, the sanitation of such places and for the maintenance of the health of the inhabitants thereof.

10. In this Act, unless inconsistent with the context, –

"scheduled native area" shall mean any area described in the Schedule to this Act; "native" shall mean any person, male or female, who is a member of an aboriginal race or tribe of Africa; and shall further include any company or other body of persons, corporate or unincorporate, if the persons who have a controlling interest therein are natives; "interest in land" shall include, in addition to other interest in land, the interest which a mortgagee of, or person having charge over, land acquires under a mortgage bond or charge; "Minister" shall mean the Minister of Native Affairs; "farm labourer" shall mean a native who resides on a farm and is bona fide, but not necessarily continuously employed by the owner or lessee thereof in domestic service or in farming operations:

Provided that –

a. if such native reside on one farm and is employed on another farm of the same owner or lessee he shall be deemed to have resided, and to have been employed, on one and the same farm;

b. such native shall not be deemed to be bona fide employed unless he renders ninety days' service at least in one calendar year on the farm occupied by the owner or lessee or on another farm of the owner or lessee and no rent is paid or valuable consideration of any kind, other than service, is given by him to the owner or lessee in respect of residence on such farm or farms.

A person shall be deemed for the purposes of this Act to hire land if, in consideration of his being permitted to occupy that land or any portion thereof –

a. he pays or promises to pay to any person a rent in money; or

b. he renders or promises to render to any person a share of the produce of that land, or any valuable consideration of any kind whatever other than his own labour or services or the labour or services of his family.

Notes

1. Quoted in Lotte Hughes, *Moving the Maasai: A Colonial Misadventure* (Basingstoke: Palgrave Macmillan, 2006), pp. 55, 59.
2. Quoted in Hughes, *Moving the Maasai*, p. 53.
3. Quoted in Hughes, *Moving the Maasai*, p. 35.
4. Quoted in Steven Pevar, "The Dawes Act: How Congress tried to Destroy Indian Reservations," OUP Blog, https://blog.oup.com/2012/02/dawes-act-congress-indian-reservations/
5. David Wallace Adams, *Education for Extinction: American Indians and the Boarding School Experience, 1875–1928*, 2nd edn (Lawrence: University Press of Kansas, 2020), pp. 31, 105.
6. R.H. Pratt, 1st Lieut. 10th Cavalry, in Charge of [Carlisle] School, to E.H. Hayt [Hoyt?], Commissioner of Indian Affairs, November 13, 1879. NARA_RG75_79_b571_1879_P1182.
7. Zitkala-Ša, "The School Days of an Indian Girl," in Zitkala-Ša, *American Indian Stories and Old Indian Legends* (Garden City: Dover Publications, 2014), pp. 22–3.
8. Zitkala-Ša, "An Indian Teacher Among Indians," in Zitkala-Ša, *American Indian Stories and Old Indian Legends* (Garden City: Dover Publications, 2014), p. 41.
9. John Fire/Lame Deer and Richard Erdoes, *Lame Deer: Seeker of Visions* (New York: Simon & Schuster, 1972), p. 228.
10. Quoted in John Milloy, "Indian Act Colonialism: A Century of Dishonour, 1869–1969," National Centre for First Nations Governance, May 2008.
11. Quoted in Milloy, "Indian Act Colonialism."
12. Quoted in The Truth and Reconciliation Commission of Canada, *A Knock on the Door: The Essential History of Residential Schools*, edited and abridged (Manitoba: University of Manitoba Press, 2016), pp. 4–5.
13. Quoted in Eric Hanson, Daniel P. Games, and Alexa Manuel, "The Residential School System," Indigenous Foundations. https://Indigenousfoundations.arts.ubc.ca/residential-school-system-2020/, accessed September 12, 2023.
14. Quoted in Stuart Macintyre, *A Concise History of Australia*, 3rd edn (Cambridge: Cambridge University Press, 2009), pp. 143, 150.
15. Quoted in Margaret D. Jacobs, *White Mother to a Dark Race: Settler Colonialism, Maternalism, and the Removal of Indigenous Children in the American West and Australia, 1880–1940* (Lincoln, NE: University of Nebraska Press, 2009), pp. 171–2.
16. Martin Meredith, *Diamonds, Gold and War: The British, Boers, and the Making of South Africa* (New York: Public Affairs, 2007), p. 495.
17. Meredith, *Diamonds, Gold and War*, p. 466.

18 Quoted in Raymond Suttner, "The African National Congress Centenary: A Long and Difficult Journey," *International Affairs*, No. 88, Vol. 4 (2012), pp. 719–38, p. 722.
19 Quoted in Meredith, *Diamonds, Gold, and War*, p. 219.
20 Quoted in Alois S. Mlambo, *A History of Zimbabwe* (Cambridge: Cambridge University Press, 2014), p. 61.
21 Quoted in Donald Jordan, "The Irish National League and the 'Unwritten Law': Rural Protest and Nation-Building in Ireland, 1882–1890," *Past & Present*, 158 (February 1998), pp. 146–71, pp. 149, 150.
22 Quoted in Anne Kane, *Constructing Irish Identity: Discourse and Ritual during the Land War, 1879–1882* (Basingstoke: Palgrave Macmillan, 2011), p. 82.
23 Quoted in Jason G. Karlin, *Gender and Nation in Meiji Japan: Modernity, Loss, and the Doing of History* (Honolulu: University of Hawai'i Press, 2014), p. 59.
24 Quoted in Michele M. Mason, "Empowering the Would-Be Warrior: Bushidō and the Gendered Bodies of the Japanese Nation," in Sabine Frühstück and Anne Walthall, eds., *Recreating Japanese Men*, (Berkeley: University of California Press, 2011), p. 75.
25 Mark Driscoll, *Absolute Erotic, Absolute Grotesque: The Living, Dead, and Undead in Japan's Imperialism, 1895–1945* (Durham: Duke University Press, 2010), p. 87.
26 Quoted in Sug-In Kweon, "Japanese Female Settlers in Colonial Korea: Between the 'Benefits' and 'Constraints' of Colonial Society," *Social Science Japan Journal*, Vol. 17, No. 2 (2014), pp. 169–88, fn. 13. https://doi-org.colorado.idm.oclc.org/10.1093/ssj/jyu004

Further Reading

David Wallace Adams, *Education for Extinction: American Indians and the Boarding School Experience, 1875–1928*, 2nd edn (Lawrence: University Press of Kansas, 2020).
Margaret D. Jacobs, *White Mother to a Dark Race: Settler Colonialism, Maternalism, and the Removal of Indigenous Children in the American West and Australia, 1880–1940* (Lincoln: University of Nebraska Press, 2009).
Anne Kane, *Constructing Irish Identity: Discourse and Ritual during the Land War, 1879–1882* (Basingstoke: Palgrave Macmillan, 2011).
Martin Meredith, *Diamonds, Gold and War: The British, Boers, and the Making of South Africa* (New York: Public Affairs, 2007).

7

Indigeneity and War, 1914–45

In December 1922, Duncan Scott, Canada's deputy minister of Indian Affairs, dispatched Royal Canadian Mounted Police (RCMP) to the Grand River Preserve of the Six Nations Confederacy of the Iroquois (Haudenosaunee) to enforce the dominion's laws banning liquor. Sent to destroy stills producing home-made hooch, the police fired shots at at least one man, Scott claiming they did so because fifty armed Indians sought to prevent the police from carrying out their duties. The incident enraged the Grand River Council of hereditary chiefs, especially Levi General, a Cayuga member known as Deskaheh, the Haudenosaunee word for chief. "They had no right to shoot any Indian," he protested. "They shot him five times … is this what you call a protection according to our treaty?"[1]

The treaty to which he referred was the agreement put in place following Britain's loss of the thirteen American colonies in 1784. It established a reserve in modern-day Ontario for those Iroquois who had allied with the British against the American colonists. Haudenosaunee chiefs had long regarded the grant of the Grand River reserve as an explicit expression of Iroquois sovereignty, an assertion contested by the British crown and, after 1867, the Canadian government. The RCMP raid was only the latest intrusion on Six Nations' sovereignty, but in many ways it proved to be the straw that broke the proverbial camel's back. It compelled Deskaheh to journey to Geneva in 1923 to put the Haudenosaunee case for self-government before the League of Nations. In his letter to the secretary-general of the League, Deskaheh described the police action as the commission of

> an act of war upon the Six Nations by making an hostile invasion of the Six Nations domain, wherein the Dominion Government then established an armed force which it has since maintained therein, and the presence thereof has impeded and impedes the Six Nations Council in the carrying on of the duly constituted government of the Six Nations people, and is a menace to international peace.[2]

Deskaheh failed in his effort to gain recognition and redress from the League of Nations, despite support from a number of member states, among them the new Irish Free State. The following year, in fact, the ministry summarily abolished the Confederacy Council of hereditary chiefs and installed a new form of government. Andrea Catapano's cousin witnessed the arrival of the Royal Canadian Mounted Police, sent to enforce the ministry's dictum against the council. "The sight of those figures thundering down the dirt road in their red uniforms on horseback stayed with my cousin until her eighties," Catapano wrote, "for it frightened her so, it sent her scurrying through the bush towards home at Martin's Corners."[3] Deskaheh's initiative may have fallen short, but the very fact of his attempt, alongside that of T.W. Ratana, a Māori spiritual and political leader seeking international recognition of the Treaty of Waitangi, marked a new moment in the relationship of Indigenous peoples and the settler governments under which they lived. Aboriginal people, having contributed significantly to Britain's war effort between 1914 and 1918 and again in 1939–45, looked to the international community for acknowledgment of their grievances, rights, and demands for autonomy.

The 1920s and 1930s were marked by an admixture of settler-state depredations against Indigenous peoples, anti-colonial disturbances, renewed pushes for political rights or independence, and spasms of violence against restive colonized populations. Opposition to colonialism took many forms, and its goals were equally varied. It included movements to obtain complete independence but also efforts to secure rights and representation within existing colonial arrangements and administrative structures. It entailed open insurrection, terrorist attacks, and nonviolent protest as well as attempts to claim and act upon citizenship rights that did not yet exist and thereby to radically transform and transcend settler colonialism from within.

***

When war broke out in August 1914, Britain mobilized virtually all of its colonial subjects. From the dominions, 630,000 Canadian enlistees and conscripts joined up, as did 417,000 Australians, 103,000 New Zealanders, and 146,000 white South Africans. Indigenous peoples from South Africa serving in the effort amounted to some 85,000; 4,000 Canadian Indian men, 2,700 Māoris, and at least 580 Aboriginal Australians enlisted as well. The contributions of colonial troops often made the difference between defeat and continued stalemate. Until Britain's new army could be recruited and trained, Indian, Australian, and New Zealand troops filled the breach following the collapse of the British Expeditionary Force in the winter of 1914–15. In the first German gas attack at Ypres in April 1915, Canadian troops stood their ground and prevented a German breakthrough on the Western Front. In that battle, Lieutenant Cameron Dee Brant, a Mohawk, was killed, a loss that the Brantford mayor memorialized in a letter to the Chiefs of the Six Nations Council and to Brant's family. "In his fall, and in the fall of other soldiers with him," the mayor wrote, "we recognize the willing sacrifice of our Indian compatriots in the defence of rights and liberties dear to every British heart. We desire to express to you our appreciation of the splendid contribution the Indians have made and will continue to make to the fighting forces of our Empire."[4]

The Great War involved a fair amount of fighting in Africa. When the German commander Paul von Lettow-Vorbeck embarked on his campaign around southern and eastern Africa, British troops were forced to follow (see Figure 7.1). More than 2 million Africans saw action in the conflict. Ten percent of them—over 200,000—lost their lives, either killed in action or

FIGURE 7.1 *Soldiers of the King's African Rifles on patrol in German East Africa, 1917.*

dying from disease or malnutrition in the horrific conditions under which they worked. Some 25,000 Africans from West Africa, 30,000 from Uganda, Nyasaland, and Kenya, and 2,400 from Rhodesia served as actual soldiers under British command, but by far the majority of them worked as carriers. Carriers—or porters—were required in such large numbers because the fighting in Africa took place in areas where roads, railways, and motorized vehicles were scarce, and where the presence of tsetse fly and other biting insects made it impossible for draught animals to survive. The heavy and unrelenting work of supply fell to human beings over the four-year period of the conflict.

Many Indigenous people regarded the Great War as an opportunity to demonstrate their worth to their governments. Others saw it as a chance to register deep discontent with the state of affairs in a settler state: a number of revolts against British, American, or dominion rule broke out during the conflict. In South Africa, in September 1914, a band of Boer commandos rebelled against the government's decision to fully support Britain in a short-lived campaign. In Canada, the Six Nations Confederacy refused to participate in the war effort because, as a sovereign nation, they claimed, they would have to be asked to do so by King George. Enlistment drives prompted resistance among some Māori groups in New Zealand and among certain Navajos, Utes, and Creeks in the US. None of these, however, proved as consequential to the continuation of settler colonial rule as the rising that took place in Ireland in the spring of 1916 in what became known as the Easter Rebellion.

* * *

Upon the outbreak of war in 1914, tens of thousands of Irishmen from north and south volunteered their services in support of Britain's fight, and many thousands gave their lives in the effort. But some Catholic Irish refused to enlist, arguing that Britain's war had nothing to do with Ireland. On the contrary, members of the Irish Republican Brotherhood insisted, Britain's war against Germany offered the Irish an opportunity that they must not let pass. They and the leaders of the Irish Volunteers, an organization seeking to create an Irish republic through revolutionary action, determined to seize it. The government had suspended home rule for the duration of the war, a policy accepted by the parliamentary leader of the Irish party, John Redmond, who sought to present the party in as cooperative a light as possible. Redmond, however, presided over a party and a set of parliamentary tactics that could no longer claim the allegiance of the Irish people, losing ground to a nationalist movement led by Sinn Féin—Gaelic for "Ourselves Alone"—for which mere home rule would no longer suffice. On the day after Easter Sunday in 1916, as the war effort against Germany foundered in a morass of mud and muddle, Irish republican forces under the leadership of Patrick Pearse and James Connolly marched to the General Post Office

(GPO) building in Dublin and overran the unarmed guard there. Another group of rebels stormed Dublin Castle, the headquarters of British rule, while others captured City Hall, the Four Courts, and St. Stephen's Green. In a dramatic declaration from the steps of the GPO, IRB commander Pearse proclaimed Ireland a republic.

The rebels had arranged with German officials to land arms and ammunition in support of the Irish rebels, but the ship carrying the weapons had been caught by the British navy and was scuttled by its captain. The rising, without sufficient arms for its participants, and—because of communications difficulties—short the 5,000 to 10,000 men expected to respond to the call to arms, sputtered out after a week, but not before the rebels captured a number of assets in Dublin. The Irish Citizen Army, headed by Michael Mallin and the Countess Constance Markiewicz, for example, took St. Stephen's Green, and then retreated under heavy fire to the College of Surgeons, where they held out for six days, with little food or fire power. Heavy fighting took place throughout the city, with casualties amounting to 450 dead and 2,500 wounded, the vast majority of them civilians. The republican cause suffered mightily in the eyes of most Irish Catholics, who declaimed against the violence and the great losses of life.

But Pearse and Connolly had never expected to defeat the British army. Their goals had been to ignite, by means of a blood sacrifice on the part of Irish manhood, nationalist feeling throughout the country. "We die that the Irish nation may live," declared one of Pearse's lieutenants. "Our blood will rebaptise and reinvigorate the land."[5] Regarded even by its protagonists as a "rhetorical gesture," the Easter Rising could boast little support among the population. Its suppression by British forces came swiftly. The army fired field artillery and naval guns on Dublin, virtually ensuring that civilians would be caught in the crossfire and killed. Army officers resorted to torture and summary executions in some instances.

The rising put down, British authorities took harsh action against the rebels and those they believed to be allied with them. Their heavy-handed response, including the mass arrests of Sinn Féiners—who had not been involved in either the planning or the carrying out of the rising—and the execution by firing squad of fifteen Volunteer leaders, mobilized Irish public opinion against their actions and in favor of independence where there had been none to speak of before. Irish MP John Dillon protested in parliament the "river of blood" released upon the innocent people of his country. "The madness of your soldiers," as he put it, served to provoke demands for self-determination amongst the majority of the Irish population in the south who had taken a neutral position in the past.[6]

* * *

Indigenous peoples who had toiled long and hard in aid of the war effort hoped they would return home to societies that would recognize their contributions in the same way as their white counterparts. In this they were profoundly disappointed. Their labor had became more and more necessary as the casualties mounted year by year, but they were never given the consideration or respect commanded by white colonists. One South African officer in France summed up the prevailing attitude towards Indigenous soldiers and laborers when he told a corps of Africans, "When you people get to South Africa again, don't start thinking you are Whites, just because this place has spoiled you. You are black, and you will stay black."[7] It might not be surprising to hear this come out of the mouth of a member of a society that had begun to legally institutionalize segregation, but the governments of Canada, New Zealand, and Australia demonstrated little more solicitation for their First Nations peoples. Upon their return home after the peace, Aboriginal peoples earned less in the way of pay and pensions than whites; provisions for postwar employment or land settlement never reached them; they couldn't gain access to basic medical care for the wounds and illnesses they suffered. Gratuitous slights accompanied the material insults suffered by those whose contributions to the war effort had been so important to securing final victory.

The loss of Indigenous lands to settlers continued throughout the war and especially into the interwar years, as the British and dominion governments introduced a variety of soldier settlement acts designed to reward and support veterans returning from the war. In Canada, a 1919 Order-in-Council gave the Ministry of Indian Affairs the power to take land from Indian reserves without permission from the Native peoples living on them; 86,000 acres of Indian land was distributed white veterans. Indian veterans were not eligible for land grants unless they were emancipated—that is, they had given up their status as Indian people and lived off the reserves. Indian people living on Vancouver Island drew upon the lessons of the Great War to register their protest against the injustice, arguing that "this is what the Kaiser would have done to us all, whites and Indians, if he had won the war."[8] Australia's Soldier Settlement Scheme, established in 1917 and updated in 1926, stipulated that the lands given to returning soldiers be crown lands, where, not incidentally, Aboriginal peoples lived. The government outright commandeered a number of Aboriginal reserves and slashed the size of others in order to make land available to white veterans. The Aboriginal people on these lands were forced to move. New Zealand's Discharged Soldiers' Settlement Act of 1915 and its amendment in 1917 took land from the Māori to accommodate Pakeha veterans. Māori soldiers theoretically enjoyed the same rights as Pakeha, but when the dust settled, only 1.7 percent of Māori veterans received land under the act, as opposed to 10 percent of Pakeha soldiers. Britain's Soldier Settlement Scheme of 1919 in Kenya gave more than 2 million acres of land to Britons and South Africans, enlarging the share of the colony held by white settlers by 33 percent. Some of the new arrivals hailed from the Anglican Ascendancy of Ireland, induced by the war for Irish independence, treated below, to uproot themselves and start again in another, far distant, settler colony.

* * *

During the interwar period, governments in Kenya and Southern Rhodesia (which split from Northern Rhodesia in 1911 and became self-governing in 1923) acted to consolidate their hold over the colonies. They passed a series of laws designed to ensure that the settlers remained profitable, often to the direct detriment of the African populations in the colonies. White settlers demanded and won advantages for themselves that entailed greater and greater intrusion into the lives of African men and women by the colonial state. The marketing board system, for example, legally obligated Africans to sell the entirety of their crops to the government marketing board at a price fixed by the board. The government then marked up the product, sold it on the world market for a significantly higher price, and pumped those profits into instruments like credit, loans, fertilizers, and equipment for white settlers. Cattle-keeping Africans faced the same discrimination: the government taxed cattle for domestic consumption—that is, African cattle—but did not tax cattle for export, which was the stock owned by white settlers. It directed the resultant tax revenues to the settlers. The two control systems often overlapped. In Kenya in 1938, the government forced the Kamba to sell their cattle for one-quarter of market value to a firm on the outskirts of Nairobi called Liebig's, a Southern Rhodesian company experienced in culling African "scrub cattle" from the Victoria and Gutu reserves in the southeast of their own country. The profits the company realized from the sale of the cattle on the world market provided funds for building a facility to chill settler beef for export. As one settler whose family raised cattle in Kamba areas at the time put it, Liebig's operated "solely for our benefit."[9]

Despite these restrictions and systemic disadvantages, many African farmers continued to produce livestock and crops, and some of them prospered. When the depression struck in 1929, the governments of Kenya and Southern Rhodesia acted to divert the wealth of these farmers to the white settlers. They did so by prohibiting Africans from growing lucrative cash crops—maize and tobacco in Southern Rhodesia, and maize and coffee in Kenya. This practice ensured that only white settlers could produce the most profitable crops, striking directly at the well-being of middle-class African farmers, and incurring their undying enmity.

In the 1920s, the development of the *kipande*—or pass—system expanded white control over labor in Southern Rhodesia and Kenya. African migrant laborers had to carry passes that provided details of their employers and wages, enabling settlers or government agents to round up those who had deserted their contracts, and then punish them for doing so. It became more difficult for Africans to leave jobs and negotiate better salaries with their employers, as their employment details were written in the *kipande* for anyone to see. Some employers withheld or destroyed the passbooks of their workers, making it impossible for them to leave to find better jobs.

In the mining centers of the Rhodesias, unemployment resulting from crashing demand for tin, copper, and other materials led workers and their families to migrate back to their villages, decimating the cities they left. Once home, they hoped to scrape together the means of subsistence from the land, but many of them failed. Food shortages in many places, along with a hostile reception by the occupiers of the land, reduced migrants to near-starvation in a number of areas. In order to prevent the arrival of migrants who might compete for scarce profits or prove to be a burden on the public's purse, the British government in Westminster ended its postwar program of encouraging and supporting the emigration of its citizens to Northern and Southern Rhodesia and Kenya, explaining that "the pressure of an unparalleled economic depression has compelled the virtual cessation of all State-aided migration and settlement."[10] Prospective settlers who might migrate on their own initiative faced new barriers: the deposit they had to pay before being allowed to enter the colonies rose considerably, as did the length of the probationary period they had to endure before they could be considered permanent residents. As a result of these policies, immigration dropped precipitously. Whereas nearly 30,000 migrants settled in the Rhodesias in the years 1926–31, only 9,000 did so between 1931 and 1936. Migrants to Kenya numbered nearly 39,000 between 1926 and 1931, but that number fell to 25,000 between 1931 and 1936. Moreover, almost as many white settlers left these colonies in those latter years, leaving the total number of whites there virtually unchanged.

Colonial governments in Kenya and Rhodesia introduced land policies that almost always disadvantaged Africans. On "native reserves," areas designated for African habitation that often contained only marginal land, authorities deliberately populated them with far more people than the reserves could support in order to induce Africans to leave them to find work on settler farms. Many did leave and made their homes on settler ranches where they provided labor or rent in exchange for a place to raise a family. Known as "squatters" in the Kenyan case, they tended to become more prosperous than their compatriots who lived on the reserves. By the end of the 1930s, some 150,000 Kikuyu squatters lived on white-owned farms. They would become important later in the Mau Mau uprising of the 1950s.

In Kenya, a number of Crown Land Ordinances made it impossible for Africans to secure land outside of the reserves to which they had been relegated and, as their population increased in size during the interwar period, the reserves became more and more crowded. A number of Kenyan activists pressed the British government to reform the system, hoping to increase the land available to Africans; in response, Britain sent a Kenyan

Land Commission to the colony in 1932 to look into the issue and take evidence from interested parties. The commission issued a report in 1934 that confirmed the racial division of land, confirming the ordinances that gave whites exclusive title to the highlands and quashing any African claims to lands inhabited by white settlers.

***

In South Africa, where prices on certain agricultural produces had fallen by more than 55 percent, marketing boards, price subsidies, low-interest loans, and even debt forgiveness could not staunch the bleeding caused by the depression. White farmers compelled their African tenants to labor longer on their lands and to pay more for the privilege of doing so. The government doubled the number of days African tenants had to work their landlords' holdings from ninety to 180; in return for working their own plots, Africans had to pay more than two-thirds of their yield to their landlords, leaving them with insufficient food to feed themselves and their families. White farmers colluded with one another to set low wages for their laborers, and tightened pass laws made it virtually impossible for Africans to leave bad situations. The 1926 Land Act and more draconian interpretations of the Cape reserve policy made it far more difficult for Africans to own land until it became virtually impossible by 1936. That year, despite vigorous African protests, the passage of the Native Trust and Land Act only enlarged the land designated for native reserves to a mere 13.6 percent of South Africa land. However, the South African government failed to meet even this benchmark until the 1980s. The responses to the depression helped turn Africans into serfs on the lands of white South Africans.

The impact of the depression on white South Africans, especially poor white farmers, had a profound political impact. In early 1933, the Nationalist Party of J.B.M. Hertzog and the South African Party under the leadership of Jan Smuts joined together to form a new United Party, with Hertzog as prime minister and Smuts holding the office of deputy prime minister. This had required compromise on Hertzog's part, a toning down of the profoundly racist policies designed to ensure white supremacy in all areas of South African life, and it angered the more extreme members of his party. Under the leadership of D.F. Malan, a number of Afrikaners broke off to form the Purified Nationalist Party in 1934; the party began to attract followers espousing doctrines alternatively labeled "Christian Nationalism" and "National Socialism." Members of Malan's party and of proto-fascist movements such as the *Broederbond*, however limited in number, held significant positions in the army, the police, the schools, and the civil service, so their impact was considerable. They persuaded white settlers that their problems had been caused by Africans, South Asians, and Jews; they initiated campaigns targeting racially mixed marriages, South Asian merchants, and the "present British-Jewish imperialist capitalist system";[11]

they influenced the passage of legislation that limited the immigration of Jews into the country; they pushed even more Africans off the land and made it ever harder for them to move about the country freely. The measures helped establish the framework for the system of segregation put in place by Smuts's government after the end of the Second World War, the system that would become out-and-out apartheid with the fall of Smuts's government in 1948.

***

In the spring of 1918, faced with an all-out offensive by the Germans on the western front, the British government revisited the question of imposing conscription on Ireland, an issue virtually guaranteed to excite massive opposition. The Irish Volunteers readied themselves to use force to prevent conscription; Sinn Féin took advantage of the threat of conscription to rally a national constituency behind it. In the general elections held in December 1918, Sinn Féin won seventy-six seats, as against the six seats held by the Irish Parliamentary party.

Home rule was rejected by the majority of the Irish electorate in the southern counties in favor of outright independence from Britain. The newly elected MPs refused to take their seats at Westminster and instead, on January 21, 1919, met in their own assembly, the Dáil Éireann, in Dublin. There they declared themselves the elected representatives of the Irish people and established an Irish republic, pledging to "ourselves and our people to make this declaration effective by every means at our command."[12]

Sinn Féin sought to gain and maintain a peaceable independence from Britain. The Irish Volunteers, by contrast, who saw in the dáil's Declaration of Independence an imprimatur, began to attack members of the police in Ireland, the Royal Irish Constabulary (RIC), counting them as "armed forces of the enemy." The Dáil had given the Volunteers no such charge, and most Sinn Féiners opposed their actions, but the Volunteers fashioned themselves into the Irish Republican Army (IRA); before long, it served as a legitimate force, a "National Army," of the new republic. Throughout 1919 they conducted boycotts against local RIC members, effectively alienating them from the general population; they assaulted the odd policemen unfortunate enough to find himself alone and unprotected; and they raided rural RIC outposts for arms, gradually forcing the RIC from the isolated posts of three to four men they held in the countryside into fewer but larger posts of eight to ten police. Attacks on the larger outposts commenced in January 1920; within six months, the IRA had damaged or destroyed forty-five barracks, while more than 400 outposts previously abandoned were burned down as a signal to the population that the British authorities could not control the countryside. Their campaign of violence and intimidation of local populations ensured that the British legal system could no longer function. Dáil courts sprang up to take their place, so that de facto civil administration fell into the hands of the republicans. When the IRA made a failed attempt on the life of Lord French, the lord lieutenant of Ireland on December 19, 1919, the British responded by increasing their military presence in Ireland and trying to chase down the gunmen of the "murder gang," as they called the IRA. For its part, the IRA formed itself into more permanent units—the "flying columns," so called, that organized and carried out larger-scaled ambushes of military and police patrols.[13]

The IRA had succeeded in registering significant RIC losses through the deaths or resignations of its constables, forcing British authorities, who were unable to replenish the ranks through recruitment in Ireland, to seek replacements from among former soldiers in the British population. Under the authority of Major-General Henry Tudor, a police force was established in May 1920. A second "Auxiliary Division" under the command of Brigadier-General Crozier, comprised of ex-officers, joined the new police force in July. These men carried out the bulk of the fighting against the IRA; it was they who conducted first unofficial and then official reprisals against the non-combatant population, garnering the hate and fear of the southern Irish that reverberates to this day at the mention of their name, the Black and Tans. The Black and Tans and Auxiliaries killed over 200 noncombatants in 1920 alone.

Between January and June 1921, when a truce between the IRA and British forces came into effect, seventeen children, five women, and sixteen unarmed men were killed in attacks carried out by Black and Tans, thirty of them in April alone. The Black and Tans and members of the armed forces meted out to the civilian population a kind and degree of violence that staggers the imagination. Weekly reports from Dublin testify to regular incidents of arson, beatings, shootings, molestation, rape, murder, and mutilation of the civilian population. Though they repeatedly denied that reprisals took place, government officials not only knew of them, they excused them, justified them, often approved of them, and may well have instigated them.

At home, the acts of reprisals against non-combatant Irish seemed to have elicited little response from the British public for almost a year. Ultimately, however, roused by increasing coverage in the press, especially by accounts of the sack of Balbriggan by British forces in September 1920, the burning of Cork, and the shooting down of a crowd of spectators at a soccer match in Dublin on what became called "Bloody Sunday," the public began to take notice, and it did not like what it saw. The conservative and liberal press alike decried the reprisals that seemed to be occurring every day. Liberal and Labour politicians denounced the reprisals and the government policies that appeared to excuse them; some Conservatives joined them in their opposition, convinced that such behavior could not serve British interests. Lloyd George believed the best way to end the conflict was to revive home rule, and persuaded his government to pass the Better Government of Ireland Act. The law gave a parliament to the twenty-six counties that made up what was regarded as "nationalist" Ireland, and another to the six counties of Ulster, where, presumably, Protestant Unionists dominated. Southern Ireland never accepted the act, but the northern counties did, consenting to the mechanism that would later partition the country into two states.

Despite its rejection of the home rule act, the IRA could not hope to defeat British forces in Ireland. It therefore agreed to negotiations between the British government and Sinn Féin to bring the war to an end in 1921. Michael Collins, an IRA commander who represented the dáil, and others representing Sinn Féin met with agents of the British government, trying in vain to impose their demands for complete independence and the establishment of a republican Ireland. The government insisted on partition for Ulster, however, and for the declaration of allegiance to the British king on the part not of a republic but of a "free state" within the British Commonwealth of Nations. The promise of the creation of a Boundary Commission to address the delineation of north from south made it possible to think that partition would be temporary. In any event, with little ability to hold out, Collins signed the treaty on December 6, 1921.

Civil war in southern Ireland ensued almost immediately. Under the leadership of Eamon de Valera, a number of IRA and Sinn Féin members refused to accept the terms of the treaty, and took up arms against Collins and his followers. For over a year, between April 1922 and May 1923, former comrades and colleagues fought against one another in a terrible round of assassination and execution of one another. Anti-treaty forces succeeded in ambushing and killing Michael Collins himself, but that didn't end the violence. Only when it became clear that de Valera's forces could not prevail did he call a halt to the fighting. As soon as the civil war ended, the newly recognized Irish parliament of the Irish Free State passed the 1923 Land Act, which arranged for more than 3 million acres to be transferred from the Ascendancy landlord class—what one member of parliament described as "descendants of Cromwellian planters"—to Irish citizens. That same member saw in the act "the undoing of the conquest of Ireland. For the conquest of Ireland was the conquest of the land of Ireland held by Irish tenure, from the people of Ireland by foreigners who held by foreign tenure from a foreign king."[14] For all intents and purposes, the land act and Irish independence marked, arguably, the end of settler colonialism in Ireland.

Legally, the formation of the Irish Free State in 1922 established the country as a dominion member of the British Commonwealth; this status left Irish nationalists with far less than they had desired in the way of freedom and the ability to engage autonomously in external affairs. The Boundary Commission had not only failed to end partition between the Free State and Northern Ireland, it had effectively cemented the division in place as more or less permanent. The government of William Cosgrave quietly but persistently pushed against the constraints of the 1922 treaty, gaining admission for Ireland to the League of Nations independently of Britain in 1923 and receiving diplomatic recognition from Washington that same year. The other white dominions, whose role in the Great War had earned them considerable stature within the British imperial structure, followed the Irish example, becoming members of the League of Nations under their own auspices and pursuing other initiatives that befit their increasing autonomy from London. At the 1926 Imperial Conference, South Africa and Canada proposed what became known as the Balfour Declaration, which established the dominions as "autonomous Communities within the British Empire, equal in status, in no way subordinate one to another in any aspect of their domestic or external affairs, though united by a common allegiance to the Crown, and freely associated as members of the British Commonwealth of Nations." Five years later, the terms were ratified in the Statute of Westminster, by which the British parliament gave up its powers to legislate for the dominions, except where otherwise specified by law.

Following the elections of 1932 in Ireland, a new government under Eamon de Valera came to power. Its platform committed it to throwing off the ties that still bound the country to Britain, establishing a full-blown republic, and uniting northern and southern Ireland in a single nation. De Valera had to move slowly and carefully, as Ireland's economic ties to Britain remained substantial and vital to the survival of the country, but he moved decisively. The Irish Citizenship Act of 1935 removed Irish men and women from the status of subjects of the British crown. The next year, de Valera removed any mention of the monarchy from the constitution. The new constitution of 1937 established the Free State as Éire and declared Catholicism the religion of the country, thus practically if not formally dissolving Ireland's ties to the British empire. It also had the effect of satisfying the desires of most Irish nationalists, dampening the sentiment for unifying the northern and southern regions of the island nation. Hardline members of the Irish Republican Army continued to press for single Irish state, resorting to violence at times to make their point, but increasingly its attempts found little support in the south, forcing the organization to look to Northern Ireland as the focus of their campaign. De Valera in fact outlawed the IRA and jailed its leadership in 1936. In 1948, the Irish parliament passed the Republic of Ireland Act, formally declaring the country's independence from Britain. It came into effect on April 18, 1949, the anniversary of the Easter Rising that had begun the process thirty-three years earlier.

South African Prime Minister J.B.M. Hertzog also worked hard to promote autonomy for the dominions. He shared Ireland's desire for a republican form of government, a possibility that was dashed by the Statute of Westminster's clause giving sovereignty to the dominions under the auspices of the British monarchy. Like many Irish Catholics, he and his nationalist followers loathed the British empire, and their political platform called for a complete severing of ties with it. They made a first step in that direction with a 1934 law, the South Africa Status Act, that asserted the divisibility of the British crown. Practically speaking, that meant that should

Britain go to war, it would not automatically follow that South Africa would as well. That would be a decision for the South African parliament.

***

As a corollary to the entrance of the US into the war in 1917, American President Woodrow Wilson issued his so-called Fourteen Points calling for the creation of a new international order, one based on principles of justice, diplomatic transparency, and the vaguely defined principle of self-determination rather than on the exercise of military power. The assertion of the right of peoples to determine their government and their national borders stood out conspicuously among the objectives, and triggered a surge of optimism amongst colonized and conquered peoples across the globe that their demands for independence and self-determination would be heard. The victorious powers at the Paris Peace Conference dashed the hopes engendered by the Wilsonian moment in the short run, but they could not stifle the impulses behind them for very long.

Native peoples of the US played a significant part in what would become a widespread Aboriginal rights movement. Native American intellectuals and activists had for over a century by 1919 turned to the languages and concepts of internationalism to make claims for freedom from the American empire that had colonized their lands. Their service in the Great War—they joined up in proportionately far greater numbers than did white Americans—brought them in contact with other colonialized and marginalized troops. *The New York Evening Herald* told readers that Indians fought because they were warriors, that they knew little or nothing about "the international aspects of the war," especially the need to defend the "self-determination of small nations." In fact, indigenous Americans well appreciated the causes for which they were fighting, as an editorial in the Spring 1917 edition of *American Indian Magazine* indicated. "The outcome of this appalling catastrophe," the editor wrote optimistically, "will be a better understanding among men and nations and a more just recognition of the rights of the small divisions of mankind."[15] Among those small divisions of humanity they included themselves, calling for the US government to confer upon them the rights and freedoms of American citizenship. In fighting for small nations abroad, argued activist Gertrude Bonnin, whose Lakota name was Zitkala-Ša, Native Americans were fighting a "just war" for their rights. "Truth and justice are inseparable component parts of American ideals," she pointed out. "As America has declared democracy abroad, so must we consistently practice it at home."[16]

Indian activists and intellectuals regularly linked their grievances to those of the small nations seeking redress in the post-1919 period. The Wilsonian moment provided a moral framework for demands for self-determination, citizenship, and rights, but it also offered scope for demands of a more material nature. Speakers at the 1919 Society of American Indians annual conference drove home the contrast between what the US had spent in Europe to assist Belgians, Poles, Armenians, and others, and its failure to honor its obligations at home. Charles Eastman, whose Santee Dakota name was Ohíye S'a, told the audience that "The United States owes us something." Thomas Sloan, an Omaha Indian, pointed out that

> This nation has given to the needy of Europe many billions of dollars. The Indians have contributed to this their share or more. It would take but a few millions of dollars to pay the claims of the Indian tribes against the government. Let us apply the justice we are carrying to the weak nations abroad to the weak nations at home.

In a follow-up article in *American Indian Magazine*, Mabel Powers, a non-Indian woman adopted into the Seneca tribe, reminded readers that "If billions of dollars and millions of lives can be spent to secure the rights of little peoples across the seas, is it not consistent to give to a little people at home an equal chance?"[17]

Indian activism in the interwar period focused a great deal on the status of treaties that had been reneged on over the course of several decades. As Laura Kellogg, who helped to establish the Society of America Indians, asked in her 1920 *Our Democracy and the American Indian*, "Have not 98 percent of your treaties with the Indian been 'scraps of paper'?" making reference here to the 1839 guarantee of Belgium's sovereignty that brought Britain into the First World War.[18] "The Red Man of America loves democracy and hates mutilated treaties," urged Bonnin in 1919.[19] Suits against the US government for redress of and compensation for violations of treaty agreements became an aspect of long-standing demands on the part of activists to recognize Indian people as full-fledged citizens of the US. Charles Eastman and others sought not "charity," but the adjudication of treaty promises made and never upheld. They adopted the language of internationalism, of the Wilsonian moment, of the law of nations, to insist that the agreements between nations they had signed on to be acknowledged and honored.

The protests and reform efforts of organizations like the Society of American Indians and the American Indian Defense Association began to have an impact on the Interior Department, where the Bureau of Indian Affairs (BIA) was located, in the 1920s. A BIA advisory Committee of One Hundred recommended in 1923 that Indian people be given citizenship; Congress passed the Indian Citizenship Act the following year, legislation that had not been sought by Native peoples and which did not have much effect on Indigenous rights. In 1926, Interior commissioned an investigation into the lives and conditions of Indian people. The report, which bore the name of Lewis Meriam, found deep and widespread failures in the areas of education, health care, employment, and housing. It urged Congress to take action to remedy the failures, especially in the realm of health care, where,

Meriam discovered, the BIA spent only fifty cents per Indian child each year. President Hoover moved to enact reforms, but the onset of the Great Depression quickly put an end to any effective amelioration.

When Franklin Roosevelt became president in 1932, he appointed John Collier, a long-time advocate for Native Americans, to head the BIA. Collier immediately took action to change policies that had long worked to efface Indian cultures. He introduced a policy of religious freedom for Indian people and revoked measures that had outlawed use of Native languages and prohibited a variety of customs, such as the potlatch and the sun dance. He encouraged tribes to return to traditional practices for healing and well-being, encouraging the renewal of offices such as that of medicine man. In 1933 Collier banned the sale of allotments in order to help stop the loss of Indian land.

Collier's most important achievement, the Indian Reorganization Act (IRA), became law in 1934. Having consulted with tribal leaders across the nation, he persuaded Congress to enact legislation that had a significant impact on Indian people. First and foremost, as they saw it, tribes had had input in the making of the bill, and one of its provisions ensured that they would have the right to vote on whether or not to participate in its reforms. It discontinued the policy of allotment; gave tribes the power to establish their own governments; increased BIA funding of businesses and educational facilities; and opened up the BIA itself to Indian employment. When put to a vote before Indian communities, 181 chose to opt in to the IRA and seventy-eight stayed out, arguing that the act did little to actually change things, as they would still be under the rule of the Bureau of Indian Affairs.

Despite its top-down nature and the continued administration of the BIA, the Indian Reorganization Act and some of Collier's other reforms did give tribal communities some degree of self-determination, if not autonomy. The abolition of allotment allowed for the return of some 4 million acres of land to reservations, and the ending of curbs on language and traditional practices would, down the road, help Indian people to revive their cultures.

***

The depredations against Indigenous peoples in Australia, New Zealand, Canada, Kenya, and South Africa gave rise to a number of resistance and/or reform movements that drew directly on Indigenous participation in the war effort to justify their demands. The League of Indians of Canada, for example, a pan-Indian organization formed in 1919, decried the residential schools that so deformed Indian children and demanded that Indian veterans receive the same kinds of postwar benefits white soldiers received. In support of its claims it hoped, "Not in vain did our young men die in a strange land; not in vain did our Indian bones mingle with the soil of a foreign land ...; not in vain did the Indian fathers and mothers see their sons march away to face what to them were unknown dangers." The experiences of war and the losses incurred therefrom, the League asserted, had compelled Indigenous people across the dominion to join together to demand their rights.

> The unseen tears of Indian mothers in many isolated reserves have watered the seeds from which may spring those desires and efforts and aspirations which will enable us to reach the state when we will take our place side by side with the white people, doing our share of productive work and gladly shouldering the responsibility of citizens in this, our country.[20]

The Ministry of Indian Affairs felt its authority sufficiently threatened to amend the Indian Act to ban tribal bands from giving money to Indian political associations. This action failed to quell Indigenous activism, leading the ministry to further amend the act in 1927, making political organizing by status Indians illegal and even forbidding Indian people from hiring lawyers to sue the Canadian government.

Aboriginal Australian John Kickett referred to his community's contributions to the war effort to denounce the inability of Aboriginal students to attend state schools and the associated abduction of children to boarding schools. "I have five of my people in France fighting," he told his member of parliament in 1918. "Fighting for our King and Country. Sir, I think they should have the liberty of going to any State school." The Aborigines' Progress Association, founded in 1923, enlisted veterans in its campaign to end the "educational" theft of children and to obtain equal rights with white Australians. The Australian Aborigine League, founded in 1933 by an Aboriginal man whose son had been killed in action, invoked his son's service in his demands for equal rights. "I am the father of a soldier who gave his life for his King on the Battlefield and thousands of coloured men enlisted in the A.I.F.," he declared in 1939. The veterans who survived the ordeals of the Great War "were pushed back to the bush to resume the status of aboriginals … the aboriginal now has no status, no rights, no land and … nothing to fight for but the privilege of defending the land which was taken from him by the white race without compensation or even kindness."[21] Before they gave their service in the next war, he insisted, Aboriginal people must have rights and status equal to those of whites.

***

In September 1939, Indigenous peoples were asked once again to support Britain in a conflict that had little to do with them. A little more than two years later, American Indians joined them following the Japanese attack on Pearl Harbor in December 1941. By 1945, more than half a million had served under the Union Jack and the American flag in the Second World War. Across the board, they performed sterling service, and rates of desertion were low. Expressions of popular discontent in the colonies certainly did take place, but overall they were few and far between, and where they occurred, were muted. Aboriginal peoples had—once again—stepped forward to meaningfully support the governments that had taken their lands and devastated their cultures.

As soon as Britain declared war on Germany in September 1939, the dominions followed suit. Canada, Australia, and New Zealand never hesitated, but in South Africa, where Afrikaner hatred of Britain and a positive disposition toward the Nazis created enormous resistance to aiding in the British war effort, the government won the motion to go to war by only thirteen votes. Ireland, which did not consider itself a dominion, despite what the British thought, declared itself officially neutral. But Éire's actual behavior during the war softened this stark assertion of separateness. It allowed British and, later, American planes to fly through its airspace, it turned over reports about German U-boat activity, it provided crucial weather reporting, it supplied equipment to help pilots navigate the area, and it participated in talks with the allies about cooperating should Germany invade the UK. Above all, it permitted the opening and operation of a recruiting center in Dublin, through which some 2,000 people passed every week on their way to Britain to help the war effort. Most of these men and women served in essential industries and agriculture.

In the US, Indian men had been identified by the draft before the attack on Pearl Harbor; when it took place, two-thirds of them, some 42,000, had already registered. Thousands more had enlisted. The 25,000 Native men and women who served in the armed forces during the war did so largely within integrated units, except in special cases such as the mobilization of the Navajo Code Talkers within the Marine Corps. Though as claimants to be part of sovereign nations, they resisted conscription as a matter of principle, Canada's First Nations men and women joined up voluntarily in significant numbers. The Royal Canadian Air Force and the Royal Canadian Navy tended to exclude them from their ranks, but in the integrated units of the army they fought alongside white soldiers, earning their respect, at least for the duration of the war. Australia at first refused to accept men not "substantially of European origin or descent" into the armed services, though once Japan threatened to invade the continent, the government changed its policy.[22] Nearly 5,000 Aboriginal people and Torres Strait Islanders enlisted, with hundreds more providing logistical support as civilian participants. Māori men and women in New Zealand joined regular integrated units but some 3,600 of them also formed the 28th (Māori) Battalion, which fought valiantly in successful battles in North Africa and the Mediterranean.

Wherever the allies called upon them, African troops distinguished themselves. In Madagascar, the King's African Rifles (KAR) set the unofficial record for rapid deployment, with the 22nd East African Brigade moving 130 miles in a single day. Their sweep through territory held by Vichy France (the collaborationist regime that worked with the Nazis) inspired British officers to conclude that African troops were "naturally" predisposed to jungle conditions.

This reputation led to their assignment in Burma two years later. In 1944, troops drawn from practically every British colony in Africa formed a major part of General Slim's 14th Army, the force ordered to advance into central Burma. In 1945 it beat the onset of the monsoon season to capture Rangoon. Much of the fighting in 1944 and 1945 took place in heavy rains and featured some of the most difficult fighting conditions in the entire war.

British officers who served with African soldiers abroad came to respect them greatly. At the front, men of all races and ethnicities fought side by side. But although British officers noted the bravery of African soldiers, they continued to believe that they were "dependent ... on the initiative of the white man in times of crisis."[23] They assumed that the men could not fight without their officers, reflecting the idyllic, paternalistic relationship that officers recall about their time in uniform with African soldiers. Back in barracks in Kenya or Southern Rhodesia, white officers and Black troops were separated. In the colonies, they never lived close to one another, and Blacks were expected to remove their hats in the presence of whites. Whites had personally seen the bravery of the King's African Rifles and other African soldiers in difficult conditions, but the comradeship of war never brought closer race relations in the colonies, where the system of racial segregation was too deeply entrenched.

The war also had a profound impact on those far from the battlefields. "Total war" required not just the fighting forces of the KAR; it demanded tremendous amounts of civilian labor to provide raw materials ranging from food to tin to agricultural fertilizers in support of the war effort. Africans suffered from compulsory labor regulations imposed on them, which were deemed legal in the midst of war. In Kenya, over 10,000 men and women carried out compulsory labor in the sisal industry alone. White settlers benefited from many of these regulations, as they owned the industries that produced other vital products like beef, maize, and coffee. With thousands of African men absent—and drought and famine conditions common in many parts of sub-Saharan Africa during the war years—many families' farms became overgrown and unworkable. Women often resorted to black market trading to survive.

Britain could count on support for the war effort from all of its sub-Saharan colonies with just one exception: South Africa. As a dominion, it enjoyed self-government, meaning that the decision about whether the country should join the war on the Allied side rested with its politicians. Many South Africans, especially Afrikaners, opposed supporting the British in the war, in large part owing to the indignities imposed on the Afrikaner population several decades earlier. Prime Minister J.B.M. Hertzog advocated neutrality (which was in fact a more moderate position than many others took, viewing South Africa and Nazi Germany as natural allies), but Deputy Prime Minister Jan Smuts was able to sway the majority in the government to support the war on the Allied side. South African whites who supported the war would only go so far, however. They opposed the possibility of

African soldiers learning to use advanced weaponry. As a result, the segregated branches of the non-white military—the Cape Coloured Corps, Malay Corps, and Native Military Corps—did not carry guns until February 1944. The recruitment of Africans into the army, consequently, fell short, for Blacks hesitated to accept the low pay and discrimination they would encounter if they joined up. Even so, 123,000 non-white South Africans served, their wartime participation contributing to a promising, if short-lived, opportunity for multiracialism. South Africa under the leadership of Smuts weakened its racialist laws after 1945; the prime minister even considered abandoning the entire system of segregation altogether. The moment didn't last, however. Smuts's support of Britain during the war brought a radicalized National Party to power in 1948, ushering in half a century of apartheid, as we will see in the next chapter.

In all the settler colonies treated in this book, Indigenous peoples gave much-needed and much-valued assistance on the home front. Men and women worked long, hard hours in factories manufacturing arms and weapons, they produced food and supplies, they provided transport, and delivered medical care. In some instances the white settler populations showed appreciation for the contributions made by Native peoples, at least during the war years themselves, and although that did not necessarily translate into immediate postwar gains for Indigenous peoples—especially not in South Africa, Kenya, or Rhodesia—it did shift the ground somewhat in terms of what might be possible in the future. For in August 1941—four months before the Japanese attack on Pearl Harbor—President Franklin Roosevelt and Prime Minister Winston Churchill had secretly met aboard a ship off the North American continent where they hammered out the text of a document known as the "Atlantic Charter." A statement of their vision of a "better future for the world" after the war, it called for lasting peace and improved living conditions and rights for all peoples. Most significantly, the Charter advocated "the right of all peoples to choose the form of government under which they will live; and ... [the] wish to see sovereign rights and self government restored to those who have been forcibly deprived of them."[24]

Colonized peoples across the Anglo settler colonies thrilled to the promises of the Atlantic Charter. They viewed them as a fair exchange for the sacrifices they had made for Britain and the US in the two world wars. They eagerly anticipated vast changes in the postwar era: the time had come, they believed, when they would no longer be fobbed off by vague promises of better working conditions or political rights. The two world wars and their impact contributed mightily to the unwillingness of Indigenous people to wait much longer for redress of the wrongs brought upon them by settler colonialism, though it would take much longer than they might have imagined.

Counterpoint: The Sámi People as Internationalists

The appeal to an international forum for redress of Indigenous rights was an integral aspect of the efforts of the Sámi people of the arctic regions of Europe to ameliorate the effects of settler colonialism, for the Sámi people had for centuries occupied lands claimed and intruded upon by four different nations: Russia, Finland, Norway, and Sweden. As native Europeans themselves, the Sámi constitute a significant exception to the conventional settler-colonial paradigm of white Europeans seizing the lands of people of color.

The Sámi peoples have inhabited Scandinavia since at least 1600 BCE, populating the northern reaches of what are today Norway and Sweden and sustaining themselves through semi-nomadic reindeer herding, fishing, and hunting. The Scandinavians, by and large, lived in the southern regions, and paid little attention to their northern neighbors. That changed in the eighteenth century, when Scandinavians began to colonize the Norwegian coast and then moved farther inland into territory upon which the Sámi grazed their reindeer. Clashes between Scandinavian settlers, who farmed the land, and Sámi herders, who sought to pasture their animals on that land, increased; in consequence, the Swedish and Norwegian governments began to intrude on the Sámi way of life. In the nineteenth century, that interference increased, and the authorities began to claim Sámi-inhabited regions as part of their territories. In doing so, they incorporated well-established tropes characterizing Sámi people as "primitive" and "uncivilized" and asserted the need to "civilize them." The national governments introduced policies designed to assimilate the Sámi through Scandinavianization, outlawing the use of the Sámi language in schools and other settings. They also imposed laws limiting the right of Sámi herders to graze their animals on lands they had used for centuries.

In 1905, Norway and Sweden ended the arrangement that had associated them within a single union for the past 100 years, introducing a border between the two states that had previously been inoperative. Sámi people who lived in the area now became citizens of two different polities; those who had had access to schools in either place no longer did; their ability to move their animals became much more difficult as border restrictions kicked in. The situation led to disputes between the two states and among the Sámi themselves.

Long concerned about securing the rights of Sámi people and now facing a situation that exacerbated their difficulties, activists believed that making progress toward ameliorating the effects of Scandinavian settler colonialism required unity among the Sámi. To that end, Elsa Laula Renberg, the leader of a number of women's associations, organized a conference in Trondheim, Norway, in February 1917. In her keynote address, she told the 100 attendees, "we have never realized how important it is for us to work together as one nation. Today, we try, for the first time, to bind ... the Sámi to each other."[25] So crucial was the cooperation of Sámi groups throughout Scandinavia to the ultimate recognition of their rights and recognition that in 1992, at the Sámi Conference held in Helsinki, delegates designated February 6 as the National Day of the Sámi.

The conference addressed three issues of importance: reindeer herding across borders and on land held by farmers, the relationship with Swedish and Norwegian settlers, and education. On the last day, the delegates made a joint statement and established a committee to further discuss the issue of reindeer herding. Subsequent national meetings were held in Sweden in 1918 and in Norway in 1919 to follow up on this and other concerns, especially those pertaining to education and to "the Law of the Lapps," which sought Sámi assimilation. Finnish Sámi created a society to preserve and promote their culture in 1932, and a number of Finnish groups held their own conference just after the end of the Second World War. It would take some time—almost forty years—before the second unified Sámi conference was held in 1956, and the Sámi of the Kola Peninsula in Russia would not join in in the overarching movement until 1992. But Trondheim had established the precedent and the principle of international cooperation, setting the stage for a vibrant Indigenous rights campaign.

Primary Source Document

Irish Declaration of Independence, 1919

Dáil Eirann Declaration of Independence

Whereas the Irish people is by right a free people:

> And Whereas for seven hundred years the Irish people has never ceased to repudiate and has repeatedly protested in arms against foreign usurpation:

> And Whereas English rule in this country is, and always has been, based upon force and fraud and maintained by military occupation against the declared will of the people:

> And Whereas the Irish Republic was proclaimed in Dublin on Easter Monday, 1916, by the Irish

Republican Army acting on behalf of the Irish people:

> And Whereas the Irish people is resolved to secure and maintain its complete independence in order to promote the common weal, to re-establish justice, to

provide for future defence, to insure peace at home and goodwill with all nations and to constitute a national polity based upon the people's will with equal right and equal opportunity for every citizen:

And Whereas at the threshold of a new era in history the Irish electorate has in the General Election of December, 1918, seized the first occasion to declare by an overwhelming majority its firm allegiance to the Irish Republic:

Now, therefore, we, the elected Representatives of the ancient Irish people in National Parliament assembled, do, in the name of the Irish nation, ratify the establishment of the Irish Republic and pledge ourselves and our people to make this declaration effective by every means at our command:

We ordain that the elected Representatives of the Irish people alone have power to make laws binding on the people of Ireland, and that the Irish Parliament is the only Parliament to which that people will give its allegiance:

We solemnly declare foreign government in Ireland to be an invasion of our national right which we will never tolerate, and we demand the evacuation of our country by the English Garrison

We claim for our national independence the recognition and support of every free nation in the world, and we proclaim that independence to be a condition precedent to international peace hereafter:

In the name of the Irish people we humbly commit our destiny to Almighty God who gave our fathers the courage and determination to persevere through long centuries of a ruthless tyranny, and strong in the justice of the cause which they have handed down to us, we ask His divine blessing on this the last stage of the struggle we have pledged ourselves to carry through to Freedom.

Notes

1 Quoted in Andrea Lucille Catapano, *The Rising of the Ongwehònwe: Sovereignty, Identity, and Representation on the Six Nations Reserve.* Dissertation presented to Stony Brook University (December 2007), p. 185.

2 "The Red Man's Appeal for Justice," https://cendoc.docip.org/collect/deskaheh/index/assoc/HASH0102/5e23c4be.dir/R612-11-28075-30626-8.pdf

3 Catapano, *The Rising of the Ongwehònwe*, p. 5.

4 Quoted in Alison Elizabeth Norman, *Race, Gender and Colonialism: Public Life among the Six Nations of Grand River, 1899–1939.* Dissertation presented to the University of Toronto (2010), p. 202.

5 See Sean Farrell Moran, *Patrick Pearse and the Politics of Redemption: The Mind of the Easter Rising, 1916* (Washington: The Catholic University of America Press, 1994), especially chapter 6.

6 Quoted in Charles Townshend, *Political Violence in Ireland* (Oxford: Oxford University Press, 1984), p. 308.

7 Quoted in Timothy C. Winegard, *Indigenous Peoples of the British Dominions and the First World War* (Cambridge: Cambridge University Press, 2012), p. 252.

8 Quoted in Winegard, *Indigenous Peoples of the British Dominions and the First World War*, p. 239.

9 Quoted in Myles Osborne, *Ethnicity and Empire in Kenya: Loyalty and Martial Race among the Kamba, c. 1800 to the Present* (New York: Cambridge University Press, 2014), p. 108.

10 Quoted in Dane Kennedy, *Islands of White: Settler Society and Culture in Kenya and Southern Rhodesia, 1890–1939* (Durham: Duke University Press, 1987), p. 77.

11 Quoted in John Higginson, *Collective Violence and the Agrarian Origins of South African Apartheid, 1900–1948* (Cambridge: Cambridge University Press, 2015), p. 308.

12 D.G. Boyce, *Englishmen and Irish Troubles. British Public Opinion and the Making of Irish Policy, 1918–22* (Cambridge: MIT PressCam, 1972), p. 43.

13 Quoted in Townshend, *Political Violence*, p. 332.

14 Quoted in Terence Dooley, *Burning the Big House: The Story of the Irish Country House in a Time of War and Revolution* (New Haven: Yale University Press, 2022), p. 241.

15 Quoted in Paul C. Rosier, *Serving Their Country: American Indian Politics and Patriotism in the Twentieth Century* (Harvard University Press, 2009), p. 52.

16 Quoted in Rosier, *Serving Their Country*, p. 53.

17 Quoted in Rosier, *Serving Their Country*, pp. 56–7.

18 Quoted in Rosier, *Serving Their Country*, pp. 55–6.

19 Gertrude Bonnin, "America, Home of the Red Man," *The American Indian Magazine*, Vol. 6, No. 4 (Winter 1919), p. 165.

20 Quoted in Winegard, *Indigenous Peoples of the British Dominions and the First World War*, p. 243.

21 Quoted in Winegard, *Indigenous Peoples of the British Dominions and the First World War*, pp. 250–1.

22 Quoted in R. Scott Sheffield and Noah Riseman, *Indigenous Peoples and the Second World War: The Politics, Eperiences and Legacies of War in the US, Canada, Australia and New Zealand* (Cambridge: Cambridge University Press, 2019), p. 55.

23 K.C. Gandar Dower, *Into Madagascar* (New York: Penguin Books, 1943), p. 41.

24 H.V. Morton, *Atlantic Meeting* (London: Methuen & Co., 1943), pp. v–xvi; David Robinson, "The Atlantic Charter Meeting: An Eyewitness Account," in Douglas Brinkley and David Facey-Crowther, eds., *The Atlantic Charter* (New York: St. Martin's Press, 1994), pp. 173–88.

25 Quoted in: Elsa Stina Larsdotter Laula Renberg, www.skbl.se/sv/artikel/ElsaStinaLarsdotterLaulaRenberg, Svenskt kvinnobiografiskt lexikon (article by Anne Heith), accessed January 31, 2025.

Further Reading

Philip J. Deloria, *Indians in Unexpected Places* (Lawrence: University Press of Kansas, 2004).

Terence Dooley, *Burning the Big House: The Story of the Irish Country House in a Time of War and Revolution* (New Haven: Yale University Press, 2022).

John Higginson, *Collective Violence and the Agrarian Origins of South African Apartheid, 1900–1948* (Cambridge: Cambridge University Press, 2015).

Dane Kennedy, *Islands of White: Settler Society and Culture in Kenya and Southern Rhodesia, 1890–1939* (Durham: Duke University Press, 1987).

Paul C. Rosier, *Serving Their Country: American Indian Politics and Patriotism in the Twentieth Century* (Harvard University Press, 2009).

R. Scott Sheffield and Noah Riseman, *Indigenous Peoples and the Second World War: The Politics, Eperiences and Legacies of War in the US, Canada, Australia and New Zealand* (Cambridge: Cambridge University Press, 2019).

Timothy C. Winegard, *Indigenous Peoples of the British Dominions and the First World War* (Cambridge: Cambridge University Press, 2012).

8

Cold War Developments, 1945–65

In October 1953, ten-year-old Yami Lester, a member of the Anangu people living in the western desert region of South Australia, got up early to prepare breakfast for his family. As he put meat on the fire, a rumbling sound filled the air, the ground shook, and a black mist blew in and covered his camp. His stepfather Kanytji, who was tending cattle a short distance away, felt a dew-like sprinkling of what felt like rain on his skin. The elders in the camp trembled at the sight and metallic smell of the big black cloud, fearful that a *manu*, or evil spirit, had befallen them.

Evil spirit, indeed. Some 200 miles north of Yami's camp, at a place called Emu Field, the British had detonated the first of what would be several atomic bombs. Without consulting his cabinet or the public, and paying no heed to the Aboriginal people who inhabited the region where the tests would be conducted, Australia's prime minister, Robert Menzies, gave Britain carte blanche to carry out nuclear weapons trials on the subcontinent between 1952 and 1963. For more than a decade, Aboriginal Australians were exposed to nuclear fallout, the victims of the nuclear arms race set off by the Cold War.

Yami and his family, along with neighboring Anangu groups, suffered immediate and longer-term injuries from what they could not know was radiation sickness. Lallie Lennon and her husband and son fell ill immediately with fever, vomiting, and diarrhea. Her daughter Jennifer started to have seizures. Lallie and her son Bruce developed rashes; she described her skin as looking like she had fallen into a fire. "Head to toe. I was a mess," she stated. Before he died, Yami's uncle developed "sores all over his body and they looked full of puss [*sic*]." Judy Mayawara saw people "vomiting green vomit. Passing green faeces." Her sister died, as did Eileen Brown's. Many older people succumbed to radiation sickness; those who survived did so with debilitating illnesses. Blindness afflicted numerous people, including Yami, Lallie, and Bruce; Yami had to be confined in a shed in order to shield his eyes from light. Some recovered their sight, though it remained weakened. Yami never did, and it saddened him to lose his old way of life. "If I had my eyes," he lamented, "I would probably still be a stockman."[1]

This nuclear testing took place on lands that had been inhabited by Indigenous peoples for millenia, lands the government regarded as remote, unproductive, and empty. The site of the first atomic bombings, Emu Field, proved too isolated to British officials, who preferred an area further south, land they named Maralinga, a northern Aboriginal word for thunder. Between 1956 and 1963, the British set off twelve atomic weapons and detonated 200 "minor" explosions designed to test weapon components. These latter in fact produced more plutonium than the bombs themselves, saturating the ground with more than 22 kilograms of plutonium-239, a deadly cancer-causing element that had a radioactive half-life of 24,000 years. Little heed was paid to the Anangu people living in the area: one family was discovered camped out next to one of the bomb craters. The single native patrol officer responsible for tracking down Aboriginal people and informing them of the danger of the tests, Walter MacDougall, had to cover a jurisdiction hundreds of thousands of square kilometers in size. When he was unable to do his job and expressed concern for people in range of the fallout, his views were dismissed out of hand. Alan Butement, the chief scientist of the Commonwealth Department of Supply, complained about "a lamentable lack of balance in Mr McDougall's outlook, in that he is apparently placing the affairs of a handful of natives above those of the British Commonwealth of Nations."[2]

A decade of relocation, nuclear testing, destruction of their hunting grounds, and despoilation of their land and sacred sites by radioactive contamination devastated the Anangu people of the Great Victorian Desert. In addition to radiation danger, Aboriginal people around Maralinga also faced extreme social, emotional, and physical hardship from being denied access to food and water resources for more than thirty years.

* * *

Two developments dominated the postwar world, decolonization and the Cold War. Decolonization began in 1947 with when India, Pakistan, Burma, and Sri Lanka—formerly called Ceylon—achieved their independence. A second stage began in 1956, when in the context of the Suez Crisis, Ghana, Malaya, and Singapore declared and won their independence. The third and largest wave of decolonization began in 1960 and swept through Africa and the Caribbean. The throwing off of colonial rule was intricately bound up with the Cold War—virtually every action taken by anticolonial actors would be regarded or responded to through the lens of the conflict between east and west—and both directly informed power relations within settler colonies. Britain characterized the rebellion of the Kenya Land and Freedom Army—better known as the Mau Mau resistance—for instance, as a communist-inspired uprising, ignoring the deep anti-settler and intra-ethnic roots of the movement. In the 1960s, its efforts to negotiate the fraught politics of white supremacist regimes in South Africa and Rhodesia in the context of Cold War proxy wars, led to those apartheid countries' exit from the British Commonwealth of Nations. Britain strove not to alienate the apartheid government of South Africa, whose uranium supplies it needed so badly for its own nuclear stockpile. The US, dealing with its own ineffective policies toward Native peoples, refrained from condemning white supremacist governments for fear of losing their anti-communist support.

Decolonization in the colonies of exploitation like India, Ghana, and Nigeria inspired and reinforced Indigenous rights movements in the Anglo settler colonies. The experiences of those Africans who had served under the Union Jack during the Second World War proved especially cogent in this regard. After giving much-needed service in all theaters of the war, veterans had come to feel that the British had betrayed them. They complained that they had been promised permits to start businesses, pensions, education, land, and other benefits, but their expectations were dashed. The words of Karigo Muchai, who had worked as a driver in the King's African Rifles, represent the experiences and feelings of many. "We Africans were told over and over again that we were fighting for our country and democracy," he pointed out,

> and that when the war was over we would be rewarded for the sacrifices we were making ... I was only trying to be given a small piece of land somewhere and to be treated a little more decently by the Kenya Government and white settlers ... These hopes and dreams of mine were quickly crushed on my return home. The army talk was false propaganda intended only to get Africans like me to risk our lives for Britain and the white settlers of Kenya ... The life I returned to was exactly the same as the one I left four years earlier: no land, no job, no representation and no dignity.[3]

British officials and settlers expected Africans to return to working in the fields, content with the lot they had had before the war, but the war had changed them profoundly. Like many veterans, Waruhiu Itote—who became a leader of Mau Mau during the 1950s (see below)—had become a "worldly" man through his service in Burma and Sri Lanka. He struck up friendships with West Africans and South Asians, and discussed the Haitian Revolution with African-American soldiers. He simply could not readjust to the discriminatory laws of colonial Kenya when he returned home, which privileged white settlers above all else. The Kenyan satirist and novelist Binyavanga Wainaina graphically described the situation faced by the returning soldiers: they "met and saw people from all over ... They saw them shit; they saw them die. They saw them sing. They ... found no mathematical principle to account for their designated roles back home."[4]

Wartime service had given hundreds of thousands of Africans a standard of living they had not known before. They had become accustomed to it and expected to develop it further once they returned home. Men in the armed forces had learned skills they planned to put to use in peacetime employment at war's end, but they were disappointed. Tens of thousands of army drivers could find no employment upon their return. Pent-up frustration and resentments over insults, assaults, and deprivations administered by colonial officials erupted in protest across virtually all of Britain's imperial holdings. Across the African continent, men like Muchai and Itote flocked to ex-servicemen's organizations and unions to protest against the grievances they felt. Strikes and demonstrations, often featuring veterans wearing their uniforms but including many more civilian men and women, broke out in cities across Africa, often resulting in widespread violence. In Southern Rhodesia in 1945; South Africa in 1946; Mombasa and Dar es Salaam in East Africa in 1947; Southern Rhodesia again in 1948—in all these places and more, mass actions against employers and colonial authorities posed profound challenges to white settler rule.

* * *

British and American officials feared that union organization, strikes, and demands for decolonization might well advantage the Soviet Union in its efforts to build up support in the colonized world in the midst of the Cold War, and the two Western nations tailored the actions they took and the decisions they made with the communist bloc always in mind. Militarily, the Cold War, epitomized by a nuclear arms race between East and West, had a profound impact on the Indigenous peoples of those lands settled by Britons and Americans. It affected Native peoples in at least three ways: as holders of lands seized for mining or as nuclear proving grounds; as "downwinders" of atomic tests; and as miners of uranium and other radioactive elements used to create nuclear stockpiles. What some have called "nuclear colonialism," and others describe as "wastelanding,"[5] began in the early 1940s, when American President Franklin Roosevelt authorized the Manhattan Project for the building of an atomic weapon. The site chosen for the top-secret undertaking, the lands around Los Alamos, New Mexico, was the ancestral home of several Pueblo, Navajo, and Apache tribes. Many of them, along with an established Hispanic community, were displaced by the US government as it seized the territory it deemed most appropriate for secrecy and security purposes. When it became clear to scientists that plutonium offered the most effective element for the fissionable material needed to create an atomic explosion, the government chose land in central Washington state to build the facilities that would produce its stockpile of the vital element. The area around Hanford was occupied by Wanapum, Nez Perce, Yakama, and Umatilla peoples, who had hunted and fished along the Columbia River for centuries and whose rights to be there had been guaranteed by treaty. They, along with 1,500 white people living in Hanford and White Bluffs, were displaced by the 40,000-acre Hanford nuclear power complex. Whites received compensation for the loss of their property; Indian people did not.

The nine nuclear reactors that yielded the plutonium for Project Y, the bomb being built at Los Alamos, produced huge amounts of atomic and other toxic waste that, absent proper storage practices, seeped into the land, the groundwater, and the Columbia River along which they sat. Where once the Indigenous people of the region had "lived in harmony with the area, with the river, with all of the environment," as Russell Jim, a member of the Yakama tribe, remembered, where "all the natural foods and medicines were quite abundant here," now "the area was an isolated wasteland, and the people were expendable."[6]

In July 1945, the scientists at Los Alamos detonated the first atomic bomb in the Tularosa Basin in New Mexico. Unsure if it would even work, they had no idea how powerful the blast would be; in the event, it far exceeded their expectations. The nuclear fallout from the explosion spread widely, settling as a white mist on hundreds of thousands of people who inhabited the region within a 250 mile radius, many of them Native American. None had been forewarned, none had been evacuated, even though the destructive effects of radioactive poisoning were well known to scientific and military officials. Three weeks later, radioactivity released by Trinity—as the test was codenamed—was measured as far away as Indiana. It ultimately made it to the Atlantic Ocean.

Within months of the atomic bombing of Hiroshima and Nagasaki, Americans heard dire warnings from military, scientific, and political leaders that their very existence depended upon the US developing new nuclear technologies. Nuclear testing thus became a regular aspect of Cold War politics in the years following the end of the Second World War. Most of it took place at the Nevada Test Site (NTS), a 1,350 square mile area in southern Nevada established in 1951. The NTS sat on land that had been recognized as belonging to the Western Shoshone people by the Treaty of Ruby Valley in 1863, land they had never ceded to the US. The government seized the area during the war, setting up a conflict with the Shoshone over land that persists to this day. Between the time of its inception and 1991, almost a thousand atomic tests were conducted at the NTS, and, although after 1963 they took place underground, all of them released massive amounts of radioactive fallout into the air. Some of the explosions—those of 1957, for instance—reached such magnitude that they spread nuclear fallout from Oregon to New England.

The Nevada Test Site had been chosen because it was ostensibly "vacant," a "wasteland" where the testing and its consequences would hardly be noticed. Indeed, for America as a whole, they were not. But the Western Shoshone and Paiute peoples who had inhabited the land for generations, along with the small number of white settlers in the region, couldn't miss them. "We'd be there early in the morning and the sky'd light up, it'd just light up, before daylight," recalled one resident. "And then we'd see them shooting up big mushroom clouds in the day. You could see the fallout coming right up the valley. You could just see it. Just kind of a smoky cloud."[7] People downwind of the explosions knew nothing of the dangers to which they were exposed, some of them, as in the case of some 250,000 US soldiers, serving as unwitting guinea pigs, as scientists and the military sought to learn about the effects of nuclear warfare.

The development and testing of nuclear weapons depended upon a reliable supply of uranium. In the early 1940s, the government knew of only one domestic source of the precious material—the vanadium mines located on the Navajo reservation in the four corners region of Colorado, New Mexico, Utah, and Arizona. Between 1943 and 1945, the Vanadium Corporation of America (VCA), which leased land from the Navajo, delivered more than 500 tons of uranium to Los Alamos. Unsure of just how much of it actually existed, government agents scoured the territory (and, as we'll see below, other parts of the globe) for sources of the critical material. By far the largest cache of what the Navajo called "yellow dirt" sat in the rocks and soil of the Yazzie Mesa, on the Arizona–Utah border. Getting the ore out of the ground provided employment to hundreds and hundreds of job-seeking Navajos, many of them just returned from serving in the military. It also unleashed radiation, heavy metals, and toxic gases such as radon into the air that would poison people and animals and contaminate the soil and the groundwater.

Scientists and government officials well knew the dangerous and deadly health effects of exposure to uranium. They did not inform the miners of them, nor did they take steps to insure their protection. Rates of all kinds of cancers soared far above the national average: fifty-six times greater in the case of lung cancer; eighty-two times for stomach cancer; 200 more times for liver cancer; sixty times for bladder or pancreatic cancer. The life expectancy of Navajo miners fell to forty-six years. Because it takes time for gene mutations to take hold and be passed down to subsequent generations, the true measure of destruction is still unknown, but it is the case that Navajo children, as of 2015 at least, present with ovarian or testicular cancer at fifteen times the national average. Indigenous inhabitants of places like the Four Corners area and southern Nevada appear to have suffered more severely than non-Indigenous settlers, likely because they depended much more on the natural world for their sustenance. Hunting and consuming contaminated animals, growing crops in contaminated soil, drinking contaminated water rendered Indigenous people more susceptible to radiation-related illnesses and deaths than those who populated cities such as Las Vegas, where they lived lives far less directly tied to the out-of-doors.

Native people discovered that the effects of nuclear testing, uranium mining, and plutonium production harmed them and their communities immeasurably and took myriad steps to address their concerns. To add injury to injury, however, many of them fell victim to a new policy of dealing with Native America known as termination, whereby the federal government sought to end its supervisory oversight of certain tribes deemed to be ready for complete assimilation into American life. Following the Second World War, many politicians and a good portion of public opinion believed that Indian people were prepared to—and deserved to—be recognized as full members of American society. Less beneficent players regarded termination as a means to gain access to the wealth held by reservations—land, minerals, water rights, fisheries. If the special status and reservations of Indian people were terminated, business interests, ranchers, farmers, mining companies, and many others would be able to exploit the resources now off limits to them. At the same time, the onset of the Cold War led many politicians to believe that the reforms established under the Indian New Deal threatened America's position vis-à-vis the Soviet Union. Land held in common, as it was on Indian reservations, they insisted, looked suspiciously like communism and was un-American. When John Collier left the Bureau of Indian Affairs in 1945, he was replaced by commissioners who viewed the relationship of Indian people to the US in profoundly different ways than their predecessor. Termination became law in a series of Congressional actions implemented in the 1950s and 1960s, whereby Indian lands in numerous states were placed under the civil and criminal jurisdiction of those states. At the same time, and in part as a result of termination, Indian people moved in unprecedented numbers to American cities where, they had been led to believe by federal propaganda campaigns, they would find all kinds of opportunities to prosper. By far the majority of them did not, and now, without the support of their natal communities or of federal assistance programs, they experienced high rates of poverty, homelessness, and disease.

For those Native Americans exposed to radiation, either through mining or atomic testing, termination could spell disaster. In 1958, for example, the Southern Paiutes of Utah, who lived directly downwind from the Nevada Testing Site, found themselves terminated as a tribe by the Bureau of Indian Affairs. It meant that they could not obtain medical care through the Indian Health Service for more than twenty years, when they were reinstated as a federally acknowledged tribe in 1970. By that time, health issues among them had spiralled wildly out of control, driven by cancer-related illnesses among adults and children alike.

***

In their struggle against the Soviet Union, the US and the United Kingdom relied heavily on South Africa. In the 1940s, America's insatiable demand for uranium to fuel nuclear arms production led the Atomic Energy Commission (AEC), the agency charged with providing the radioactive element, to search high and low for sources that could be tapped. One of the most promising appeared to be the mines of South Africa, the extraction of gold from which generated a significant amount of uranium, certainly far more than the US believed it had access to at home at that time. For its part, Britain's nuclear initiative literally depended on the uranium it imported from South Africa.

In addition, the Americans saw in the republic a major ally in deterring Soviet advances in Asia and Africa and collaborated with South Africa in its Atoms for Peace program starting in 1957. These strategic needs led both the US and the United Kingdom to apologize for the system of apartheid that a white supremacist government imposed on South Africa in 1948, and to justify their resistance to international efforts to end it.

For much of the first half of the twentieth century, the South African government had eroded the rights of non-whites in South Africa. In 1948, a Dutch Reformed Church minister named Daniel François Malan won a surprising victory in the elections of that year; he instituted the formalized segregationist system called apartheid. Often translated as "separateness"—and given colloquial expression as "apart"/"hate"—apartheid divided the population of South Africa along the lines of race. The structural backbone of apartheid—the Population Registration Act of 1950—brought a rigidity to the oddly fluid and not legally defined notions of race that had governed South African society previously. The act stipulated that every citizen of the nation would be classified by race, either a "white person, a coloured person, or a Native."[8] (South Asians would come to comprise a fourth group—see Figure 8.1.) Underlying all of the apartheid legislation was the desire of Afrikaners to assert and maintain their control over all of South Africa by settling Black and coloured Africans on land set apart from whites. Under the Group Areas Act (1950), the Bantu Authorities Act (1951), the Natives Resettlement Act (1954), and the Bantu Self-Government Act, implemented by Natives Affairs Minister (and later Prime Minister) Hendrik Verwoerd, some 3.5 million Africans were forcibly relocated to Bantustan "homelands," territories that offered little in the way of arable or pasturable land or employment. Rural Africans struggled to survive on lands that were ostensibly "sovereign" and "independent," designations the Nationalist government used to justify excluding Africans from citizenship and voting rights in South Africa.

The racial designations under the Population Registration Act tore families apart. The Groups Area Act of 1950 magnified the social dislocation created by racial classifications, stipulating that different racial groups had to live in different areas (a process that the Native Lands Act of 1913 had begun). Whites rarely had to move from the lush suburbs they inhabited, but coloured and Black Africans did. The "removals" became notorious, as when Cape Town's District 6 was declared a "white" area in 1968 and 60,000 Black and coloured Africans lost their homes. In Sophiatown, outside Johannesburg, another 60,000 Africans lost their homes and property to bulldozers making room for the white suburb of Triomf. Gajida Jacobs, who lived in District 6, recalled the day "when they chucked us out of Cape Town. My whole life came changed!" she lamented, weeping.

> They broke us up. They broke communities up. The happiness they took from us. They took our happiness from us! ... that was my whole life

tumbling down! I don't know how life continued ... You know, far away from family. All the neighbors were strangers. That was the hardest part of my life .... They destroyed us when they did this thing.[9]

Indignities abounded. The Mixed Marriages Act of 1949, which banned marriage between different racial groups, noted that "racial appearance and social habits" were important considerations. Officials used the "pencil test," for example, to determine whether a person's hair was so tightly curled that they might be considered "Black." If less curly, he or she might earn the designation "colored." Bureaucrats sitting on Race Classification Boards in Johannesburg came up with guidelines asserting that "a soccer player is a Native, a rugby player is a Coloured" to assist them in their work. Under the act, comedian Trevor Noah was "born a crime," as he put it in the title of his memoir of childhood, for his mother was African and his father white.[10]

In 1950, the apartheid government passed the Suppression of Communism Act, a sprawling piece of legislation that defined communism as any program that sought change "by the promotion of disturbance or disorder" or any action that animated "feelings of hostility between the European and the non-European races ... calculated to further" disorder. Under this act, the government could designate virtually any activity undertaken in opposition to its policies as communist, and subject any perpetrators to imprisonment. Indeed, South Africa's government made liberal use of the Suppression of Communism Act of 1950 to ban or restrict the movement of anyone who had apparent "communist" leanings, but the extensive use of the legislation enabled the nation to blame its racial problems at the door of communism. The country's anti-communist stance also provided Britain and the US the cover they needed to delay (and in the case of Britain, altogether avoid) imposing sanctions on South Africa during the years of apartheid.

The formal installation of a white supremacist regime sparked widespread opposition. The African National Congress (ANC), founded in 1912, led the African response first to segregation and then to apartheid. Known initially as the South African Native National Congress (until 1923), the ANC early on attracted a significant proportion of the educated, Christian elites who spent their evenings reading poetry, writing letters, and discussing political voting patterns, sometimes with white liberals who shared their views. Malan's victory in 1948 demonstrated that the ANC's moderate approach in the pre-war years had fallen far short of what was needed to combat massive discrimination against Africans. As workmen put up signs in parks, on beaches, and at public toilets reading "Net blankes"—"Whites Only"— younger members of the ANC became increasingly angry. Such future luminaries as Nelson Mandela, Oliver Tambo, and Walter Sisulu mobilized the ANC Youth League, formed in 1944, to protest these actions. Everyone agreed that a more active approach than the old ANC had espoused was vital, and when it took longer to materialize than some activists could

FIGURE 8.1 *Sign of Apartheid.*

tolerate, they formed the breakaway Pan Africanist Congress (PAC) in 1959 to pursue more militant actions.

Inspired by Mahatma Gandhi's non-violent resistance to the British in India, the ANC instituted the Defiance Campaign in 1952. Black, coloured, and South Asian men and women openly and flagrantly defied the nation's racialist laws. The campaign sought to overburden the police and judicial systems of the country; jailtime become a badge of honor, especially in the Eastern Cape, where much of the opposition was centered. In 1955, at the Congress of the People, 3,000 delegates crafted and issued a short statement called the Freedom Charter, a document espousing the groups' vision for a multi-racial nation. "South Africa belongs to all who live in it," it declared.

African and coloured women played a central role in the struggle for a free South Africa through the ANC Women's League (ANCWL). The ANCWL played a particularly important role in the Defiance Campaign of 1952, with women everywhere enraged when the government decided to apply pass laws to them as well. Women believed the laws threatened their homes: as Alice Kunene put it, "The Pass Laws means the death of our children. The oppression of the Pass Laws is going to bring destruction to our homes." By July 1956, 50,000 women had taken part in thirty-eight separate pass law protests across the country, in a process that culminated on International Women's Day in Pretoria. Outside the Union Buildings— the seat of the government—as many as 20,000 women gathered from across the nation. They wrote and signed notes to Prime Minister Johannes Strijdom, then stood in "perfect silence for half an hour, before breaking into a triumphant rendition of the ANC anthem [and South Africa's national anthem today], 'Nkosi sikeleli Afrika': 'God bless Africa.'" One of the songs written to commemorate the protest ran: "Strijdom, you have tampered with the women, You have struck a rock."[11]

Townships like Alexandra were hotbeds of opposition. Demonstrations and political events were common, despite government orders, and, in the 1950s, Alexandra's residents participated in a series of famous bus boycotts. To protest price increases on government buses, they walked upwards of ten miles each way to get to work. Music played an important role in the anti-apartheid movement. Vuyisile Mini, a labor union member and singer from the Transkei, wrote one of the enduring songs of the 1950s. Entitled *Pasopa Verwoerd*, it offered an upbeat and cheerful rhythm accompanied by clapping and tapping of feet. But the tune belied its warning: "Watch out Verwoerd, the black man is coming." *Pasopa Verwoerd* and many other anti-apartheid songs were deliberately written and sung in Afrikaans. Their singers wanted the police and apologists for apartheid to know precisely what they were singing. Other songs in Xhosa or Zulu were incomprehensible to most whites, conveying deep meanings that were invisible in their English or Afrikaans translations.

African resistance to apartheid changed dramatically in 1960 when, at a town called Sharpeville, just south of Johannesburg, police opened fire on several thousand African protestors organized by the PAC to resist the country's racist pass laws by setting their passbooks on fire. The police killed sixty-seven and wounded 186, and outlawed the ANC and PAC, driving them underground. The "Sharpeville Massacre" marked the moment when the ANC and PAC embarked upon armed resistance to the government through their militant wings, Umkhonto we Sizwe (Spear of the Nation) and Poqo ("alone," "pure"), respectively. The ANC was in the midst of planning a campaign of sabotage when government forces raided its secret meeting place in 1963; Nelson Mandela and nine other leaders were tried for attempting to overthrow the state. Mandela told the court at trial that "Africans want to be allowed to own land in places where they work ... and not be confined to living in their own ghettos ... African women want to be with their men folk and not be left permanently widowed in the reserves."[12] He and seven others received guilty verdicts and were sentenced to life imprisonment in 1964. The newly formed Bureau of State Security, shorthanded BOSS, rounded up other activists and effectively crushed the ANC and any other resistance to the white supremacist state over the next decade.

***

The formation of a white-supremacist settler government in South Africa aroused envy among the white settlers of Kenya, who saw in the principles of "separate development" under apartheid a blueprint for their own security in a changing world. In the years following the end of the Second World War, they devoted much of their time and energies in the legislative council shoring up and advancing their positions vis-à-vis Africans, legally, economically, and politically. The efforts of 29,000 white settlers to prevent 5 million Africans from making political gains rankled; the actions the settler state took to block African access to land set off an explosion in Kenya during the 1950s that shattered the dream of an expanded white settler state and ended the colonial presence entirely.

Known as the Mau Mau movement, it has come down to us in the guise of a clear and straightforward battle of dreadlocked African fighters in the forests of central Kenya conducting a campaign against white settlers and the British troops that protected and defended them. Certainly Mau Mau constituted an anti-colonial resistance struggle, but the situation was far more complex than the simple narrative of African rebels rising up against white settlers suggests. The impact of colonialism over the previous half-century had been uneven, and had created class distinctions among Africans. Many educated, wealthy Africans had prospered under British rule, and they were as much the targets of anger—and often even more so—as colonial officials or white settlers.

Mau Mau erupted among the Kikuyu of central Kenya, the colony's most populous ethnic group. At its roots lay a multitude of social problems created—and exacerbated—by the settler colonial system over the previous half-century. At the heart of the problems stood land, a fundamental element within Kikuyu culture, the importance of which cannot be overstated: one was not considered a man in his own right without owning a piece of land. But since the 1920s, the Native reserves had become progressively more crowded as two generations of fathers had subdivided their property among their sons, reducing the size of plots with each successive generation. As this had taken place, many wealthy and educated Kikuyu had gathered up small pieces of land to add to their burgeoning properties. Poor people lacking land had left the reserves and taken up residence on the vast European farms of Kenya's "White Highlands," where they worked for the settlers in exchange for a place to live. By the 1940s, many of these "squatters" had been residents of European farms for more than two decades.

Kenya's settlers had done well for themselves during the war. The allied war effort demanded food and other products considered vital for the war effort, and the legislative council passed laws in 1942 that forced Africans to work for free in such enterprises, the majority of which were owned by settlers. Settlers became so prosperous that in the mid- to late-1940s they could afford to purchase tractors and mechanized farming equipment, thus seriously reducing the need for squatters, whom they drove from their farms. With nowhere else to go to find land on which they might farm or graze their animals, some 100,000 Kikuyu squatters were stripped of their cattle and forcibly returned "home" to the reserves—places from which many had been absent for more than twenty years. There they were met by residents who insisted that the squatters had long ago forfeited any claims to land they might have held in the past. Chiefs and elders on the reserves who had amassed a great deal of land and wealth gave the newly arrived squatters the cold shoulder. They showed no more inclination than white settlers had to address the difficulties squatters faced; in fact, they often enforced regulations on the reserves that served to make squatters' lives even more precarious. Their lack of sympathy and often open antagonism toward poorer Kikuyu infuriated the returnees.

The returning squatters had few options: some might find a scrap of land to work on; others might take up employment on the land of their wealthier brethren; but the majority ended up in Nairobi. There they built temporary shelters in the ever-expanding slums, where they tried to eke out a living. It was there in the urban wastelands of Nairobi that the movement that became Mau Mau brewed among discontented, disenfranchised, poor Kikuyu who had no realistic means of establishing livelihoods. Members of "the movement"—only later would it take on the name "Mau Mau"— began meeting in secret and administering oaths to bind themselves together. They united on behalf of a vision of a renewed, ordered Kikuyu society in which the inequalities they faced were eliminated.

In 1952, Mau Mau activists in Nairobi and central Kenya began killing individuals they believed had betrayed their people. They chose victims who were known as "loyalists," Kikuyu who had been loyal to the settler government, and who had often become wealthy from years of association with it. For much of 1952, the colony's governor, Sir Philip Mitchell, did little to stem the violence, both because he was ill and because he did not want to end his career besmirched by bloodshed. By the time his replacement, Evelyn Baring, arrived in October 1952, much of central Kenya had fallen into near-total lawlessness, a state epitomized by the murder of one of the government's most prominent loyalist chiefs. Mau Mau warriors had killed Waruhiu wa Kung'u in broad daylight in his Hudson town car on October 7, 1952, demonstrating that the government could not protect even its most important supporters. Baring declared a State of Emergency on October 20, 1952, by which the government utilized extra-legal powers to repress dissent; Baring's administration also used the decree to silence the vibrant African press. Soon after, the government rounded up 183 men it believed were the ringleaders of the organization, including Jomo Kenyatta, Kenya's future president. The arrest of wealthy intellectuals like Kenyatta demonstrated how little the government understood about Mau Mau: its members were poor, disenfranchised Kikuyu, not wealthy elites like Kenyatta.

Between late 1952 and mid-1954, Mau Mau fighters operating from bases in the two forests of central Kenya fought a series of running engagements with British troops and their loyalist allies: the Kenya Regiment, which was made up of white settlers; the Kenyan Police; the King's African Rifles; and the Home Guard. Dedan Kimathi, Stanley Mathenge, and Waruhiu Itote, three men who had fought under the Union Jack during the Second World War, led well-organized Mau Mau raids on their targets. They typically took place at night. Gangs left the forest under cover of darkness to carry out their missions, which usually involved attacking a Home Guard post or raiding a police station for ammunition before melting back into the deep, heavily wooded forests where government forces could not track them. They enjoyed great success against better-equipped and -armed troops. Occasionally they carried out raids against isolated white settler farms, incursions that gave rise to wildly exaggerated pronouncements in the British and settler colonial press about Blacks slaughtering whites. But settlers were rarely their targets: only thirty-six settlers died during the period Mau Mau operated while more than 20,000 Kikuyu died at the hands of the rebels. The British hanged 1,090 "terrorists" at the gallows in the most extensive use of capital punishment in British imperial history. Thousands more Mau Mau men and women were imprisoned, where they faced horrific conditions. Following a gun battle with the British, for instance, Elizabeth Gachika was shot and captured. She was sent, her wounds untreated, to a Kamiti prison, where "hard core" Mau Mau women were detained. There, ill-fed and poorly clothed, she was forced to do hard labor, digging up trees, quarrying stone, and carrying it long distances on her head to supply the road-building undertaken by colonial officials. Infractions of the rules brought down harsh punishments: beatings, rape, withholding of food. As another detainee described Kamiti, it "was a hell prison. Some were dying, some were beaten to death, sometimes they died after work. We were happy when someone died because we said 'Now she is free.'"[13]

Unable to rapidly defeat Mau Mau by force of arms, the British used tactics we saw in the South African War half a century earlier. They built an extensive system of "detention and rehabilitation" camps—concentration camps—in which more than 80,000 suspected Mau Mau were held. British staff and loyalists carried out torture—including rape, castration, and murder—in the camps. Paolo Nzili, for example, was badly beaten and then castrated during nine years of imprisonment. "I felt completely destroyed and without hope [in the camps]," the 85-year old man later despaired.[14] But even in these restrictive and appalling conditions, Mau Mau fought back: detainees smuggled letters out of the camps to sympathetic members of parliament in Britain, and appealed to the colony's laws to demand better treatment.

Kenyans who sided with the government were rewarded during the 1950s, winning land taken from Kikuyu suspected of aiding the Mau Mau rebels. We see evidence of this in the "villagization" process imposed by British authorities. In order to cut off Mau Mau's lines of logistical support, the British enclosed Kikuyu villages in barbed wire and imposed a curfew on them. As many as a million Kikuyu lived in these villages, in which the Home Guard and other loyalists enjoyed nearly unrestricted power. When the Emergency ended, men returned home from the detention camps to find their wives impregnated, their land seized, and their cattle confiscated. They had no recourse against the loyalists who had stolen their livelihoods and dishonored their wives. Colonial development and welfare programs, too, offered benefits to those who remained "loyal." While those who sided with Mau Mau could expect to have their land seized, those who opposed the movement received agricultural assistance, loans, and voting rights.

The British defeated Mau Mau militarily in late 1954, though the Emergency stayed in place until December 1959. By that time, following revelations of brutality committed against detainees by colonial forces, Britons at home had raised difficult questions about the conduct of the army, and about torture and killings in the detention camps. Despite vociferous white settler opposition, the Colonial Office moved towards reform, issuing new constitutions in the 1950s that provided for greater African representation in the legislative council. For many Kenyans, this did not go far enough, and they continued to demand and agitate for "one man, one vote." An exhausted postwar British government saw little purpose in trying to sustain a white settler population vastly outnumbered by Africans seeking control over their own lives, and during a series of contentious meetings in London during the early 1960s, British politicians and Kenyan leaders finally hammered out an agreement. The British government and the World Bank provided loans with which to buy out white settlers, 10 percent of whom had already left the country in 1961 alone. Through a number of smallholder settlement schemes, most especially the Million Acres Scheme established in 1962, land ownership became de-racialized, and some 35,000 landless Kenyan families were established on 1 million acres of land previously held by white settlers. Many of the latter made their way to apartheid South Africa and white supremacist Southern Rhodesia, making the transition to African rule much easier. Jomo Kenyatta, as head of the Kenya African National Union political party, would lead Kenya to full independence in 1963.

***

Where South Africa installed a white supremacist settler government and Kenya saw the establishment of independence, Southern Rhodesia, populated by a population of hardy white settlers that rarely took kindly to outside interference in its affairs, occupied a kind of middle ground between the two outcomes. After Northern Rhodesia and Nyasaland won their independence from Britain in 1964, the white supremacist government of Ian Smith pressed for Rhodesia's liberation from British rule. The British government in London refused to consider it without Africans' legal and electoral rights first being secured in some sort of system that guaranteed majority rule and adherence to the principle of one person, one vote. Smith and his followers, regarding African leaders as the stalking horses of communism and fearful of losing their property and privileges, baulked at this condition. In 1964 and

1965, the British government tried both to seek accommodation with and to impose increasingly harsh strictures on the Rhodesian government. By late 1965, with the impasse unresolved, white Rhodesians lost patience with negotiations and determined to act unilaterally. On November 11—Armistice Day—Prime Minister Ian Smith, a former British fighter pilot, took to the airwaves to make a unique and dramatic declaration of independence. The Unilateral Declaration of Independence, or UDI as it came to be called, surprised British ministers. They had believed they could negotiate a firm timetable to Black majority rule, but Smith refused to consider it. He and his supporters claimed that Rhodesia would not only defend its white minority population against "uncivilized" and "savage" Africans, it would also stand as a vital holdout against a Soviet-inspired takeover of its government.

Britain responded to the UDI by imposing sanctions against Rhodesia, but the rogue nation—never formally recognized by any other country—navigated them with ease, in large part because of assistance from South Africa. South Africa had declared itself a republic in 1961, ending its status as a British dominion and withdrawing from the commonwealth. Following the Sharpeville massacre, the country had become an international pariah. In 1964, the International Olympic Committee banned South Africa from participating in the Olympics, though international rugby and cricket organizations took longer to ban it from competition, as we'll see below. South Africans regarded Rhodesia as a natural ally. Staunchly anti-communist and firmly under the control of white minority rule, the two nations regarded themselves as a bulwark against the development of socialism and communism in southern Africa.

Africans responded to the UDI with an intensified guerrilla campaign against the Rhodesian government. The guerrilla forces developed out of the two prominent African political parties in the colony, the largely Shona Zimbabwe African National Union (ZANU) headed by Ndbaningi Sithole and later Robert Mugabe, and the Ndebele-dominated Zimbabwe African People's Union (ZAPU) of Joshua Nkomo. Each had their own militant wings—ZANLA and ZIPRA, respectively—which competed against and clashed with one another on occasion. The "Rhodesian Bush War," as it became known, was a long, drawn-out affair. The settler government's forces, well-trained and highly capable as they were, ultimately could not prevail over a movement that enjoyed mass African support. As white settler numbers remained relatively static over the next decade, the African population rose steadily, till it was only a matter of time before Smith's government could no longer maintain control. We'll see how it played out in the next chapter.

* * *

Indigenous rights movements gained strength and momentum in the years following the Second World War by drawing upon international organizations such as the UN to put forward and buttress their claims to equality. What one scholar describes as "international shaming" played a powerful role in bringing settler societies to question the legitimacy and morality of their discriminatory practices.[15] We see this phenomenon at work in the case of New Zealand in the late 1950s and 1960s when it confronted South Africa's policy of apartheid in the realm of international sport. In the summer of 1958, the New Zealand Rugby Football Union (NZRFU) agreed to play a tournament in South Africa two years hence. It soon became clear that no Māori players would be allowed to accompany the team to the segregated dominion, which in 1948 had established a formal regime of apartheid. The All Blacks, as the team was called, would be all white.

The All Blacks had fielded all-white teams when it toured South Africa in 1928 and 1949. The Rugby Union's surrender to South African segregationist policies had prompted expressions of dismay from Māori footballers and political and community leaders, but the incidents had been sporadic and short-lived. This time was different. Over the next two years, protests escalated from pronouncements of outrage on the part of church officials and Māori men and women to mass demonstrations and civil disobedience on the part of New Zealanders of all stripes. Māori and Pakeha campaigners initially targeted the discrimination against Māori players by the NZRFU and the failure of the New Zealand government to intervene to overturn its decision, but, as time passed, protesters increasingly declaimed against the South African system of apartheid as well. Poet Allen Curnow satirized the situation with a bit of doggerel (Whineray was the team captain). "On the tour, on the Tour, on the Tour,/You can play if you're racially pure./All Whites together, we're Birds of that Feather,/That's how we got picked for the Tour./ Oh, we're Whineray's Whites, and we champion the Rights/Of Rugby to trample rough-shod/Upon Conscience and Creed, while it follows the Lead/Of a double damned Dutch Reformed God."[16]

More vociferous protests followed after South African police fired on a crowd of Africans in the township of Sharpeville on March 21, 1960, killing sixty-seven and wounding more than 400 peaceful men and women demonstrating against the pass laws that restricted their movements and curtailed their freedoms. The Sharpeville Massacre, as it came to be called, brought worldwide attention to the abuses inflicted on African peoples by the system of apartheid; in New Zealand, it intensified sentiment against the NZRFU and the government. In April, for instance, fifteen men and women occupied the pitch in Wellington where the All Blacks were conducting trials. They held banners reading "No Bloody S.A. Apartheid for New Zealand," and when the police tried to remove them, "several put up vigorous resistance sending constables' helmets flying."[17] Massive street marches and demonstrations sprang up in cities throughout New Zealand; monster petitions bearing thousands upon thousands of signatures were introduced to parliament.

These protests had not seen their like before. Although they failed to dissuade the Rugby Union from participating in the South African tour with an all-white All Blacks team in 1960, they did ensure that no such repeat would follow. When, in 1965, the South African president declared that he expected the All Blacks team scheduled to tour his country in 1967 to conform to the traditions and customs of South Africa, newspapers and protest groups rallied around a "no Māoris, no tour" campaign. The Rugby Union hesitated to respond in like manner and, in fact, when the invitation to tour the apartheid nation arrived, refused to divulge its terms. Māori MP Matiu Rata took to the floor of parliament in late 1965 to urge the government to cancel the tour if Māori players were to be excluded from the team. In early February 1966, the prime minister intervened to declare that "in this country we are one people; as such we cannot as a nation be truly represented in any sphere by a group chosen on racial lines."[18] Three weeks later the Rugby Union accepted the now inevitable: on February 25 its council determined that it could not accept South Africa's invitation as it was currently issued. South Africa, in turn, would not budge from its apartheid policies, and the 1967 rugby tour was cancelled.

This kind of international coordination to challenge settler colonialist policy would become far more prevalent in the years after 1967, when the global Indigenous movement turned its attention and gave the bulk of its energies to initiatives seeking to regain the lands Native peoples had lost to white settlers over the past four centuries.

Counterpoint: The Creation of Israel: The Indigenous as Settler Colonists

At the end of November 1947, the UN voted to accept Great Britain's plan to partition its mandate colony of Palestine into two separate states, one Jewish—Israel—and the other Arab; the city of Jerusalem would become an international entity independent of both. According to Resolution 181, as the UN plan was called, Israel would comprise 56 percent of the mandate territory, while the Arab state made up 42 percent of it, despite the fact that the Arab population outnumbered Jews by more than two to one. The international enclave of Jerusalem, Bethlehem, and immediate surrounding territory came to 2 percent of the total land mass. The plan never went into effect, as civil war between Arabs and Jews broke out almost immediately, and upon the Jewish People's Council's declaration of Israeli independence on May 15, 1948, Egypt, Transjordan, Syria, and Iraq invaded the newly created state. When the war ended ten months later, Israel had taken some 60 percent of the land set aside for Palestinians by Resolution 181; it drove out most of the Arabs who had lived there. In turn, Arab states expelled the Jews living among them.

The horrific Hamas attack on Israeli citizens on October 7, 2023, and Israel's subsequent all-out invasion of Gaza set off a ferocious debate about Israel's status as a settler colony. As one scholar framed the question, "are Jews 'indigenous' or settler colonists in Palestine?" His answer? "They are both ... Israeli Jews are settler colonialists with a historical memory of indigenous origin."[19] Jews have lived in the lands claimed by Palestinian nationalists for 3,000 years. They were expelled from them twice. In 586 BCE Nebuchadnezzar's forces destroyed Solomon's Temple in Jerusalem and exiled the Jews to Mesopotamia and Persia. Fifty years later the Persian emperor Cyrus allowed them to return to Judea. The second exile took place in the first and second centuries CE, after Jewish revolts against Rome resulted in their defeat. While some Jews remained in the region, most of them lived in a widely disseminated Jewish diaspora throughout the Middle East and Europe, where they created vibrant cultures of their own even as they persisted in maintaining deep imaginative ties to Palestine. Diasporic Jews faced centuries of discrimination and frequently deadly anti-Semitic assaults on their persons and property. The dream of returning to Israel from exile animated the thoughts and lives of millions of them.

Toward the end of the nineteenth century, following vicious anti-Jewish pogroms in Europe, Theodor Herzl founded a movement—Zionism—to find a homeland for Jews. The British government, in the Balfour Declaration of 1917, designated Palestine as that place, and when it won the former Ottoman territory as a mandate colony following the end of the First World War, proceeded to allow some Jews entrée into the territory. Jewish immigration to Mandate Palestine continued steadily for over a decade by the 1930s, the numbers of settlers spiking as first the Bolshevik Revolution and the subsequent civil war gave rise in Ukraine to a pogrom against Jews that killed as many as 200,000; Russian Jews saw the writing on the wall and left in large numbers as well. After the United States in 1924 and then the Soviet Union at the end of the decade imposed significant restrictions on the immigration of Jews to their countries, Palestine became the destination for most Jews seeking to leave Europe. The vast majority settled in the urban centers of Tel Aviv, Haifa, and Jerusalem, despite the Zionist movement's intentions of settling Jews on the land. The Nazis' rise to power in Germany in 1933 set off a new wave of immigration (the so-called fifth *aliya*) to Palestine. Between November 1931 and December 1936 more than 210,000 Jews left Europe for Palestine; by December 1939 another 90,000 arrived. The massacre of millions of Jews during the Holocaust moved the majority of the members of the UN to create the state of Israel as a refuge.

That refuge came under attack from Arab states a numbers of times after the first Arab–Israel war in 1948. In 1967 and again in 1973, Israel fought off armed invasions by neighboring countries; it faced terrorist attacks on its civilian populations on a regular basis. Following the Six Day War of 1967, Israel occupied the territories of Gaza and the West Bank, land the UN had designated for Palestinians in 1947. (Israel left Gaza in 2004, dismantling the settlements built there and forcibly removing the settlers who inhabited them.) It continued to displace Palestinians from their lands, giving them over to Jewish settlers in the West Bank in ever increasing numbers. Under the governments of Benjamin Netanyahu, settler colonialism grew dramatically; by the beginning of 2023, 144 Israeli settlements officially existed within the West Bank, with another hundred or so "outposts," or unrecognized settlements, driving up the number of Israeli settlers. Palestinians there face discrimination and violence on a daily basis, which have intensified severely since the 2023 Hamas attack and Israel's invasion of Gaza.

Primary Source Document

Southern Rhodesia's Unilateral Declaration of Independence, 1965

Prime Minister Ian Smith: Announcement of Unilateral Declaration of Independence, November 11, 1965

Now I would like to say a few words to you. Today, now that the final stalemate in negotiations has become evident, the end of the road has been reached.

It has become abundantly clear that it is the policy of the British Government to play us along with no real intention of arriving at a solution which we could possibly accept. Indeed, in the latest verbal and confidential message delivered to me last night we find that on the main principle which is in dispute the two Governments have moved further apart.

I promised the people of this country that I would continue to negotiate to the bitter end and that I would leave no stone unturned in my endeavours to secure an honourable and mutually accepted settlement.

It now falls to me to tell you that negotiations have come to an end. No one could deny that we have striven with might and main and at times bent over backwards to bridge the gap which divides us from the British Government.

... Let no one believe that this action today marks a radical departure from the principles by which we have lived, or be under any misconception that now the Constitution will be torn up and that the protection of the rights of all peoples which are enshrined in that Constitution will be abrogated and disregarded.

Neither let it be thought that this event marks a diminution in the opportunities which our African people have to advance and prosper in Rhodesia. Far from this being the case, it is our intention, in consultation with the chiefs, to bring them into the Government and administration as the acknowledged leaders of the African people on a basis acceptable to them.

It is our firm intention to abide by the Constitution. Indeed, we have never asked for anything other than independence on the basis of the present Constitution, and only such amendments are included as are necessary to adapt it to that of an independent country.

With regard to the position of Members of Parliament, judges, civil servants, and members of the armed forces, as well as the police, provision has been made for all of them to carry on their duties, and all are deemed to have complied with the requirements of the New Constitution. They will continue to carry on their normal work. All present laws shall continue to operate and the courts will enforce them in the normal manner, We are doing no more than assuming the right which various British Ministers have in the past indicated were ours. And in fact this Constitution was the one which would carry us to independence.

Let no one be persuaded that this action marks a change in our attitude towards our neighbours in Africa, to whom we have ceaselessly extended the hand of friendship and to whom we have nothing but goodwill and the best of intentions.

We have never sought, nor will we ever seek, to interfere or in any way attempt to influence their policy and their internal affairs. All we ask in return is their goodwill in permitting us to look after what are, after all, our own private and domestic matters ....

There can be no solution to our racial problems while African nationalists believe that, provided they stirred up sufficient trouble, they will be able to blackmail the British Government into bringing about a miracle on their behalf by handing the country over to irresponsible rule.

There will be no happiness in this country, while the absurd situation continues to exist where people such as ourselves, who have ruled ourselves with an impressive record for over 40 years, are denied what is freely granted to other countries, who have ruled themselves in some cases for no longer than a year.

There can never be long-term prosperity, which is so necessary for the nurturing of our endeavours to improve the standard of living and increase the happiness and better the lot of all our people, whilst the present uncertainty exists.

No businessman could ever seriously contemplate massive long-term investment in a country in which chaos and confusion will always be future possibilities.

Whatever the short-term economic disadvantages may be, in the long term steady economic progress could never be achieved unless we are masters in our own house ....

That some economic retributions will be visited upon us there is no doubt. Those who seek to damage us do not have any great concern for the principles to which they endlessly pay lip service; for if they really believed in these principles, which they ceaselessly proclaim, then they could not possibly deny the many disasters which have been brought about by the premature withdrawal of European influence from countries in Africa and Asia who were nowhere near ready for it.

There is no doubt that the talk of threats and sanctions is no more than appeasement to the United Nations, the Afro-Asian bloc, and certain members of the Commonwealth; and undoubtedly some action will be taken.

But I cannot conceive of a rational world uniting in an endeavour to destroy the economy of this country, knowing, as they undoubtedly do, that in many cases the hardest hit will be the very people on whose behalf they would like to believe they are invoking these sanctions. We for our part will never do anything in the nature of taking revenge on any neighbouring African State for what other countries may do to us ....

We may be a small country, but we are a determined people who have been called upon to play a rôle of world-wide significance.

We Rhodesians have rejected the doctrinaire philosophy of appeasement and surrender. The decision which we have taken today is a refusal by Rhodesians to sell their birthright. And, even if we were to surrender, does anyone believe that Rhodesia would be the last target of the Communists in the Afro-Asian bloc?

We have struck a blow for the preservation of justice, civilization, and Christianity; and in the spirit of this belief we have this day assumed our sovereign independence. God bless you all.

Source: from the *East Africa and Rhodesia Newspaper*, November 18, 1965, pp. 204–5.

Notes

1 Quoted in Yalata and Oak Valley Communities, with Christobel Mattingley, *Maralinga: The Anangu Story* (London: Allen & Unwin, 2025), pp. 39–42.
2 Quoted in National Museum Australia, "Maralinga," 2024, https://www.nma.gov.au/defining-moments/resources/maralinga.
3 Quoted in David Killingray and Martin Plaut, *Fighting for Britain: African Soldiers in the Second World War* (Woodbridge: James Currey, 2010), p. 221.
4 Binyavanga Wainaina, *One Day I Will Write About This Place: A Memoir* (Minneapolis: Graywolf Press, 2011), p. 252.
5 See Valerie Kuletz, *The Tainted Desert: Environmental and Social Ruin in the American West* (New York: Routledge, 1998); Traci Brynne Voyles, *Wastelanding: Legacies of Uranium Mining in Navajo Country* (Minneapolis: University of Minnesota Press, 2015).
6 Quoted in Atomic Heritage Foundation, "Native Americans and the Manhattan Project," 2022, https://ahf.nuclearmuseum.org/ahf/history/native-americans-and-manhattan-project/, accessed January 31, 2025.
7 Population Registration Act of 1950, https://www.sahistory.org.za/sites/default/files/archive-files2/leg19500707.028.020.030.pdf, accessed January 31, 2025.
8 Quoted in Sarah Alisabeth Fox, *Downwind: A People's History of the Nuclear West* (Lincoln: University of Nebraska Press, 2014), p. 53.
9 Interview with Mrs. Gajida Jacobs, in David M. Gordon, *Apartheid in South Africa: A Brief History with Documents* (Boston: Bedford St. Martin's, 2017), pp. 141, 142.
10 See Trevor Noah, *Born a Crime: Stories from a South African Childhood* (London: One World Books, 2019).
11 Cherryl Walker, *Women and Resistance in South Africa* (London: Onyx Books, 1982), pp. 189–201.
12 Nelson Mandela, "Statement during the Rivonia Trial," David M. Gordon, *Apartheid in South Africa: A Brief History with Documents* (Boston: Bedford St. Martin's, 2017), pp. 88–9.
13 Quoted in Cora Ann Presley, *Kikuyu Women, the Mau Mau Rebellion, and Social Change in Kenya* (Ann Arbor: University of Michigan Press, 1992), p. 143.

14 "Mau Mau Uprising: Kenyans Win UK Torture Ruling," *BBC News*, October 5, 2012, http://www.bbc.com/news/uk 19843719, accessed September 17, 2014.
15 Peter H. Russell, *Recognizing Aboriginal Title: The Mabo Case and Indigenous Resistance to English-Settler Colonialism* (Toronto: University of Toronto Press, 2005), p. 138.
16 Allen Curnow, *On The Tour or God Amend New Zealand, to T. H. Pearce Esq, Manager of the 1960 All White Rugby Team* (Pilgrim Press, 1960).
17 Quoted in Trevor Richards, *Dancing On Our Bones: New Zealand, South Africa, Rugby and Racism* (Wellington: Bridget Williams Books, 1999), pp. 19, 25.
18 Quoted in Richards, *Dancing On Our Bones*, p. 34.
19 Barnett R. Rubin, "False Memories: How Zionism's Dreams of Liberation became Entangled with Colonialism," *Boston Review* 2024. https://www.bostonreview.net/authors/barnett-r-rubin/, accessed January 31, 2025.

Further Reading

Caroline Elkins, *Imperial Reckoning: The Untold Story of Britain's Gulag in Kenya* (New York: Henry Holt, 2005).

Sarah Alisabeth Fox, *Downwind: A People's History of the Nuclear West* (Lincoln: University of Nebraska Press, 2014).

Trevor Noah, *Born a Crime: Stories from a South African Childhood* (London: One World Books, 2019).

Peter H. Russell, *Recognizing Aboriginal Title: The Mabo Case and Indigenous Resistance to English-Settler Colonialism* (Toronto: University of Toronto Press, 2005).

9

Land Back, 1960s–Present

In 1966, Marie Smallface, a member of the Kainai Reserve in Alberta, Canada, journeyed to Zambia to work in a girls' camp and then moved on to the capital city, Lusaka, at the time a hotbed of anti-colonial activity. There she met Jacob Marule, a member of the African National Congress who was agitating against South African apartheid from the relative safety of Lusaka. She married him, and after four years of involvement in anti-colonial activity and development, moved back with him to Canada in the autumn of 1970. Smallface-Marule went to work as an assistant to George Manuel, a member of the Neskonlith Indian Band who worked at the National Indian Brotherhood in Ottawa. Under the influence of Smallface-Marule and her husband, Manuel began to incorporate an international perspective into his political activities on behalf of Canada's First Nations people. As he put it, she was "the first person to be able to show me, from direct and personal experience, the close relationship and common bonds between our own condition as Indian people, and the struggles of other aboriginal peoples and the nations of the Third World." Manuel's immersion in global Indigenous activism received further reinforcement when he ventured to Australia and New Zealand in 1971, where he encountered people living in much the same conditions as Native people at home. He noted that "just as much as the Māoris and the Aborigines, the Indian people in Canada are dark people in a White Commonwealth." Unusual for his time, his outlook extended beyond the Indigenous peoples of the white commonwealth countries to include those of African states as well. "We share with the Māori and Aborigine, and I suspect also with many different African peoples," he declared, "not only this common struggle but also the very real progress we have made in the past decade."[1]

The following year, Manuel accompanied Canada's delegation to the UN Conference on the Human Environment in Sweden as an advisor. Jacob Marule, attending as a representative of the ANC, introduced him to a number of other Indigenous men and women in attendance, including members of the local Sámi community, who found in Manuel a man eager to share information on Indigenous rights. He and the Sámi activists agreed that they should plan an international conference for Indigenous peoples. Their contacts, determination, and hard work paid off, culminating in a conference attended by Indigenous representatives of nineteen different countries who met together on Vancouver Island in October 1975. In the course of the proceedings, they established the World Council of Indigenous Peoples (WCIP).

Smallface-Marule and Manuel envisioned the WCIP as a promoter of Indigenous rights at the international level, and steered it toward advocacy of the claim that Indigenous peoples had the right to self-determination. They looked to the United Nations as the body best positioned to deliver justice in this regard, and although the WCIP did not survive beyond the late 1990s, its activism and political program did much to bring about the 2007 UN Declaration on the Rights of Indigenous Peoples (UNDRIP).

More than two decades in the making, the declaration—a legally non-binding resolution calling upon UN member states to recognize the rights of Indigenous peoples to self-determination; possession of their own governing institutions; protection of their cultures; and ownership of their lands, among other enumerated rights—passed the General Assembly of the UN on September 13, 2007, by a vote of 143 to 4. The four no votes came from the United States, Australia, New Zealand, and Canada. These settler nations ultimately changed their positions in subsequent years, recognizing and acceding to the moral—though not legally binding—imperative of the international Indigenous communities, but their initial denials revealed the extent to which the demands for self-determination threatened their core foundations. A good deal of that perceived threat centered on Indigenous demands for the restitution of lands taken from them during centuries of settler colonialism. Not surprisingly, given that the expropriation of land stands at the very heart of settler colonialism, demands for the return of those lands took center stage in nearly all the countries we have treated; all of the other issues Indigenous activists demanded be addressed, whether cultural or political, bore directly on the repossession of traditional territories. "Once you lose your land," as Tamzyn Pue, a leader of the Ngati Maru in Taranaki, New Zealand, put it, "you lose your culture, you lose your [language], you lose your identity, you lose everything."[2]

Where Indigenous populations constituted a majority of the inhabitants of Anglo settler colonies, such as Ireland, Kenya, Rhodesia, and South Africa, they were able to assert political control and begin the process, however haphazard or ineffective, of returning seized lands to the descendants of the dispossessed. In places like Canada, the United States, Australia, and New Zealand, where settler colonialism resulted in the widespread destruction of the Aboriginal inhabitants and rendered them part of a permanent minority, the demand for the return of land has spawned an international Indigenous movement generally known as Land Back. As we saw at the beginning of the chapter, Australia joined New Zealand, Canada, and the United States in initially rejecting the UN Declaration on the Rights of Indigenous Peoples in 2007. The commonwealth, along with the three other settler nations, changed its position within a few years, unable to withstand the public pressure put on it by the international community and mollified by the fact that UNDRIP was not legally binding upon its signatories. In the meantime, Indigenous communities found ways to acquire ancestral territory that did not involve either legislation or court rulings, often buying land on the open market.

***

The Rhodesian Bush War against Ian Smith's white supremacist government, begun in the early 1960s and intensified after the Unilateral Declaration of Independence in 1965, took a major toll on the country. Gradually, South Africa's support for the settler government waned, the African guerrilla forces increased in size, and the Rhodesian economy began to collapse. Under these pressures, parliament amended the Land Tenure Act in 1977, limiting the portion of Rhodesian land whites could own to half a million acres, and Smith reluctantly acquiesced to negotiating for peace, sitting down with the rebel leaders and British officials to discuss opening the government to Africans. Talks produced a multi-racial government under the leadership of Bishop Abel Muzorewa, which in 1979 ended the racially based system of land ownership. The so-called Lancaster House Agreement, which ended the settler regime in Rhodesia, protected white interests by stipulating that white-owned land could not be seized for a period of ten years. The problem was one that confronted a variety of African nations at independence, Rhodesia among them: wiping away settlers' legal title to land would make companies wary of investing in Zimbabwe, and, besides, settlers had the resources and expertise to remain successful and continue sustaining Zimbabwe's economy. The Lancaster Agreement stipulated that property could only be acquired according to a "willing seller, willing buyer" scheme based on market values. Britain provided £44 million for the government to buy some 20 million acres of land on which to settle landless Africans, but progress proved difficult. The arrangement left nearly three-quarters of Rhodesia's most productive land in the hands of white settlers by the end of the decade, with perhaps 50,000 African families occupying around 7.5 million acres.

The Republic of Zimbabwe came into existence on April 18, 1980. The elections of that year gave Robert Mugabe's ZANU-PF party a large majority in parliament, making him prime minister. Once in power, Mugabe, like many other leaders of independent African states, quickly transitioned Zimbabwe to one-party rule. When the land restrictions provision of the Lancaster Agreement expired in 1990, the Zimbabwean government altered the constitution to permit compulsory seizure of white-owned land. It also passed the Land Acquisition Act of 1992, which empowered it to limit the size of white farms and to purchase them at less than market prices. Even with these new powers, the government's redistribution of land to African families faltered; much of it went to Mugabe's friends and political supporters rather than to landless Africans. Only some 2.5 million acres were settled by poor families between 1990 and 1997, and most of that was not fertile enough to support productive farming.

In the late 1990s, Zimbabwe's economy faced serious difficulties. Drought, corruption, poor economic policy, and Mugabe's decision to join a war in Congo combined to cause food shortages, popular discontent, and economic instability. Mugabe was under pressure to do something about white-owned land, much of which came from veterans of the Rhodesian Bush War, who argued that they had sacrificed much in the conflict but had received no reward for their efforts. As war veterans—many of whom were too young to have actually fought in the war—increasingly blamed Mugabe for their poverty, he declared that his government would seize 1,500 white-owned farms for redistribution, and demanded that Britain provide the funds to buy out white farmers. The funds Britain had promised in 1980 had long ago run out, and the program itself expired in 1996. Now, in the late 1990s, Tony Blair's Labour government refused to accept responsibility for what Mugabe described as problems caused by colonialism. As Clare Short, the foreign secretary, wrote to the Zimbabwean government, "we do not accept that Britain has a special responsibility to meet the costs of land purchase in Zimbabwe ... We are a new government from diverse backgrounds without links to former colonial interests. My own origins are Irish, and as you know, we were colonised, not colonisers,"[3] she noted, raising the issue of Ireland's settler colonial past in defense of her government's denial of responsibility for Rhodesia's.

Britain's refusal spurred Mugabe to new action. Regarding Cecil Rhodes' disbursement of millions of acres (over 15 million even before the commencement of the twentieth century) as directly responsible for Zimbabwe's travails, the prime minister pressed forward with a new land redistribution scheme called the "fast track" program. "In Zimbabwe," Mugabe declared to the UN in September 2000, "and only because of the color line arising from British colonialism, 70 percent of the best arable land is owned by less than 1 percent of the population who happen to be white, while the black majority are congested on barren land. We have sought to redress this inequity," he maintained, "through a land reform and resettlement program" designed to bring about "economic and social justice."[4] Between June 2000 and October 2003, the government seized about 4,300 white-owned farms, causing white farmers to flee the country and investors to pull out their money. Their exodus sped up following the passage of "indigenisation" laws that required all companies to demonstrate at least 50 percent Zimbabwean ownership. Few enterprises remained productive. The Zimbabwean dollar began a freefall that ended in its disuse in favor of the US dollar and South African rand, with inflation officially measured in mid-2008 at a peak of 231 billion percent.

***

The South African government's crackdown on the ANC and PAC in the years following 1963 profoundly weakened the anti-apartheid movement, leaving it without leadership and momentum. Into this void in the 1970s stepped a variety of ordinary men and women, led by African student groups, clergy, and unions. Over the next two decades, student boycotts, bus boycotts, massive strikes, uprisings in the townships and homelands, and international sanctions confronted the apartheid government with serious challenges. As the African and South Asian populations grew in size, the number of white residents fell dramatically, finally reaching a nadir of 10 percent of the total population. Violence in the cities and homelands; an economic downturn exacerbated by regular industrial actions taken by increasingly militant labor unions; near-constant protests and sabotage; and a UN embargo on weapons to the country made it impossible for the apartheid regime to govern South Africa. In 1989, it acceded to the inevitable and began to negotiate with the African National Congress for reforms that would recognize Africans' rights to political and legal equality. Between 1989 and 1993, the government of F. W. De Klerk held talks with the ANC's leader, Nelson Mandela, arriving at an agreement to hold national elections open to people of all races. Africans went to the polls on April 27, 1994; on May 10, 1994, Mandela was sworn in as president of South Africa.

From the time of its founding in 1912, the ANC had considered the return of land to Africans one of its primary aims. As negotiations with De Klerk proceeded, the issue of land restitution received careful consideration; ANC leaders regarded access to land a central element in creating a system of equality and saw landlessness as a marker of inequality. Private individuals held by far the vast majority of the land in South Africa; some 72 percent of it was in the hands of white people while Africans owned a tiny percentage. With the transition to full democracy, the government now faced an issue of mind-boggling complexity. How should the land be distributed? What land? To whom? And how should it be acquired? Who would pay for it? Would it be paid for at all? The thorny legal, political, economic, and moral problems raised by these questions plague the government to this day.

The 1996 constitution set out the principles according to which land distribution should take place: people who could prove that they had lost their rights to their land after 1913, the date marking the Native Land Act, could claim restitution. The state, not landowners, would be the body against which the claims were to be made, and landowners were entitled to just and equitable—read market value—compensation. The entity created to handle the process, the Reconstruction and Development Programme

(RDP), hoped to see 30 percent of agricultural land returned to dispossessed people within the first five years of the new government's tenure. It never came close. As of 2017, little progress had been made in redistributing land. Whites still owned the bulk of residential and agricultural land and Africans still had little access to it.

More than 26,000 claims had still to be adjudicated, which, as the constitutional court declared, would take nearly 150 years. And that was just for claims made by 1998, the cutoff date mandated by the constitution. If further claims were to be considered, it would take more than 700 years for the process to be completed.

Effective land reform has proven elusive, even for those who won their cases. Many Africans now occupying formerly white-owned farms have not had the wherewithal to work them productively. Lacking the resources necessary to purchase expensive equipment and without the skills necessary to manage an operation capable of competing on the global market, many African-owned agricultural enterprises have failed. More fundamentally, critics charge, the underlying assumptions governing land restitution undercut the ANC's original intentions. If land redistribution was meant to help redress the inequities and ills imposed by the white settler state and exacerbated by apartheid, a new philosophy would have to prevail. Setting 1913 as the date after which African dispossession would be considered left out over a century of earlier land seizures by white settlers, leaving the descendants of millions of Africans high and dry. Asking Africans to pay market value for white-owned property when they had no means of doing so meant that no progress could be made. Instead, argues Tembeka Ngcukaitobi, an attorney with the high court of South Africa, the state should take action to ensure that three principles be addressed: "correcting historical wrongs, confronting the persisting inequities of the present, and securing an equality-based future." To that end, the government would have to consider compulsorily taking land not being used for productive purposes from private individuals who acquired African land through conquest or other violent means. It would have to give that land—urban as well as agricultural—to those in need who would work it productively. Current constitutional provisions would need to be amended to enable such a program of land redistribution to be established, but as Ngcukaitobi reminds us, the whole point of the 1996 constitution was "to dismantle the colonial and apartheid state."[5]

South Africa's democratic government is only thirty years old at the time of this writing. Having never sat in parliament or run a government agency when they won power in a democratic election in 1994, Africans faced an overwhelming task of governing a country in chaos. Mandela and the ANC inherited a daunting set of problems as the country transitioned from a system of white supremacy to one of non-racial democracy. Expectations ran high, and could not have been met by even the most experienced politicians and bureaucrats in the best of economic times. Neither pertained. The fact that the new government was able to avoid civil war, establish a stable democratic system, implement the rule of law, and bring electricity, running water, housing, and telephones to millions of people who had not known them before, constitutes, as one prominent historian of South Africa put it, "one of the finest achievements of the twentieth century."[6]

***

The initiatives to build a global movement that emphasized self-determination for Indigenous peoples emerged from the civil rights struggles that marked the 1960s and 1970s in every settler nation treated in this book. This is not to say that the issues and concerns of Indigenous peoples mirrored those of other groups demanding reforms of society, and the differences among groups could sometimes create tensions. In the United States, for instance, Indian activist Vine Deloria, Jr. declared in his seminal work, *Custer Died for Your Sins* (1969), that the agenda promoted by African Americans seeking legal equality with whites was misguided, and not one Indian people should pursue. "The problem," he proclaimed, "is not one of legal status, it is one of culture and social and economic mobility." Equality meant sameness, he argued, and fell far short of what African Americans and Native Americans really needed to seek—peoplehood. Peoplehood depended upon acquiring "cultural independence," which in turn could not be attained "without a land base." That is why, Deloria explained, Indian activists focused their efforts on regaining the land Indian people had lost to white settlement; their campaigns reflected "the urge of peoples to find their homeland and to channel their psychic energies through their land into social and economic reality. Without land and a homeland no movement can survive." He urged African Americans to support the efforts of people like Stokely Carmichael in the Black power movement, leaders who understood that the object of the civil rights movement had to be not legal equality but self-determination.[7]

Deloria had been the executive director of the National Congress of American Indians (NCAI) in the mid-1960s, an organization dedicated to ending and reversing the policy of termination, which, as you will recall from the last chapter, removed legal recognition of certain tribes and resulted in the loss of a great many economic resources. One aspect of the work of the NCAI and the National Indian Youth Council (NIYC) involved suing a number of states for violating treaties that had protected Native fishing and hunting rights. Their efforts contributed to the rise of what became called "red power," an Indian protest campaign exemplified by the establishment of the American Indian Movement (AIM) in 1968. Eschewing what they regarded as the cautious and ineffectual policies of earlier Native organizations, AIM members sought out confrontation with local, state, and federal authorities, embarking upon a series of occupations and marches that frequently ended in violence.

One of the first of these direct action demonstrations took place in November 1969, when some ninety Indian people occupied Alcatraz Island in San Francisco Bay. Hailing from tribes from across America, and calling themselves Indians of All Tribes, they claimed the island as a reservation and for a year and a half demanded that the United States government live up to its treaty obligations. The occupation ended with the arrest of a number of activists in June 1971, but not before inspiring other direct actions and confrontations. AIM followers, whose numbers had burgeoned in response to Alcatraz and other protests, marched on Washington, DC, in November 1972 in what they called the "Trail of Broken Treaties." They seized the headquarters of the Bureau of Indian Affairs and held it for six days, issuing a twenty-point list enumerating their demands. The best known and most violent interaction between AIM and local, tribal, and federal agents took place in the winter of 1973 on the Pine Ridge Reservation in South Dakota, the site of the Wounded Knee Massacre of 1890. AIM members had come to Wounded Knee at the request of a group of Sioux men and women who sought their help in dealing with a corrupt and abusive tribal leadership on the reservation. For more than two months, AIM and dissident Pine Ridge Indians faced off against local and tribal police, US marshals, and FBI agents trying to end their siege; gunfire rang out every day as the two sides battled one another. A federal marshal was badly wounded and two Indian men were killed. The television and newspaper coverage of the siege brought previously unimagined public attention to the grievances of Indian people and particular scrutiny to the conditions at Pine Ridge, which the US government promised to address in its successful efforts to end the confrontation in early May 1973.

AIM's confrontational approach didn't appeal to all people seeking change for Native people, but it did bring public attention to matters they cared about and that made AIM a significant influence. A year before the establishment of the World Council of Indigenous Peoples (WCIP) on Vancouver Island in 1975 (cited above), AIM played a major role in a conference held on the Standing Rock reservation, attended by 5,000 delegates from ninety-seven different Indigenous nations. The delegates formed the International Indian Treaty Council under AIM's auspices and charged it with the responsibility of garnering UN recognition of Indigenous peoples and the treaties made with them. Again, land repatriation stood at the heart of the matter, and not just for Indian people. As Russell Means, one of AIM's leaders, noted, "in the history of the world the successful struggles for independence ... all involve land, *all* involve land—whether it's in Africa or Asia or Southeast Asia ... or in the Middle East, or in Ireland and the United States or Canada."[8]

One of the best-known legal actions for the return of Native land was the Sioux nation's claim for the Black Hills, first made in 1920. In

1980, the Supreme Court ruled that Congress had violated the 1868 Fort Laramie treaty by seizing the Black Hills, and awarded the Sioux $100 million in compensation. "A more ripe and rank case of dishonorable dealings will never, in all probability, be found in our history," the justices lamented in handing down their decision. But the Sioux didn't want the money. They wanted the Black Hills, which they held sacred and regarded as a source of their very cultural identity. They rejected the cash award with the succinct declaration, "the Black Hills are not for sale."[9]

Subsequent land claims cases have seen considerable success, especially since 2010, when the US government settled a 1996 suit brought by Blackfeet member Elouise Cobell on behalf of 300,000 Indian people. The federal government pledged to provide $1.9 billion to purchase former Indian lands lost to the allotment process in the late nineteenth century; as of late 2022, some 3 million acres had been transferred to tribal governments. Three million acres of returned land constituted a drop in the bucket in the context of the hundreds of millions of acres lost to forced dispossession, allotment, and dishonest treaties, but as Cris Stainbrook, president of the Indian Land Tenure Foundation, put it, the Cobell settlement "hasn't solved the problem, but [it] really put a dent in it."[10]

Much—though not all—of the land buybacks took place in the mountain West, where the biggest bang for the buck could be realized owing to lower land valuations than in the rest of the country. The Blackfeet, Crow, Oglala Sioux, Navajo, Umatilla, Cayuse, and Walla Walla people added significant acreage to the territories they possessed in Montana, South Dakota, Arizona, Oregon, and Washington, respectively. Other buyback initiatives in Oklahoma, Minnesota, Oregon, Washington, California, and the Dakotas involved purchasing land from private parties such as Ted Turner, utilizing funds from non-profit organizations, a number of which are affiliated with environmental NGOs. Under the leadership of Secretary of the Interior Deb Haaland, a Laguna Pueblo woman appointed by President Joseph Biden, a significant amount of public land—Canyon de Chelly in Arizona and Glacier Bay National Park in Alaska, to name just two—has been placed under the stewardship of Native tribes.

Recently, David Treuer, a member of the Ojibwe tribe and a scholar, called for the return of the national parks to Native Americans. "All 85 million acres of national-park sites should be turned over to a consortium of federally recognized tribes in the United States," he wrote in *The Atlantic* in 2021.

> The total acreage would not quite make up for the General Allotment Act, which robbed us of 90 million acres, but it would ensure that we have unfettered access to our tribal homelands. And it would restore dignity that was rightfully ours. To be entrusted with the stewardship of America's most precious landscapes would be a deeply meaningful form of restitution. Alongside the feelings of awe that Americans experience

while contemplating the god-rock of Yosemite and other places like it, we could take inspiration in having done right by one another.[11]

* * *

The Black power movement in the United States inspired a similar development in Australia, where Aboriginal people were beginning to demand self-determination. As in the United States, self-determination involved recognition of Aboriginal rights to decide for themselves how their ancestral lands would be utilized and claims to the actual land itself that had been taken by white settlers. Successive Australian governments refused those claims and derided efforts to bring suits in court for their return as "frivolous and vexatious."[12] Prime Minister William McMahon reiterated in his 1972 Australia Day speech that while Aboriginal communities might lease lands they had once lived on, provided that they "have the intention and ability to make reasonable social and economic use of the land," those lands remained the property of the commonwealth.[13] Aboriginal land rights claims, he made clear, would go nowhere. That night, a number of young Aboriginal activists made their way surreptitiously to the parliament building in Canberra. When people arrived for work that morning, they found an umbrella set up on the lawn in front bearing a sign that identified it as the "Aboriginal Embassy." Michael Anderson, one of the leaders of the protest, declared to reporters that "the land was taken from us by force ... we shouldn't have to lease it ... our spiritual beliefs are connected with the land."[14]

Over the next days, weeks, and months, Indigenous people from all over Australia, white sympathizers from unions and anti-apartheid organizations, and students from Australian National University streamed into what became an encampment on the parliament lawn. In February, Anderson issued a formal demand for land and self-determination that would have to be met before the embassy would disperse; the government responded with a declaration that legislation would be brought that would enable it to remove the protesters by force if they would not go peaceably. For months a stalemate ensued, with increasing numbers of protesters arriving at the site and the government able to do little to resolve the situation owing to significant political support for the embassy in the legislature and across the country.

Everything changed on the morning of July 20, when the government ordered a surprise raid on the tents that had been set up on the lawn. One hundred and fifty police officers marched onto the grounds, tore up the tents, and battled with the occupants. Arrests were made only in a few instances but injuries to the protesters were numerous. Some had to be hospitalized. The protesters removed themselves to the nearby university, where they made plans for what to do next. On July 23, some 200 activists—elderly Aboriginal men and women among them—marched back to the parliament building to set up a new tent encampment on the lawn, and were met by 360 police officers. Violence once again ensued, worse than that of three days earlier, prompting one observer to describe the incident as "one of the most violent confrontations in the history of Canberra." Embassy leaders declared that they would set up the tents yet again, despite the fear that it could turn into "Australia's Sharpeville," invoking the 1960 massacre of South Africans at the hands of the apartheid police. The Aboriginal activists were willing to take the risk, noting that "people had reached the stage where they were prepared to die for the issue" of land rights.[15]

In the event, the protesters and the government resolved the standoff peacefully, and the tents were dismantled with little fanfare. The memory and import of the embassy nevertheless remained a crucial element of settler/Indigenous politics. Aboriginal individuals and groups continued to press their cases in court and before the legislature, though little came of their efforts over the next two decades. A breakthrough occurred on June 3, 1992, when Australia's high court ruled in the *Mabo* decision that the doctrine of *terra nullius* (literally, the land of no one), the principle upon which settler law and policy had rested since the arrival of the first convicts in 1788, should not stand, setting off a legal bombshell in settler/Aboriginal relations. The court's rejection of *terra nullius* meant, at least in theory, that Aboriginal people's ownership of land at the time of white settlement should be legally recognized; that Aboriginal people could turn to Australian law to make claims for the return of or compensation for lands taken from them by settlers and the settler state. "Dispossession is the darkest aspect of the history of this nation," wrote two members of the court. "The nation as a whole must remain diminished unless and until there is an acknowledgement of, and retreat from, those past injustices."[16] In December the following year, parliament passed the Native Title Act, 1993, legislation that sought to codify the process whereby land claims could be made. The act didn't go far enough for Aboriginal leaders but set off a campaign by mining corporations to panic white Australians into thinking that their rights to property ownership were under attack. By the mid-1990s, a right-wing populist backlash led by Pauline Hansen and subscribed to by National Party leader and then Prime Minister John Howard led to significant losses for the Aboriginal movement's efforts to get land back. Howard's government enacted legislation that seriously undercut the Natives Title Act, giving special consideration to white pastoralists and farmers and mining operations to circumvent restrictions on their access to Aboriginal territories. Nevertheless, as of 2000, Aboriginal people owned some 16 percent of the Australia continent, most of it in the remotest parts of the continent. Aboriginal Australians continue to this day to pursue a land back policy, seeking to lay claim to homelands they had held for thousands of years before white settlers arrived on their shores and took them from them (see Figure 9.1).

FIGURE 9.1 *Australians demanding land back for Aboriginal peoples in Melbourne, 2023.*

There was one place where ceding land back to Aboriginal people raised no objections at all—Maralinga. In 1962, the Australia prime minister had told the Anangu people that when the nuclear testing at Maralinga ended, they would get their land back. That promise came to fruition in 1984, some eighteen years after the British had packed up their weaponry and their armed force personnel and departed the area they had contaminated so completely with plutonium and other varieties of nuclear waste. Anangu leaders knew what their mob faced, though perhaps not how long the clean-up process would take. They flew to London in 1991 and again in 1992 to put their case before the British government; in 1995, Britain paid out AU $45,250,000 for decontamination and compensation. Another fourteen years would pass before the last two sections of Maralinga were deemed habitable, and in 2014 the Anangu people were finally granted unimpeded access to their ancestral lands, lands that atomic testing had saturated with plutonium-239—a highly toxic chemical with a half-life of 24,000 years—for over a decade at the height of the Cold War.

* * *

As was true in Australia, the aims and initiatives of the American civil rights movement, buttressed by the UN's campaign on behalf of Indigenous rights worldwide, resonated powerfully in New Zealand among young Māori people, and, as in Australia and the United States, activists gave their attention to the issue of returning land to the Māori. The Māori Affairs Amendment Act of 1967 had enlarged the ability of the government to take Māori land even if its owners refused to sell, prompting opponents to call it the "land grab act." Outrage against it and other long-standing grievances brought together a coalition of younger and more seasoned Māori activists, who manifested their anger in the Māori Land March of 1975. Led by octogenarian Whina Cooper, the president of the Māori Women's Welfare League, and chanting "not one more acre of Māori land," 5,000 demonstrators made their way 660 miles south to Wellington, standing in silence in front of parliament as the rain poured down on them. The ruling Labour government paid attention, and in response passed the Treaty of Waitangi Act that very year, acknowledging the legitimacy of the original agreement made between Māori and Pakeha people in 1840. The legislation set up a Waitangi Tribunal through which claims under the treaty would be heard and recommendations made to the government.

Two years later, in 1977, the National government excited further ire by its decision to sell disputed land claimed by Māori people at Bastian Point in Auckland to developers. For a year and a half, protesters occupied the property, generating a great deal of television coverage that had the effect of presenting and explaining Māori grievances to the Pakeha viewing public. When the government sent in police and troops to end the occupation, television cameras captured and broadcast the shocking scenes of the reading of the Riot Act and the arrest of 222 demonstrators, outraging many white New Zealanders who had not before then realized the plight Māori people faced, and galvanizing Pakeha support for redress of past wrongs. When Labour returned to power in 1984, it extended the scope of the Waitangi Tribunal to include claims going back to 1840, vastly expanding the number of Māori land claims that could be brought before it. Litigants wasted no time in bringing them forward.

* * *

The existence of the Treaty of Waitangi provided a path to land claims successes that Australian Aborigines did not possess. Treaty agreements also eventually benefited Canadian First Nations people and Native Americans as they sought to recover lands. The process was often lengthy and the results uneven, to be sure, but as treaty rights were increasingly recognized by the courts, Native North Americans made progress in realizing their demands for the return of or compensation for the loss of their lands. In Canada, the Calder decision in 1973 legally recognized, for the first time, Aboriginal title, paving the way for the government's Comprehensive Land Claim Policy of that year. The vehicle by means of which First Nations and Métis land claims are negotiated and settled, the policy permits two kinds of claims: the first, comprehensive claims, deal with demands for ancestral lands made by Indigenous groups that did not sign treaties with the Canadian government.

Specific claims, by contrast, are made by Aboriginal groups that assert violations of treaties with the government or violations of the provisions of the Indian Act. In both instances, resolution is generally reached through the payment of monetary compensation rather than return of actual land itself, and, in those instances, acceptance of the compensation requires the plaintiffs to surrender their rights to the land. These stipulations remain deeply dissatisfying to many First Nations peoples, though others have pursued cases despite the shortcomings. Between 1975—when the Inuit people of Nunavik and the Cree of Eeyou Istchee accepted compensation from the Province of Quebec and the federal government for the damage done by the James Bay hydroelectric project—and 2017, twenty-five settlements had been reached; as of 2020, some 140 First Nations, Métis, or Inuit groups were talking with the federal government to address their comprehensive claims.

Slowly, if haphazardly, land itself has been granted as part of a settlement. In a suit brought by the Blueberry River, Doig River, Halfway River, Salteau, and West Moberly First Nations in the early 2000s, for example, the British Columbia and federal governments acknowledged that their predecessors had violated Treaty 8, signed back in 1899. That document had guaranteed each member of the five First Nations 160 acres, access to their hunting grounds, and any income they might realize by working the land, promises that were continually reneged on. When the British Columbia supreme court came down on the side of the plaintiffs' claims in 2021, the provincial and federal governments agreed to terms. "Honoring Treaty 8 is a key part of our work to advance reconciliation ... and reconnect these five Nations with their land," David Eby, BC's prime minister, declared. "By settling these treaty land entitlement specific claims, we're restoring the rightful amount of land that was promised under the treaty and all the benefits that should have flowed at the time to those Nations." In addition to stopping old-growth logging, limiting how much resource corporations can extract from the land, introducing measures to protect wildlife, and paying into a C$200 million fund intended to "heal" the land after decades of industrial depredation, the provincial government will return just under 110,000 acres of land to 3,300 members of the five First Nations. The federal government will contribute C$800 million to the Nations in compensation for the treaty whose terms it admitted Canada had "broken."[17]

***

If, as anthropologist Patrick Wolfe theorized, settler colonialism is a structure, not an event—that is, that it creates the architecture within which a society operates and which does not go away—does it mean that settler colonialism never ends? Or can we find instances in which it does cease to exist as a meaningful framework within which Indigenous people live their lives? If so, what conditions would have to be met to make that determination? Does gaining independence through decolonization, as first Ireland and then Kenya, Zimbabwe, and South Africa did, mark the shift from a settler colonial regime to another? Or is that a necessary but not sufficient development to establish the claim? Does it also require the recovery of dispossessed lands? What about the achievements of the "land back" movement in returning some territory to Indigenous peoples in places like Australia, New Zealand, Canada, and the United States. In the absence of recognition of Indigenous self-determination, or sovereignty, does that suffice to end at least some instantiations of settler colonialism?

It seems clear that both sovereignty and repossession of lost lands are necessary components of a settler decolonization scheme. Ireland appears to have achieved that end, even without the inclusion of Northern Ireland within its boundaries, having won independence from Britain, established its own government, and acquired through legislative means lands formerly held by the settler Anglo-Ascendancy. You'll remember the assertion of the Irish member of parliament upon the passage of the Land Act of 1923: it marked the end of the conquest of Ireland by English settlers. One might argue that Kenya, Zimbabwe, and South Africa have seen a partial resolution to settler colonialism, having attained independence and self-government. In Kenya and Zimbabwe, on the one hand, white settlers left in fairly considerable numbers, ceding their domination, if not complete influence, over the social, cultural, economic, juridical, and political structures of the state. South African whites, on the other hand, having lost political control, still retain a significant interest in those very institutions, putting settler decolonization further out of reach than we might see in the other two African nations. Nevertheless, the possibility exists in all three states that decolonization could be achieved sometime down the proverbial road. If land back policies were put in place that had the effect of making a meaningful transfer of land from white settlers to Indigenous African peoples, the combination of self-determination—or sovereignty—and repossession of land could mean the end of settler colonialism. However unlikely it is that so momentous an event would come to pass any time soon, the possibility does exist. That is because Africans, like the Irish, constitute a majority in their countries and thus the ability, politically, to make great change.

The situation faced by the minority populations of Aboriginal Australians, Māori, Native Americans, and First Nation Canadians makes the prospect of settler decolonization unlikely, even theoretically. The concept of Indigenous sovereignty is frequently envisaged as a choice between two absolute possibilities—Native people are either "inside" the nation or "outside" of it. Being "in" a fully sovereign United States, Canada, Australia, or New Zealand necessitates that they surrender any claims to Indigenous self-determination; being sovereign and self-determining means they are apart from the settler nation, and such a scenario is regarded as necessarily requiring the end of settler sovereignty. Such a scenario presents an impasse that is inherently unresolvable: Americans, Canadians, New Zealanders, and Australians aren't going anywhere, or giving up their status as sovereign nations; Indigenous movements across the world have demonstrated that Native people will not cease to demand recognition as self-determining people with the right to reclaim stolen lands. But as a number of activists and scholars have suggested, the choice between being "in" or "out" is a false one; they argue that Indigenous peoples within these countries might consider carving out a "third space" between the alternatives of obtaining full sovereignty, on the one hand, and giving up the possibility of any self-determination or assertion of authority whatsoever, on the other. As one scholar described such a situation, a third space of sovereignty would entail the settler-state and Indigenous peoples establishing "a multilayered political system wherein settler and indigenous polities can coexist, overlap, and interweave jurisdictions."[18]

Activists have pursued a variety of means of making that potential third space a reality. In North America, the Idle No More movement (Canada) and the NDN Collective (United States) seek to establish nation-to-nation relationships between tribal governments on the one hand, and the federal government on the other. The 1982 recognition of First Nation sovereignty in the Canadian constitution and treaties between the Indigenous entities and the governments of each country do, to some extent and in certain instances, recognize tribal authority, but, in actual practice, the power of Native people to exercise self-determination even on their own lands often does not exist. One glaring example of this deficiency in the United States would be the inability of tribal police and courts to prosecute laws against non-Indians for offenses committed on their lands.

In New Zealand, the Independent Working Group on Constitutional Transformation, made up of representatives from a number of Māori organizations meeting together between 2012 and 2015, proposed one-, two-, and three-sphere models of constitutional arrangements that would give meaningful authority to Māori people: a three-sphere model consisting of a Māori assembly, the New Zealand parliament, and a joint deliberative body; a single-sphere model comprised of Māori and New Zealand representatives making decisions together in a constitutionally mandated assembly; and a two-sphere model of a Māori assembly and the New Zealand parliament. Aboriginal Australians called in the 2017 "Uluru Statement from the Heart" for the establishment of a committee—the Makarrata Commission—that would manage and superintend agreements between the Australian government and Australian First Nations, and for a constitutional amendment that would guarantee a First Nations Voice in parliament. The attorney who helped draft the language described the Voice initiative as a "safe and responsible middle path,"[19] reflecting the desire for a third space among Indigenous peoples. The referendum for Voice was put to Australian voters in October 2023, but fell far short of the votes it needed to be enacted.

This loss devastated First Nation Australians, who overwhelmingly voted for it, and speaks volumes about how difficult it is and will continue to be to secure a third space—a middle way—for Indigenous sovereignty. The tenacity of settler colonialism in those countries whose Native people do not enjoy a majority remains a formidable obstacle to the amelioration of its wide-ranging, long-lasting, and powerful impacts.

Counterpoint: Tatars Take Land Back—and Lose it Again

Beginning in 1989, Tatars began to return to the Crimean peninsula, from which they—or more likely their parents and grandparents—had been deported by the Soviet government in 1944. Given fifteen minutes to gather their belongings, the Indigenous population of the peninsula was packed into cattle cars and hauled off to the Urals and to Soviet Central Asia. According to Tatar sources, which are disputed by the Russian government, nearly half of them died en route or within the first three years in the "special settlement system" in which they were confined, forced to provide labor for the Soviet administration until Khrushchev's denunciation of Stalin and the dismantling of the special settlement system in 1956 allowed for their release. Barred from moving back to Crimea, most settled in Central Asia, gaining employment, building homes, raising families, and establishing some degree of political power. They did not, however, forget where they had come from and Tatar activists continually pressed for repatriation to the peninsula.

With the fall of the Soviet Union, the Russian government relented, allowing Tatars to return to Crimea. After years of a mostly prosperous existence in Central Asia, they migrated back to what most of them considered their "homeland" in droves. Entire neighborhoods, collective farms, and large extended families organized themselves for the journey, piling into automobiles and boarding trains and making their way west as quickly as they could. In 1987, for example, only 17,400 Tatars lived in Crimea; by the time 1993 came to a close, some 260,000—more than half of the total Crimean Tatar population of the former Soviet Union—did so. Possessed of powerful memories of a blessed land instilled in them by the first generation of the 1944 deportation, the Tatars returned to a place that little resembled the idealized landscape they expected, inhabited by Slavic peoples largely hostile to their presence. Upon arrival, they seized and occupied the lands of old and unused state or collective farms, living in tents, cobbling together shacks, or squatting in rundown buildings until they could build settlements on land they viewed as central to their identity as Tatars. When Russian authorities tried to stop them, many threatened to self-immolate, crying "Homeland or Death." Their willingness to give up everything they had known in Central Asia, to remove themselves to a life of much less comfort and a considerably lower standard of living, to die in pursuit of their claims had the effect of forcing the Russian and then Ukrainian governments to back off. Settlements grew up quickly, though, owing to a lack of funding, many of them still lacked the most basic of infrastructural needs like running water, electricity, and even sewers. But such is the tie to land and to place for the Tatars, they have persisted. A woman by the name of Saniye recounted to an interviewer how she and her husband, Seidjalil Asanov, had "left behind a six-room house in Tajikistan. There was a garden, an orchard with grapes and figs, an aisle of flowers—it was so beautiful," she recalled. Now that they live in a flimsy shack made of sheet metal, burlap, and wood, surrounded by dust, mud, and weeds, they couldn't be happier. "We're living in the homeland," she beamed. Still another individual put it, "Give me a rotting homeland, but a homeland all the same."[20]

On March 2, 2014, Russian troops invaded Crimea, taking back the land the Kremlin had ceded to the Ukrainian Soviet Socialist Republic in 1954. Six weeks later, Vladimir Putin's government demanded the return of all lands taken illegally from Crimea, a pronouncement that hit particularly close to home for Tatars, who had seized the lands they now lived on back in the 1990s. Russian troops and police raided and disbanded Tatar political organizations and local vigilantes spray-painted Tatar houses with swastikas. Fearful for their lives and future, many Tatars nevertheless determined to stay put. One man asserted, "Our people are peaceful, but if they threaten us, our men will defend the community. It is better to die here than leave again." Another said, "What we can say definitively as Tatars is there is nowhere else for us to go. We were removed once before by force. We endured genocide. We came home again. And we will never leave again."[21] Despite these protestations, many did leave. Some 20,000 Tatar men and women fled to Ukraine in 2014–15, having been dispossessed of their homes. And soon after the Russian invasion of Ukraine in 2022, 10,000 Tatar men, most of draft age, similarly escaped Crimea to avoid being conscripted into the Russian army. So intimately tied to the land now claimed and held by Russia, Tatar identity has been deeply fractured by Russia's actions, and it is difficult to see how, if at all, it might rebuild itself.

Primary Source Document

United Nations Declaration on the Rights of Indigenous Peoples, 2007

United Nations Declaration on the Rights of Indigenous Peoples

The General Assembly, Guided by the purposes and principles of the Charter of the United

Nations, and good faith in the fulfilment of the obligations assumed by States in accordance with the Charter, Affirming that indigenous peoples are equal to all other peoples, while recognizing the right of all peoples to be different, to consider themselves different, and to be respected as such, Affirming also that all peoples contribute to the diversity and richness of civilizations and cultures, which constitute the common heritage of humankind, Affirming further that all doctrines, policies and practices based on or advocating superiority of peoples or individuals on the basis of national origin or racial, religious, ethnic or cultural differences are racist, scientifically false, legally invalid, morally condemnable and socially unjust, Reaffirming that indigenous peoples, in the exercise of their rights, should be free from discrimination of any kind, Concerned that indigenous peoples have suffered from historic injustices as a result of, inter alia, their colonization and dispossession of their lands, territories and resources, thus preventing them from exercising, in particular, their right to development in accordance with their own needs and interests, Recognizing the urgent need to respect and promote the inherent rights of indigenous peoples which derive from their political, economic and social structures and from their cultures, spiritual traditions, histories and philosophies, especially their rights to their lands, territories and resources, Recognizing also the urgent need to respect and promote the rights of indigenous peoples affirmed in treaties, agreements and other constructive arrangements with States, Welcoming the fact that indigenous peoples are organizing themselves for political, economic, social and cultural enhancement and in order to bring to an end all forms of discrimination and oppression wherever they occur, Convinced that control by indigenous peoples over developments affecting them and their lands, territories and resources will enable them to maintain and strengthen their institutions, cultures and traditions, and to promote their development in accordance with their aspirations and needs, Recognizing that respect for indigenous knowledge, cultures and traditional practices contributes to sustainable and equitable development and proper management of the environment, Emphasizing the contribution of the demilitarization of the lands and territories of indigenous peoples to peace, economic and social progress and development, understanding and friendly relations among nations and peoples of the world, Recognizing in particular the right of indigenous families and communities to retain shared responsibility for the upbringing, training, education and well-being of their children, consistent with the rights of the child, Considering that the rights affirmed in treaties, agreements and other constructive arrangements between States and indigenous peoples are, in some situations, matters of international concern, interest, responsibility and character, Considering also that treaties, agreements and other constructive arrangements, and the relationship they represent, are the basis for a strengthened partnership between indigenous peoples and States, Acknowledging that the Charter of the United Nations, the International Covenant on Economic, Social and Cultural Rights and the International Covenant on Civil and Political Rights, as well as the Vienna Declaration and Programme of Action, affirm the fundamental importance of the right to self-determination of all peoples, by virtue of which they freely determine their political status and freely pursue their economic, social and cultural development, Bearing in mind that nothing in this Declaration may be used to deny any peoples their right to self-determination, exercised in conformity with international law, Convinced that the recognition of the rights of indigenous peoples in this Declaration will enhance harmonious and cooperative relations between the State and indigenous peoples, based on principles of justice, democracy, respect for human rights, non-discrimination and good faith, Encouraging States to comply with and effectively implement all their obligations as they apply to indigenous peoples under international instruments, in particular those related to human rights, in consultation and cooperation with the peoples concerned, Emphasizing that the United Nations has an important and continuing role to play in promoting and protecting the rights of indigenous peoples, Believing that this Declaration is a further important step forward for the recognition, promotion and protection of the rights and freedoms of indigenous peoples and in the development of relevant activities of the United Nations system in this field, Recognizing and reaffirming that indigenous individuals are entitled without discrimination to all human rights recognized in international law, and that indigenous peoples possess collective rights which are indispensable for their existence, well-being and integral development as peoples, Recognizing that the situation of indigenous peoples varies from region to region and from country to country and that the significance of national and regional particularities and various historical and cultural backgrounds should be taken into consideration, Solemnly proclaims the following United Nations Declaration on the Rights of Indigenous Peoples as a standard of achievement to be pursued in a spirit of partnership and mutual respect:

Article 1

Indigenous peoples have the right to the full enjoyment, as a collective or as individuals, of all human rights and fundamental freedoms as recognized in the Charter of the United Nations, the Universal Declaration of Human Rights and international human rights law.

Article 2

Indigenous peoples and individuals are free and equal to all other peoples and individuals and have the right to be free from any kind of discrimination, in the exercise of their rights, in particular that based on their indigenous origin or identity.

Article 3

Indigenous peoples have the right to self-determination. By virtue of that right they freely determine their political status and freely pursue their economic, social and cultural development.

Article 4

Indigenous peoples, in exercising their right to self-determination, have the right to autonomy or self-government in matters relating to their internal and local affairs, as well as ways and means for financing their autonomous functions.

Article 5

Indigenous peoples have the right to maintain and strengthen their distinct political, legal, economic, social and cultural institutions, while retaining their right to participate fully, if they so choose, in the political, economic, social and cultural life of the State.

Article 6

Every indigenous individual has the right to a nationality.

Article 7
1. Indigenous individuals have the rights to life, physical and mental integrity, liberty and security of person.
2. Indigenous peoples have the collective right to live in freedom, peace and security as distinct peoples and shall not be subjected to any act of genocide or any other act of violence, including forcibly removing children of the group to another group.

Article 8
1. Indigenous peoples and individuals have the right not to be subjected to forced assimilation or destruction of their culture.
2. States shall provide effective mechanisms for prevention of, and redress for:
    (a) Any action which has the aim or effect of depriving them of their integrity as distinct peoples, or of their cultural values or ethnic identities;
    (b) Any action which has the aim or effect of dispossessing them of their lands, territories or resources;
    (c) Any form of forced population transfer which has the aim or effect of violating or undermining any of their rights;
    (d) Any form of forced assimilation or integration;
    (e) Any form of propaganda designed to promote or incite racial or ethnic discrimination directed against them.

Article 9
Indigenous peoples and individuals have the right to belong to an indigenous community or nation, in accordance with the traditions and customs of the community or nation concerned. No discrimination of any kind may arise from the exercise of such a right.

Article 10
Indigenous peoples shall not be forcibly removed from their lands or territories. No relocation shall take place without the free, prior and informed consent of the indigenous peoples concerned and after agreement on just and fair compensation and, where possible, with the option of return.

Article 11
1. Indigenous peoples have the right to practise and revitalize their cultural traditions and customs. This includes the right to maintain, protect and develop the past, present and future manifestations of their cultures, such as archaeological and historical sites, artefacts, designs, ceremonies, technologies and visual and performing arts and literature.
2. States shall provide redress through effective mechanisms, which may include restitution, developed in conjunction with indigenous peoples, with respect to their cultural, intellectual, religious and spiritual property taken without their free, prior and informed consent or in violation of their laws, traditions and customs.

Article 12
1. Indigenous peoples have the right to manifest, practise, develop and teach their spiritual and religious traditions, customs and ceremonies; the right to maintain, protect, and have access in privacy to their religious and cultural

sites; the right to the use and control of their ceremonial objects; and the right to the repatriation of their human remains.
2. States shall seek to enable the access and/or repatriation of ceremonial objects and human remains in their possession through fair, transparent and effective mechanisms developed in conjunction with indigenous peoples concerned.

Article 13
1. Indigenous peoples have the right to revitalize, use, develop and transmit to future generations their histories, languages, oral traditions, philosophies, writing systems and literatures, and to designate and retain their own names for communities, places and persons.
2. States shall take effective measures to ensure that this right is protected and also to ensure that indigenous peoples can understand and be understood in political, legal and administrative proceedings, where necessary through the provision of interpretation or by other appropriate means.

Article 14
1. Indigenous peoples have the right to establish and control their educational systems and institutions providing education in their own languages, in a manner appropriate to their cultural methods of teaching and learning.
2. Indigenous individuals, particularly children, have the right to all levels and forms of education of the State without discrimination.
3. States shall, in conjunction with indigenous peoples, take effective measures, in order for indigenous individuals, particularly children, including those living outside their communities, to have access, when possible, to an education in their own culture and provided in their own language.

Article 15
1. Indigenous peoples have the right to the dignity and diversity of their cultures, traditions, histories and aspirations which shall be appropriately reflected in education and public information.
2. States shall take effective measures, in consultation and cooperation with the indigenous peoples concerned, to combat prejudice and eliminate discrimination and to promote tolerance, understanding and good relations among indigenous peoples and all other segments of society.

Article 16
1. Indigenous peoples have the right to establish their own media in their own languages and to have access to all forms of non-indigenous media without discrimination.
2. States shall take effective measures to ensure that State-owned media duly reflect indigenous cultural diversity. States, without prejudice to ensuring full freedom of expression, should encourage privately owned media to adequately reflect indigenous cultural diversity.

Article 17
1. Indigenous individuals and peoples have the right to enjoy fully all rights established under applicable international and domestic labour law.
2. States shall in consultation and cooperation with indigenous peoples take specific measures to protect indigenous children from economic exploitation and from performing any work that is likely to be hazardous or to interfere

with the child's education, or to be harmful to the child's health or physical, mental, spiritual, moral or social development, taking into account their special vulnerability and the importance of education for their empowerment.
3. Indigenous individuals have the right not to be subjected to any discriminatory conditions of labour and, inter alia, employment or salary.

Article 18
Indigenous peoples have the right to participate in decision-making in matters which would affect their rights, through representatives chosen by themselves in accordance with their own procedures, as well as to maintain and develop their own indigenous decision-making institutions.

Article 19
States shall consult and cooperate in good faith with the indigenous peoples concerned through their own representative institutions in order to obtain their free, prior and informed consent before adopting and implementing legislative or administrative measures that may affect them.

Article 20
1. Indigenous peoples have the right to maintain and develop their political, economic and social systems or institutions, to be secure in the enjoyment of their own means of subsistence and development, and to engage freely in all their traditional and other economic activities.
2. Indigenous peoples deprived of their means of subsistence and development are entitled to just and fair redress.
...

Article 25
Indigenous peoples have the right to maintain and strengthen their distinctive spiritual relationship with their traditionally owned or otherwise occupied and used lands, territories, waters and coastal seas and other resources and to uphold their responsibilities to future generations in this regard.

Article 26
1. Indigenous peoples have the right to the lands, territories and resources which they have traditionally owned, occupied or otherwise used or acquired.
...

Article 28
1. Indigenous peoples have the right to redress, by means that can include restitution or, when this is not possible, just, fair and equitable compensation, for the lands, territories and resources which they have traditionally owned or otherwise occupied or used, and which have been confiscated, taken, occupied, used or damaged without their free, prior and informed consent.
...

Article 31
1. Indigenous peoples have the right to maintain, control, protect and develop their cultural heritage, traditional knowledge and traditional cultural expressions.
....

Article 32
1. Indigenous peoples have the right to determine and develop priorities and strategies for the development or use of their lands or territories and other resources.
...

Article 33
1. Indigenous peoples have the right to determine their own identity or membership in accordance with their customs and traditions. This does not impair the right of indigenous individuals to obtain citizenship of the States in which they live.
...

Article 34
Indigenous peoples have the right to promote, develop and maintain their institutional structures and their distinctive customs, spirituality, traditions, procedures, practices and, in the cases where they exist, juridical systems or customs, in accordance with international human rights standards.
...

Article 37
1. Indigenous peoples have the right to the recognition, observance and enforcement of treaties, agreements and other constructive arrangements concluded with States or their successors and to have States honour and respect such treaties, agreements and other constructive arrangements.
...

Article 44
All the rights and freedoms recognized herein are equally guaranteed to male and female indigenous individuals.
...

Notes

1 Quoted in Jonathan Crossen, "Another Wave of Anti-Colonialism: The Origins of Indigenous Internationalism," *Canadian Journal of History/Annales canadiennes d'histoire*, Vol. 52, No. 3 (2017), pp. 533–59, pp. 539, 537.

2 Quoted in Fabiola Cineas, "New Zealand's Māori Fought for Reparations—and Won," *Vox*, January 17, 2023. https://www.vox.com/the-highlight/23518642/new-zealand-reparations-maori-settlements, accessed January 30, 2025.

3 Richard Bourne, *Catastophe: What Went Wrong in Zimbabwe?* (London: Zed Books, 2011), p. 145.

4 Quoted in Annie Schleicher, "Land Redistribution in Southern Africa," *Online NewsHour*, April 14, 2004. https://web.archive.org/web/20040501103309/http://www.pbs.org:80/newshour/bb/Africa/land, accessed January 30, 2025.

5 Tembeka Ngcukaitobi, *Land Matters: South Africa's Failed Land Reforms and the Road Ahead* (Cape Town: Penguin, 2021), pp. 219, 226.

6 Leonard Thompson, *A History of South Africa*, revised edn (New Haven: Yale University Press, 1996), p. 241.
7 Quoted in Vine Deloria, Jr., *Custer Died for Your Sins: An Indian Manifesto* (New York: Macmillan Publishing Company, 1969), pp. 174, 179, 180.
8 Quoted in Nick Estes, *Our History is the Future: Standing Rock versus the Dakota Access Pipeline, and the Long Tradition of Indigenous Resistance* (London: Verso, 2019), pp. 225–6.
9 Quoted in Estes, *Our History is the Future*, p. 242.
10 Quoted in Felicity Barringer, "Native American Land Return Movement Makes Gains, Faces Obstacles," Bill Lane Center for the American West Newsletter, November 22, 2022, https://andthewest.stanford.edu/2022/native-american-land-return-movement-makes-gains-faces-obstacles/, accessed January 31, 2025.
11 David Treuer, "Return the National Parks to the Tribes," *The Atlantic*, May 2021. https://www.theatlantic.com/magazine/archive/2021/05/return-the-national-parks-to-the-tribes/618395/, accessed January 30, 2025.
12 Quoted in Stuart Macintyre, *A Concise History of Australia*, 3rd edn (Cambridge: Cambridge University Press, 2009), p. 236.
13 Quoted in Robert Trumbull, "Aborigines in Australia Given New Land Rights," *New York Times*, January 26, 1972. https://www.nytimes.com/1972/01/26/archives/aborigines-in-australia-given-new-land-rights.html, accessed January 31, 2025.
14 Quoted in S. Robinson, "The Aboriginal Embassy: An Account of the Protests of 1972," *Aboriginal* History, Vol. 18, No. 1/2 (1994), pp. 49–63, p. 51.
15 Quoted in S. Robinson, "The Aboriginal Embassy," pp. 58, 59, 60.
16 Quoted in Macintyre, *A Concise History of Australia*, pp. 288–9.
17 Quoted in Leyland Cecco, "Canada to Pay $800m to Settle Land Dispute with Five First Nations," *The Guardian*, April 17, 2023. https://www.theguardian.com/world/2023/apr/17/canada-first-nations-land-claims-dispute-settlement, accessed January 30, 2025.
18 See Kevin Bruyneel, *The Third Space of Sovereignty: The Postcolnial Politics of US-Indigenous Relations* (Minneapolis: University of Minnesota Press, 2007), p. 218. See also Lorenzo Veracini, *Settler Colonialism, A Theoretical Overview* (Basingstoke: Palgrave Macmillan, 2010).
19 Quoted in Naaman Zhou, "The Failure of Australia's Attempt to Create an Indigenous Voice to Parliament," *The New Yorker Magazine*, October 19, 2023. https://www.newyorker.com/news/daily-comment/the-failure-of-australias-attempt-to-create-an-indigenous-voice-to-parliament, accessed January 30, 2025.
20 Quoted in Brian Glyn Williams, *The Crimean Tatars: From Soviet Genocide to Putin's Conquest* (New York: Oxford University Press, 2015), p. 146; Greta Lynn Uehling, *Beyond Memory: The Crimean Tatars' Deportation and Return* (Basingstoke: Palgrave Macmillan, 2004), p. 229.
21 Quoted in Williams, *The Crimean Tatars*, p. 160.

Further Reading

Richard Bourne, *Catastophe: What Went Wrong in Zimbabwe?* (London: Zed Books, 2011).

Vine Deloria, Jr., *Custer Died for Your Sins: An Indian Manifesto* (New York: Macmillan Publishing Company, 1969).

Nick Estes, *Our History is the Future: Standing Rock versus the Dakota Access Pipeline, and the Long Tradition of Indigenous Resistance* (London: Verso, 2019).

Tembeka Ngcukaitobi, *Land Matters: South Africa's Failed Land Reforms and the Road Ahead* (Cape Town: Penguin, 2021).

INDEX

A
Aboriginal Australians 68–70, 122–3
Aboriginal peoples 7, 152
Aboriginal Tasmanians 59–60
Aborigines' Protection Society 84–5
Acadians 48
Act of Settlement (1652) 20, 21
Adams, David Wallace 115
African National Congress (ANC) 181–3, 201–2
African peoples (South Africa, Zimbabwe, and Kenya) 7
Alcatraz Island protest 204
Alexander VI, Pope 4, 8
All Blacks (rugby) 189–90
allotment 114–18
American Colonization Society (ACS) 108–9
American Indian Movement (AIM) 203–4
American Indian or Indian people 7
Americoes 108–9
Amherst, Sir Jeffrey 49
Anangu people 173–4
Anderson, Michael 206
apartheid 180–3
Armstrong, William 94
Arthur, George 69
Asanov, Saniye and Seidjalil 214
assimilation 3
Atlantic Charter 166
atomic bomb 176–7
Australia 66–70, 103–5, 122–4, 152, 163, 206–8, 211–13
Australian Aborigine League 163

B
Bacon, Nathaniel 40
Baker, Eugene 98
Balfour, Arthur 137
Banks, Joseph 66, 68
Baptiste, Sister Marie 121
Baring, Evelyn 185
Barkley, Edward 15
Basutos 101
Berkeley, William 39–40
Biden, Joseph 205
Bingham, Richard 11–12
bison destruction 97–8
Black and Tans 157
Black Hawk War 95
Black Hills 204–5
blackness 4–5
Blair, Tony 200
Boedecker, Henry 114
Boers 54, 76, 78, 83, 100–1
Bonar Law, Andrew 138
Bonnin, Gertrude 160, 161
Botha, Louis 130
Braddock, Edward 48
Bradford, William 42
Brant, Cameron Dee 148–9
Brant, Joseph 52
Britain 60–1, 163–4, 166, 174–6
British North America Act of 1867 118
British South Africa Company (BSAC) 132–3
Brown, Eileen 173
Browne, E. D. 113
Burgoyne, Iris 124
Burma 165
Busby, James 106

C
Calleja, Félix 80
Canada 89–93, 118–22, 147–8, 152, 162–4, 197–9, 209–12

INDEX

Canberra protest 206–7
Cape Liberalism 102–3
Cape Town, South African 53–4
Carlisle Indian Industrial School 115, 117
Carmichael, Stokely 203
Carroll, James 125
Carson, Sir Edward 138
The Case of Ireland's being Bound by Acts of Parliament in England Stated (Molyneux) 24
Catapano, Andrea 148
Catholics 4, 6, 72–5
Caulfield, Sir Toby 19
Cetshwayo 127
Charles I, King of England 18, 19, 20
Charles II, King of England 20–1, 40
Chelmsford, Lord 127
Cherokees 47, 52, 95
Chickasaws 96
Chivington, John 96
Choctaws 94–5
Christians 4, 6
Churchill, Winston 166
Cobell, Elouise 205
Cochecho massacre 35–6
Collier, John 162, 179
Collins, Michael 158
Connolly, James 150–1
Cook, James 66, 68
Cooper, Whina 209
Cornwallis, Edward 48
Cortés, Hernán de 27
Cosgrave, William 158
country marriages 62
Creeks 47, 65–6, 95
Creek War 95
Crimea 214
Cromwell, Oliver 20
Crozier, Brigadier-General 157
Custer, George 98, 99

D
Davitt, Michael 135, 136
Dawes Act 114–15
Deakin, Alfred 122–3
De Bry, Theodore 37
Declaration of Independence 51, 52
Declaratory Act 24–5

Defenders 71
De Klerk, F. W. 201
Deloria, Sam 6–7
Deloria, Vine, Jr. 203
Deskaheh 147–8
Devereau, Walter, First Earl of Essex 14–15
Dharug 67
Dillon, John 151
Dingane 100–1
Doctrine of Discovery 4, 6, 8–10
Dominion Lands Act 118
Dragging Canoe 52
Dudley, Robert, Earl of Leicester 14
Dutch East India Company 53

E
Earl of Kingsborough 73, 74
Earl of Tyrconnel 22
Easter Rebellion 150–1
Eastman, Charles 161
Easton Treaty 48–9, 51
Eby, David 210
Eliot, Charles 134
Eliot, Rev. John 43
Elizabeth I, Queen of England 11, 14, 16, 17
Emmet, Thomas 73
enfranchisement 119
England, seizure of Ireland 12–27
English Pale 13, 14
Eora 66–7

F
Ferdinand VII, King of Spain 80
First Nations People 7, 118–22, 209–10
Fitzgerald, Lord Edward 73
Fort Garry 91–3
French, Lord 157
French and Indian War 47–51
Frere, Sir Bartle 127

G
Gachika, Elizabeth 186
George III, King of England 51, 52, 55
George V, King of England 131, 150
Ghost Dance 117
Gilbert, Sir Humphrey 15

Gilisho, Kirapusho Ene 113
Gladstone, William 128, 136, 137
Glorious Revolution 22
Graces 18
Gradual Enfranchisement Act (1869) 119–20
Grant, Cuthbert 63
Great Trek 83–4
Great War 148–53, 160
Grey, Sir George 1–2
Guerin, George 121

H
Haaland, Deb 205
Handsome Lake 64
Hansen, Pauline 207
Hariot, Thomas 37
Harrison, William Henry 65, 93
Haudenosaunee 44, 52–3, 147
Henry II, King of England 12, 13
Henry VIII, King of England and Ireland 13, 27
Hertzog, J. B. M. 155, 159, 165
Herzl, Theodor 191
Hidalgo y Costilla, Miguel 79–80
Hobson, William 106
Hokkaido 138–9
Hoover, Herbert 162
Hornaday, William 97
Houghers 25
Howard, John 207
Hull, William 65

I
Indian Act (1876) 119–20
Indian removal from US 93–100
Indian Reorganization Act (IRA) 162
Indians 27–8, 35–55
Indigenous peoples 2–3, 5–8, 6–7, 151–2
Ireland 11–27, 14, 70–5, 135–8, 150–1, 156–9
Irish Brigade 88–9
Irish Catholics 85–7
Irish Declaration of Independence (1919) 168–9
Irish famine 87–8
Irish Penal Laws 29–32
Irish Republican Army (IRA) 156–8

Iroquois 47
Israel 190–2
Itote, Waruhiu 175, 176, 185–6

J
Jackson, Andrew 65–6, 93
Jacobs, Gajida 180–1
James I, King of England 17, 37
James II, King of England and Scotland 21, 22–3
Jameson, Leander Starr 132–3
James VI, King of Scotland 17
Japanese settler colonialism 138–40
Jefferson, Thomas 51, 93
Jeffreys, Herbert 40
Jim, Russell 177

K
Kalenjin people 134
Kamba people 134
Kancamagus, Chief 35–6
Kelley, Robin 3
Kellogg, Laura 161
Kenya 113–14, 134–5, 153–4, 165, 183–7, 211
Kenyatta, Jomo 185, 186
Khoikhoi 53–4
Khrushchev, Nikita 213
Kickett, John 163
Kikuyu people 134, 184–5, 186
Kimathi, Dedan 185–6
King Philip's War 44–5
King's African Rifles (KAR) 165
Korea 139–40
Kunene, Alice 182

L
Lake, Gerald 73, 74
Lakota 117–18
Lalor, James Fintan 135–6
Lame Deer 117
Lancaster House Agreement 199
Land Back (Indigenous) 198, 211
    Australia 206–8
    Canada 209–10
    New Zealand 208–9
    Rhodesia/Zimbabwe 199–201
    South Africa 201–3
    United States 203–6

land wars (Ireland) 135–7
League of Indians of Canada 162–3
Lee, Richard Henry 51
Lennon, Lallie 173
Lester, Yami 173
Lettow-Vorbeck, Paul von 149
Liberia 108–9
Lloyd George, David 157
Lobengula 131–3
Los Alamos, New Mexico 176–7
Loyalists 61–2

M
Maasai 113–14, 134
Macdonald, John A. 119, 120
MacDougall, Walter 174
MacDougall, William 91–2
MacKenzie, Ranald 98, 99
Madison, James 65
Malan, Daniel François 155, 180, 181
Mallin, Michael 151
Manchuria 139–40
Mandela, Nelson 181, 183, 201, 202
Manuel, George 197–8
Māoris (New Zealand) 7, 105–8, 124–6, 152, 164, 189–90, 208–9, 212
Mapike, Thomas 131
Maritz, Gerritt 83
Markiewicz, Constance 151
Marshall, John 4
Marule, Jacob 197
Mary II, Queen of England 21–3
Mary of Modena 21
Mashonaland 131–2
Massasoit 41–2
Matabeleland 131–3
Mathenge, Stanley 185–6
Mau Mau 174, 175, 184, 185–7
Mayawara, Judy 173
McMahon, William 206
Means, Russell 204
Menzies, Robert 173
Meriam, Lewis 161–2
Metacom 43, 44
Métis 62–3, 91–3, 121–2, 209–10
Mexico 79–81
Milner, Sir Alfred 129

Mini, Vuyisile 183
Mitchell, Sir Philip 185
Moffat, John 131
Mohawks 44
Mohegans 42, 43–4
Molyneux, William 24
Mootian, Thomas Ole 113
Morelos, Father José María 80
Msane, Saul 131
Muchai, Karigo 175, 176
Mugabe, Robert 188, 199–200
Muzorewa, Abel 199

N
Napier, Sir George 101
Narragansetts 42, 43–4
Natal 101–2
National Congress of American
    Indians (NCAI) 203
National Indian Youth Council
    (NIYC) 203
Native Americans 7, 114–18, 160
Native Lands Act 130, 131
Native Schools Act 125
Natives' Land Act (South Africa)
    140–3
Navajo Code Talkers 164
Navajos 178
Ndebele 132–3
Nebuchadnezzar 191
Neolin 49
Netanyahu, Benjamin 192
Newcastle, Lord 48
New England settlers 43
New Spain 27–8
New Zealand 105–8, 124–6, 152, 189–90, 208–9, 211–12
New Zealand Rugby Football League
    (NZRFU) 189–90
Ngata, Apirana 125
Ngcukaitobi, Tembeka 202
Nine Years' War 16, 17
Nkomo, Joshua 188
Noah, Trevor 181
Nolan, Peter 136
North, Lord 71
Northern Rhodesia 153, 154
Norway 167–8

nuclear testing/colonialism 173–4, 176–9
Numbered Treaties 118
Nzili, Paolo 186

O
Ocaneechis 40
O'Connell, Daniel 85–6
O'Connor, Arthur 73
Ohio Country 47, 48, 49, 64–5
Ojibwes 61
O'Malley, Grace 11–12
O'Neill, Conn 13
O'Neill, Hugh, Earl of Tyrone 16
O'Neill, Sir Brian McPhelim 15
O'Neill, Sir Phelim 18–19
Opechancanough 39
Osceola 95

P
Paiute people 177, 179
Pakeha people 124–6, 209
Palestine 190–2
Pan Africanist Congress (PAC) 182, 183
Parnell, Charles 136
pays d'en haut 47, 48, 49
Pearse, Patrick 150–1
Pedis 127–8
Peel, Robert 87
Penacooks 35–6
peoplehood 203
Pequots 42
Percy, George 38
Philip, John 78
Phillip, Arthur 66
Pilgrims 41–2
Pine Ridge Reservation 204
Pitt, William 71, 75, 86
Plaatje, Sol 131
Plantation of Ulster 17
Plymouth settlers 41, 42, 43, 44
Pocahontas 37
Pontiac 49–50
possessive individualism 84
Potlatch Law 120
Power, Ambrose 26
Powers, Mabel 161
Powhatan 37, 39

Poynings' Law of 1494 24
Pratt, Richard Henry 115
Proclamation Act of 1763 118
Protestants 72–5
Pue, Tamzyn 198
Puritans 41–2, 44–5
Putin, Vladimir 214

R
Raleigh, Sir Walter 36
Rata, Matiu 190
Ratana, T. W. 148
Raven 52
Redmond, John 150
Red Sticks 65
Reform Act of 1832 84, 85, 86–7
Renbert, Elsa Laula 167–8
Retief, Piet 83–4
Rhodes, Cecil 131–3, 200
Rhodesia 132, 134, 153–4, 187–8, 199–201. *See also* Zimbabwe
Riel, Louis 91–3, 121, 122
Rolfe, John 38
Roman Catholic Church 13, 17–23, 25
Roosevelt, Franklin 162, 166, 176
Ross, John 95
Royal Irish Constabulary (RIC) 156–7
Royal Proclamation of 1763 50, 55–7
Rubusana, Walter 131
Russell, Lord John 85, 88
Russia 213–14

S
Sámi people 167–8
Samoset 41
San 54, 76, 78
Sand Creek massacre 96
Sauk 95
Sayengeraghta 53
Scandinavia 167–8
Schomberg, Marshal 23
Scott, Duncan 147
Scott, Thomas 92
Scott, Winfield 95
Scullabogue massacre 74
Second World War 163–6
Selkirk, Lord 63
Seminoles 95

Settlement of South Australia 81–2
settler colonialism 2–3, 4–8, 210–11
Seven Years' War 47–51
Sharpeville Massacre 183, 189
Sheridan, Philip 99
Sherman, William 97, 99
Shona 133
Short, Clare 200
Shoshone 177
Sidney, Sir Henry 14, 24
Sinn Féin 156
Sisulu, Walter 181
Sithole, Ndbaningi 188
Six Nations 147, 149, 150
Sloan, Thomas 161
Smallface-Marule, Marie 197–8
Smith, Ian 187–8, 199
Smith, John 37
Smith, Sir Thomas 15
Smuts, Jan 130, 155, 156, 165–6
Smythe, Thomas 37
South Africa 53–4, 75–9, 126–34, 152, 155–6, 159–60, 165–6, 174–5, 179–83, 188, 189–90, 201–3, 211
Southern Rhodesia 153–4, 165, 187
Southern Rhodesia's Unilateral Declaration of Independence (1965) 192–4
Soviet Union 213
Squanto 41
Stainbrook, Cris 205
Stalin, Joseph 213
Stamp Act 51
Standing Bear, Luther 116
Stephen, James 89
Strijdom, Johannes 183
Susquehannas 40
Sweden 167–8
Swift, Jonathan 24

T
Taiwan 139, 140
Tambo, Oliver 181
Tasmania 59–60, 68–9
Tatars 213–14
Tecumseh 65
Tenskwatawa 64–5

terra nullius 207
tobacco 38–9
Trail of Tears 94
Transvaal 128–9
Treaty of Fort Laramie 96–7
Treaty of Medicine Lodge 96–7
Treaty of Paris 49–51
Treaty of Waitangi 106, 107, 110–11
Treuer, David 205
Trevelyan, Charles 87
Tudor, Henry 157
Turner, Ted 205
Tuscarora War 45–6

U
Ukraine 214
Ulster 16–19
United Irishmen 71–5
United Nations Declaration on the Rights of Indigenous Peoples (UNDRIP 2007) 198–9, 214–20
United States 93–100, 160–2, 166, 203–6, 211–12
uranium 178–9

V
Valera, Eamon de 158, 159
Veracini, Lorenzo 5
Verwoerd, Hendrik 180
Victoria, Queen of England 132
Virginia Company 37–9
Voortrekkers 83–4

W
Waggoner, Josephine 99, 100
Wahunsenacawh 37, 39
Wainaina, Binyavanga 175
Wakefield, Edward Gibbon 85
Waldron, Richard 35–6
Walker, Ranjinui J. 6–7
Wampanoags 35–6, 41–2
War of 1812 64–6
Waruhiu wa Kung'u 185
Washington, George 48, 51, 52
Wentworth, Thomas 18
Whiteboy movement 26, 86
William, Prince of Orange 21–3, 72
Williamite-Jacobite War 22–3

Wilson, Sir Henry 138
Wilson, Woodrow 160
Winthrop, John 42
Wolfe, Patrick 2, 3, 210
Wolfe Tone, Theobald 71, 74
Wolseley, Joseph 93
Wood, William 99
World Council of Indigenous Peoples (WCIP) 198
World War I. *See* Great War
World War II. *See* Second World War
Wounded Knee Creek 118

X
Xhosa 1–2, 54–5, 76–7

Y
Yamasee War 45–6

Z
Zimbabwe 199–201, 211. *See also* Rhodesia
Zionism 191
Zitkala-Ša 116–17
Zulus 101, 127–8